Henry Venn, Saint Francis Xavier

The missionary life and labours of Francis Xavier taken from his own correspondence :

with a sketch of the general results of Roman Catholic missions among the heathen

Henry Venn, Saint Francis Xavier

The missionary life and labours of Francis Xavier taken from his own correspondence :
with a sketch of the general results of Roman Catholic missions among the heathen

ISBN/EAN: 9783741158292

Manufactured in Europe, USA, Canada, Australia, Japa

Cover: Foto ©Andreas Hilbeck / pixelio.de

Manufactured and distributed by brebook publishing software (www.brebook.com)

Henry Venn, Saint Francis Xavier

The missionary life and labours of Francis Xavier taken from his own correspondence :

PREFACE.

THE history of modern Roman Catholic Missions to heathen countries forms an important subject of inquiry with all who take an interest in the progress of Christianity. One of the most remarkable periods in this history is that which extends from the middle of the sixteenth to the middle of the seventeenth centuries. It was then that Jesuit Missionaries and some of the ablest men appeared in the field. The great influence and wealth of Portugal were at that time exerted to give effect to the work of evangelizing India, Japan, China, and America. It is difficult to calculate the number of Missionaries which the Church of Rome maintained during that period in all parts of the known world. Long after the work had declined, by the expulsion of the Portuguese from their Eastern supremacy, Niecamp, who wrote a History of the Danish Mission in South India, states, that when the first two Protestant Missionaries were sent out (in 1706), the number of Romish Missionaries then in the East was estimated at two thousand.

Yet our information of Roman Catholic Missions is very meagre and unsatisfactory. The sources of information are either various collections of letters of

Missionaries, or dry compilations from those letters. But these sources of information cannot satisfy any one who desires a clear knowledge of this subject. He will seek for histories of Missions written from the field of labour by the labourers themselves, or by those who have witnessed the work abroad: or the Journals and collected letters of individual Missionaries. Since Missions were taken up in earnest by the Protestant Church, at the close of the eighteenth century, the press, in England and America, has teemed with such Missionary histories and biographies. Numerous volumes have been written by Missionaries themselves, or by their relatives and others. In such books we see the living man and his real work. As soon, therefore, as my attention was turned to the subject of Romish Missions, I sought out for some such authentic biographies, memoirs, or histories of Romish Missionaries. Wherever I inquired, the Life of Xavier was presented to me, and no second work of that class could be named. I searched public libraries and booksellers' shops without success. I made inquiries personally at the head-quarters of Romish Missionaries in France, namely, the Institute of the Faith at Lyons, but was assured that the Life of Xavier was the only biography of any authority: the same answer was returned to a friend who made the inquiry at the College of the "Propaganda" at Rome; and my friend was further informed that it was contrary to the principles of the Romish Church to permit the unauthorized publication of the personal history of its Missionaries.

I was hence led to study the life of Xavier as the only authentic source from which an internal view of the life and labours of a Romish Missionary can be obtained.

The life of Xavier has another title to consideration. Many prevailing sentiments of the present day, even in Protestant countries, respecting Missions, find their counterpart in some of the most striking features in the history of Francis Xavier, such as a craving for the romance of Missions; the notion that an autocratic power is wanted in a Mission, such as a Missionary Bishop might exercise; a demand for a degree of self-denial in a Missionary bordering upon asceticism. These, and many such sentiments, are often illustrated by a reference to the life and success of Xavier. The delusive character of such sentiments cannot fail to appear on a careful study of the truth of Xavier's history.

Independently of the general interest of the subject, the history of Francis Xavier may claim special attention at this time, in connection with Japan, now brought, after a lapse of more than two centuries, into intercourse with Europe; for his name will ever be associated with the first attempt to evangelize that country.

These considerations have induced me to bestow upon Xavier's letters, and upon various contemporaneus documents, a careful investigation, the result of which is presented to the public in the following pages.

The work has been undertaken under a deep sense of the dignity of the Missionary subject; and of the sacred obligation of exercising the candour enjoined by the

Lord of Missions, in his rebuke of some of his own Apostles, who would have repudiated the acts of all "who followed not with them." Yet there are more solemn interests than those of Christian candour at stake in the consideration of Xavier's history, which will develop themselves in the progress of this undertaking, and will, it is hoped, justify the amount of time and thought which the investigation has occupied. The work is commended to the divine blessing in the humble prayer that it may conduce to the advancement of the truth of the Gospel, and to the Mission of that truth throughout the whole world.

CONTENTS.

CHAPTER I.

XAVIER'S LIFE BEFORE HIS DEPARTURE FOR INDIA.

SECT. 1. Introduction	1
SECT. 2. Xavier's early history before his designation to India	6
SECT. 3. Xavier's preparation for his departure to India	11

CHAPTER II.

FIRST THREE YEARS OF MISSIONARY LIFE IN INDIA.

SECT. 1. Xavier's arrival in India—Goa	20
SECT. 2. Xavier's Missionary labours on the Fishery Coast	29
SECT. 3. Xavier's abandonment of India—inconsistencies of Xavier's character	68

CHAPTER III.

LEGENDARY LIFE OF FRANCIS XAVIER	83

CHAPTER IV.

XAVIER'S VISIT TO THE SPICE ISLANDS OF THE INDIAN ARCHIPELAGO	102

CONTENTS.

CHAPTER V.

XAVIER A DIRECTOR OF JESUIT MISSIONS IN THE EAST, AND A ROYAL COMMISSIONER FROM THE KING OF PORTUGAL.

SECT. 1. Xavier's direction and management of the Jesuit Missions in the East . . 122

SECT. 2. Xavier the Royal Commissioner of King John III. of Portugal . . . 147

SECT. 3. Xavier's confession, after seven years' labour, of the failure of his endeavours to convert the heathen . . . 155

CHAPTER VI.

XAVIER'S LABOURS IN JAPAN.

SECT. 1. Xavier's preparations for his visit to Japan 167

SECT. 2. Xavier's arrival in Japan, and first account of the people 178

SECT. 3. Conclusion of Xavier's labours in Japan . 188

SECT. 4. Legends of Xavier's labours in Japan 210

CHAPTER VII.

INTERNAL DISSENSIONS OF THE MISSION IN INDIA . . 214

CHAPTER VIII.

XAVIER'S ATTEMPT TO REACH CHINA—DEATH AND CHARACTER.

SECT. 1. Xavier's voyage to China, and Death 231

SECT. 2. Xavier's personal character reviewed 250

CONTENTS.

CHAPTER IX.

THE FAILURE OF ROMISH MISSIONS TO THE HEATHEN.

SECT. 1. Sources of information respecting Romish Missions	262
SECT. 2. Vast extent of Romish Missions	269
SECT. 3. Failure of the principal Romish Missions since the time of Xavier—South India	277
Ceylon	291
Japan	294
China	300
Abyssinia	308
Paraguay and the Philippine Islands	312
SECT. 4. Concluding Remarks	319

CHAPTER I.

Xavier's Life before his departure for India.

SECTION 1. *Introduction.*—SOURCES OF INFORMATION—BIOGRAPHIES—XAVIER'S LETTERS—METHOD PURSUED IN THIS WORK.

SECTION 2. *Xavier's early history.*—RESIDENCE IN THE UNIVERSITY OF PARIS—BIAS TOWARDS PROTESTANTISM—ASSOCIATION WITH IGNATIUS LOYOLA—THE JESUIT SOCIETY—KING OF PORTUGAL PROPOSES TO SEND JESUIT MISSIONARIES TO INDIA.

SECTION 3. *Preparation for India.*—JOURNEY TO LISBON—EMPLOYMENTS IN LISBON—PORTUGUESE POWER IN THE EAST—XAVIER'S COMMUNICATIONS WITH THE KING OF PORTUGAL AND THE VICEROY OF INDIA ON HIS FUTURE PROCEEDINGS—EXTRAORDINARY POWERS CONFERRED ON XAVIER BY THE POPE AND THE KING OF PORTUGAL.

SECTION 1.—*Introduction.*

LOOK at the apostolic life and labours of St. Francis Xavier!—is frequently uttered as a taunt against Protestant Missionaries by Romanist writers, and is too often echoed by Protestant authors of repute.

But where shall we obtain any certain knowledge of the life and labours of Xavier? Shall we turn to his biographies? The earliest of these was a short sketch of Xavier's life and labours, drawn up by Emmanuel Acosta, a Jesuit Father, out of the notices which had been given in "Letters from India." This narrative was published by Maffeus in his volume of the letters and acts of the Jesuits in the East, 1573.

Tursellinus, a Jesuit Father, who had no personal knowledge of India, wrote a life of Xavier in Latin, in 1596, forty-four years after Xavier's death. In 1682, a French Jesuit, Father Bohours, wrote a life in French, of which James Dryden, the brother of the poet, gave an English translation. These are the most celebrated biographies of Xavier. But if any one tolerably acquainted with the subject will apply to these works the usual tests of credibility, he will soon detect such irreconcilable contradictions between Xavier's own letters and the assertions of his biographers, together with such loose statements, and so many geographical mistakes as to destroy all confidence in the competency or the historical fidelity of the authors.

There is, however, one existing portrait bearing throughout an evident stamp of truthfulness, and enlivened with such vivid colouring, that it is impossible to contemplate it without a satisfactory conviction that we see the very man, and are made acquainted with the main facts of his history. That portrait is drawn by Xavier's own hand in a copious collection of original letters. Many of these letters were written to friends in Europe, with the avowed intention of putting them in full possession of all that he did, and of all that happened to him. Other letters were written to fellow-labourers in the same field with himself. So that we are furnished in this collection with a complete, though not a formal, autobiography.

No one ever had a juster estimate of the proper character of correspondence between friends, or a greater zest in its prosecution. Some of Xavier's correspondents in Europe were in the highest positions, such as John III., King of Portugal, and Ignatius Loyola. His letters to such persons would be most carefully prepared. Other letters were written to intimate friends and Jesuit associates, and contained the genuine effusions of his heart. As the communications between Europe and India were then confined to the annual fleets, Xavier's letters were mostly annual letters: several letters were written at one time, repeating the same events in varied language. The letters would at this day be termed Missionary Journals or Reports. They are written with great clearness and freedom of style. They enter into minute details, they furnish graphic descriptions of passing scenes, and reflect the varied feelings and the spirit of the writer. They breathe throughout a fervent devotion to God, and an ardent zeal for bringing the heathen into the fold of the visible Church of Christ.

"When you write to us in India" (said Xavier, in a letter to two of his friends), "do not write shortly, or in a mere perfunctory style. We wish to learn from you particulars respecting each of our brethren, what they are about, what is their health, what are their thoughts, what their hopes, what the fruit of their labours. Do not regard this as a burden when there is only one opportunity in the year for receiving and sending letters to India. Let your letters occupy us a full week in reading. We promise to do the same with you." (Bologna I. 9. French, No. 9.)

Xavier's letters have been collected and preserved with superstitious reverence by the Jesuit Fathers. A few were published in the numerous collections called "Epistolæ Indicæ." But Tursellinus first printed them as a separate volume in 1596, which contained Latin translations of fifty-two Spanish and Portuguese originals. Sixty-five years later—in 1661—Peter Possinus, also a Jesuit, published a volume of "new letters," translated, as he states, from Spanish and Portuguese autographs. He gives, in his preface, this story. A Jesuit friend, Alex. Philippucius, after having suffered for two years and a half excruciating pain, and being past all hope of recovery, prayed at last to Francis Xavier; and before noon on the same day was miraculously cured. Philippucius, out of gratitude to his "Healer," determined to follow his example, and go to India as a Missionary; and, before doing so, to procure the publication of as many of Xavier's letters as could be found. For this purpose the archives of Rome, of Lisbon, and of Goa were searched; and the result was, the collection of ninety new letters in addition to those previously published by Tursellinus.

In 1795, an edition of Xavier's letters in the Latin translations was published at Bologna, by a very careful editor, who was himself a Jesuit Father, said to be Roch Manchiaca. In this edition the letters are arranged in chronological order; and reasons are given in the "prolegomena" for the dates assigned to each letter, and for regarding some which had been admitted into other collections as spurious. This collection contains 146 letters, and is in every respect the standard edition. A French translation of this edition was published at Brussels in 1838.

The method which it is proposed to pursue in this volume, in order to obtain a correct view of the life and labours of Francis Xavier, is, first to weave into a narrative the facts contained in the letters, supplying from the biographers only a few connecting links. Such a narrative, as far as it goes, must be authentic. We shall afterwards inquire what additional information the biographers supply beyond the statements in Xavier's own letters, and apply the narrative as a test of the accuracy of such additional information.

The main object of the work will be to investigate Xavier's Missionary character, and the results of his Missionary labours in the East. The extracts of letters will be given in a free translation of the Latin. The references are to the Bologna and to the French editions. In the former the letters are arranged in four books; in the French edition the letters are numbered consecutively throughout.

Section 2. *Xavier's early history before his designation to India.*

The first letter in the collection of Xavier's letters bears the date of Paris, 24th March 1535. Xavier was then residing in the University of Paris as a Master of Arts and a Reader in Aristotelian Philosophy. The letter was written to his eldest brother in Spain, to solicit from him pecuniary assistance, and to vindicate himself and his friend, Ignatius Loyola, from certain calumnies by which his brother had been prejudiced against them. The letter describes at great length his love for his brother, as well as the trials and difficulties to which he had been himself subjected in consequence of his distance from his family. It expresses unbounded admiration and affection for Ignatius Loyola, and the debt of gratitude which Xavier owed to Loyola for two special benefits, namely, for having, on several occasions, procured him money in seasons of distress, and for having rescued him from the influence of Protestant teachers. He writes:—" I declare in my conscience, and, as it were, under my hand and seal, that my obligations to him are far greater than a whole life devoted to his service can repay, or even partially satisfy. For in the serious difficulties into which my poverty has cast me, as I have often explained to you, in consequence of my distance from you, he has always come opportunely to my relief, either with a supply of his own money, or through his friends: but the benefit he has conferred of highest value is that of fortifying my youthful imprudence against the deplorable dangers arising from my familiarity with men breathing out heresy, such as are many of my contemporaries in Paris in these times, who would insidiously undermine faith and morality, beneath the specious mask of liberality and superior intelligence." (I. 1. Fr. 1.)

Xavier was twenty-nine years of age when he wrote this letter, having been born the 7th April 1506, at the Castle of Xavier, in the kingdom of Navarre, at the foot of the Pyrenees. On his mother's side he was related to the kings of Navarre and the family of the Bourbons. He was now living in the college of St. Barbe, where he had an intimate friend named Lefevre. This friend was first gained over to the confidence of Loyola, and to the adoption of those spiritual exercises by which the future founder of the order of Jesuits proposed to reach the highest degrees of religious attainments. Xavier for a time resisted this influence, but at length yielded himself to it with the ardour which is displayed in his letter to his brother.

Xavier's early acquaintance with Protestant truth appears to have exercised some influence on his future life. In India he was removed from the personal influence of Ignatius Loyola, and from the more powerful associations of Romish superstition; and his mind seems at times to have exhibited the more healthy tone of religion which he had witnessed amongst the early friends from whom Loyola had beguiled him.

His standard of spiritual religion was far higher than that of his associates. He was ever dissatisfied that he could not bring up his followers to this standard. But he had turned away from Protestant truth, by which alone it can be reached. He sought to attain the same standard by a system of mental and bodily discipline, which in a few cases, such as his own, may succeed in fostering religious sentiments, and a salutary self-control, but which, in its general tendency, forms the well-known character of the Jesuit.

In the year 1534, on the Feast of the Assumption, Loyola had imparted to six of his friends, including Xavier and Lefevre, a project of forming an association for converting unbelievers. The seven friends took a vow to renounce all worldly possessions, and to make a journey to Jerusalem; or, if that expedition were not possible, to throw themselves at the feet of the Pope, to serve the church in any place which he might select.

After this association had been formed, Xavier remained about two years in Paris. Ignatius Loyola left Paris in 1535, and was himself the bearer of the letter to which we have alluded to the brother in Spain. That letter earnestly entreated the brother to receive Loyola as a friend, and to repose a full confidence in his spiritual advice.

Loyola did not return to Paris, but enjoined his associates to meet him at Venice in the early part of 1537. Xavier left Paris in the November previous, and travelled on foot as a mendicant friar, practising various bodily austerities. From Venice they proceeded to

Rome, and obtained the sanction and benediction of the Pope for their mission to the Holy Land. The war between the Turks and Christians prevented, however, the execution of this project. It was therefore determined, with the sanction of the Pope, that they should disperse themselves amongst the most celebrated Universities of Italy to revive the tone of religion. Xavier was chiefly stationed at Bologna.

Three years were thus spent by the associates in Italy. Their number increasing, Loyola determined to form them into an ecclesiastical order, under the title of " the Company of Jesus." In addition to their vows of perpetual poverty and celibacy, they now added one of implicit obedience to the Superior of the order, whose authority was to be absolute.

Events now occurred which decided unexpectedly the future labours of Xavier. John III., King of Portugal, possessed a splendid dominion in the East. He was zealous for the propagation of Christianity in these possessions. Many years before Xavier's time numerous priests, friars, and Missionaries had been sent out for this purpose, especially those of the Franciscan order. There was a bishop at Goa, the seat of the Indian government, who had his vicars at the Moluccas and Malacca, at Ormuz in the Persian Gulf, at Diu in Guzerat, at Mozambique and Sofala, in East Africa. There were Missionaries labouring in Travancore, on the Coromandel Coast, in Ceylon, and in the Moluccas; but the King had not been satisfied with the progress of Christianity. He was led to believe that the new order of Jesuits would prove more efficient Missionaries than their predecessors. This idea was suggested to him by John Gaven, who had formerly been Principal of St. Barbe's College at Paris, and therefore well knew the qualifications of Xavier, Loyola, and Lefevre. Gaven was now connected with the Portuguese embassy at Rome; and he proposed that the Pope should be applied to by the King of Portugal to send these three men to India. The King entered so heartily into the proposition, that he applied, through his ambassador, for the whole number of the associates; and the Pope sanctioned the application. They had already taken a vow to proceed to any part of the world which the Pope might select; but this unexpected call to the East Indies did not approve itself to Ignatius Loyola; and, at this early stage of Jesuitism, it was shown how qualified is the obedience of a Jesuit to the Head of the Church when his own views are crossed. Loyola had been captivated by the romance of a Mission to the Holy Land; but India had no paramount charms in his apprehension. He therefore demurred to the migration of the whole body of associates, and selected two of the number for that Mission, namely, Simon Roderick and Nicholas Bobadilla. These two were the least eminent of the party. The former was a Portuguese subject, and had been educated at Paris at the expense of the King, and therefore could be scarcely withheld from obeying the royal summons. The two Missionaries designate were appointed to proceed to Lisbon, and Bobadilla was to accompany the Portuguese ambassador in his journey home to Portugal; but both were seized with fever on the eve of their departure. In this emergency, Ignatius consented to the substitution of Xavier as the Missionary to return with the ambassador to Portugal. In the course of a few days from the first notice of his designation to India, Xavier took leave of the Pope, of Ignatius, and of his other friends, and started from Rome for Portugal, in the suite of the ambassador, on the 16th March 1540.

SECTION 3. *Xavier's preparation for his departure to India.*

Xavier's journey from Rome to Lisbon, in the suite of the Portuguese ambassador, occupied more than three months. The cavalcade was very numerous, and religious exercises were daily performed. In a letter from Bologna (31st March 1540), Xavier sends to Loyola a very touching expression of his affection, connected with an important Missionary remark. "We have no resource to console us in our separation but the frequent interchange of letters. For my part I will never lay myself open to the charge of negligence; convinced of the wisdom of the remarks you made upon my departure, that the colonies must be attached to the Metropolitan Church as daughters to their mother. I have determined, in whatever part of the world I may be, whether alone or with the members of our Society, to keep up my intercourse with you by letter, and to cherish the most intimate relations with you and with our house in Rome, and to send you an exact and detailed account of all my actions, as daughters are accustomed to do in writing to their mothers." (I. 2. Fr. 2.)

Xavier relates an incident on the journey which affords a specimen of his power of graphic description, and shows at the same time how ready he was to recognise a miracle in a providential deliverance. Writing to Loyola from Lisbon, he says:—" Whilst on our journey through Italy it pleased the Lord to manifest his power in a wonderful manner towards one of the servants of the ambassador who accompanied us. It was the same man whom you saw at Rome, and who, after postponing his purpose of entering the monastic life, at last relinquished it altogether through a sinful indolence. A great river of uncertain depth opposed our progress. This man rushed forward on horseback to try the depth of the unknown channel, impelled by his rashness, notwithstanding our remonstrances. He had proceeded but a short distance when the force of the current overcame the strength of the horse, and both horse and rider were swept down the stream, while the whole company remained on the bank looking on with consternation. They were carried in an instant as far off as your residence is from the Church of St. Louis. Then the Lord God was pleased to hear the fervent prayer of his servant the ambassador, and of us all, supplicating with tears the preservation of the unfortunate man, now beyond all human help. The Lord answered the prayer, and, by a manifest miracle, delivered the lost man from imminent destruction. The man was master of the horse to the ambassador, and when he was carried headlong down the whirlpool, he doubtless wished himself in a monastery rather than where he was. His conscience, at that moment, chiefly tortured him with the recollection of a lost opportunity which he then in vain desired to recover. This he afterwards confessed to me, and entreated all to take warning from his case." (L. 3. Fr. 3.)

It is stated by the biographers, that, during this journey, the cavalcade passed near the castle of Xavier, where Xavier's aged mother was lying at the point of death, but that the son refused to visit the mother, though pressed to do so by the ambassador. This is represented as an act of self-denial and a trait of high virtue. But how much higher an exercise of Christian heroism is the parting interview between an affectionate son and his parents, when, for the love of Christ, they submit to the separation. The conduct attributed to Xavier is, however, scarcely consistent with his generous character, and with the circumstances of his age, and long separation from his family.

Simon Roderick and Nicholas Bobadilla, who had recovered their health, and Paul Camerte, who had lately been received as an associate into the Society at Rome, joined Xavier at Lisbon, to proceed with him to India. The Missionary party was, however, detained at Lisbon for ten months.

Six of Xavier's letters describe the events during the ten months' detention at Lisbon. Xavier was at once introduced to the King, who became deeply interested in the scheme of the company of Jesus, and encouraged Xavier to labour for the religious improvement of the Court of Portugal. All the young nobility and pages of honour, connected with the palace, were required to attend the confessional of the Jesuit Fathers; so that the Court of Portugal, in the days of its greatest temporal splendour, wore the appearance, says Xavier, of a religious institution. Often the whole day, and far into the night, was spent in hearing confessions from members of the court.

The question was soon raised whether it would not be better to retain Xavier and his associates in Portugal, than to transfer their labours to India. "The king," Xavier writes, July 26, 1540, "is not decided to send us to India, because he thinks we may as well serve God here. Two of the bishops insist upon our departure, grounding their opinion upon the hope, that, if we go, some of the Kings of India may be converted to Christianity. For ourselves, we are daily occupied in seeking coadjutors, and I hope the way is gradually becoming clear for obtaining them. If we remain here we shall found religious houses, and we shall more easily obtain associates here than in India. If we go, and our Lord God vouchsafes us a few years of life, we shall found, by his help, similar establishments in the midst of India and Ethiopia." (I. 4. Fr. 4.)

The Missionary party soon increased to six in number, and the question, whether they should be detained in Portugal or proceed to India, was decided by dividing the party. Three, including Simon Roderick, were to remain in Portugal; while Fathers Xavier and Paul Camerte, and a lay assistant named Francis Mansilla, were to go to India.

Simon Roderick was not, however, lost to India. He was appointed by the King Principal of the College at Coimbra, which was made an instititution for the support of one hundred Jesuit associates, which number was soon afterwards doubled. At this college Jesuit Missionaries were prepared for India, so that, in a few years, a large and regular supply was obtained to follow in the wake of Xavier.

Xavier's letters, written at this period, are full of his prospects and hopes of success in India.

John III. of Portugal was very powerful in naval resources. He maintained an exclusive right against all other nations of Europe of trading with the East by way of the Cape of Good Hope. He was invested by the Pope with rights of sovereignty over all countries east of the Cape. The general name of "India" then comprised the regions of East Africa, Arabia, Persia, Hindostan, China, and the Indian Archipelago. The territory actually possessed by Portugal consisted only of numerous settlements upon the coasts, where factories were established, and forts erected, garrisoned by Portuguese soldiers. A fleet of armed ships commanded the seas, protected the trade, and supported the garrisons. A Viceroy resided at Goa, and each of the other settlements had its local governor. The King retained all the appointments, civil, military, and commercial in his own power, directed all affairs, and was possessed of all the revenues.

It was only natural, therefore, that Xavier should have great confidence in the influence which he should possess, as one selected and commissioned by the King for advancing Christianity amongst the natives, especially as it was well known the King took the liveliest interest in the success of this Mission, and was to receive direct accounts from the Missionary respecting this and all other Indian affairs.

Xavier writes, on the eve of his departure:—" We leave loaded with favours by his Majesty, and are to accompany the Viceroy whom he sends this year to India, and to whom he has specially commended us. We sail in the same vessel with him. That officer entertains so much affection for us that he has reserved to himself the whole care of providing for our wants, and has forbidden us, or any one else on our behalf, to think of providing furniture, or whatever may be requisite for the voyage. He has already determined that we are to be daily guests at his own table. I mention these things, not to display the honour and advantage, such as it is, as if this delighted us, which we should much rather be without; but that you may understand what just hopes we have of great assistance in the conversion of the natives, through the exuberant affection towards us of the highest authority in India. That conversion we desire with our whole heart; and you, out of your zeal for God's glory, will rejoice at, and congratulate us on, the blessed opportunity of carrying the name of Jesus Christ before the heathen Kings of those regions, where it is abundantly clear that the Viceroy of Portugal has the highest authority and respect." " In a private conversation which I had with the Viceroy three days ago, he told me that there was an island in India of pure heathen, without any mixture of Jews or Moslems, in which he hoped for a great and immediate fruit of the preaching of the Gospel: that he had no doubt, from what he had observed of the habit of their minds, but that the King, and, in a short time, the whole island, would openly embrace the religion of Christ." (I. 8. Fr. 8.)

The name of the Viceroy was Martin Alphonso de Soza. He had previously held office in India, and was regarded as an eminently just and upright governor: the island to which he alluded was probably Manaar, on the coast of Ceylon.

Personal vanity was not an element in the character of Xavier. His exultation in the royal patronage, and his confidence in his own personal influence, only reveal his dependence upon an arm of flesh, rather than upon the inherent power of divine truth, as God's instrument for the conversion of the world. "Those," writes Xavier, " who are acquainted with India assure us that as soon as the natives of India have for guides and teachers such as we are, that is, those whose whole conduct is above the suspicion of avarice, they will receive the religion of Christ. If we carry with us into that country the spirit of mortification, the absolute renunciation of worldly advantages, the perfect disinterestedness of which we here give a pattern, there is no doubt, they say, but that in a few years we shall have made the conquest of two or three kingdoms; that the natives will be induced to trust us in proportion as they see clearly that we are not moved by any temporal motives, but simply by the desire of saving their souls." (I. 3. Fr. 3.)

Xavier was instructed, before his departure, by the King himself, in the state of India, and upon the methods he should use, under his royal authority, to establish the faith. The King also gave him four briefs which he had obtained for him from the Pope; the first conferred on Xavier the quality of Papal Nuncio to the new world: another gave him all the powers which the Church of Rome could give for the propagation of the faith in the East: a third recommended him to the care of David, King of Ethiopia: the fourth was addressed to all the princes and governors of the islands and continents between the Cape of Good Hope and the mouths of the Ganges. The King also furnished him with a general order to his officers to provide the Missionaries with every thing requisite for their maintenance. Though Xavier bears the name of a Missionary, how little was there in common between his position and that of the simple Missionary of the present day! Selected by a powerful sovereign to go out under his special patronage and protection, as his envoy for religious matters, to his eastern dominions; receiving a special commission and benediction from the chief Pontiff of the Church; the representative of the newly appointed order of the Jesuits; selected, under such august auspices, to supersede the existing Missionary agencies in the East; travelling from Rome through Europe to his post of embarkation in the suite of the ambassador of the King of Portugal; sailing with the new Viceroy, and a guest at his table;—it is difficult to conceive more splendid worldly attractions to any enterprise, and greater temporal advantages for its prosecution, than those which accompanied the call of Xavier to become "the Apostle of India."

CHAPTER II.

First three years of Missionary life in India.

SECTION 1. *Arrival in India and labours at Goa.*—ARRIVAL AT GOA—STATE OF RELIGION IN GOA—COLLEGE OF THE FAITH—MISSIONARY INSTITUTIONS FOR TRAINING NATIVE TEACHERS—DELIGHT IN THE PROSPECT OF MISSIONARY LABOURS.

SECTION 2. *Xavier's Missionary labours on the Fishery Coast.*—DESTINATION TO THE FISHERY COAST—LABOURS AMONG THE FISHERMEN — MULTITUDES BAPTIZED — SUPPOSED MIRACLE — CHARACTER OF THE BRAHMINS — GLOWING REPORTS OF SUCCESS IN HIS LETTERS TO EUROPE—SPIRITUAL JOYS IN HIS WORK—CONTRADICTORY STATEMENTS IN HIS LETTERS TO MANSILLA—DISGRACEFUL CONDUCT OF CHRISTIANS—THREATS OF THE INQUISITION—THE GREAT KING OF TRAVANCORE—THE RAVAGES OF THE BADAGES—BAPTISM OF MORIBUND INFANTS—QUESTIONABLE REPORT OF 10,000 BAPTISMS IN ONE MONTH.

SECTION 3. *Xavier's abandonment of India in despair of success.*—WARLIKE EXPEDITION AGAINST THE KING OF JAFFNAPATAM—XAVIER'S DISAPPOINTMENT BY ITS FAILURE—REMOVAL TO MADRAS—ABANDONMENT OF INDIA—INCONSISTENCIES OF XAVIER'S CHARACTER — REPUTED, AND ACTUAL, NUMBERS OF CONVERTS.

We now enter upon a review of the Missionary career of Francis Xavier in the East. His labours extended over ten years and a half, from his arrival in India, May 1542, to his death on the coast of China in December 1552. These labours may be divided into four periods.

The first, comprising Xavier's labours in South India for rather more than three years.

The second, his voyage to the Chinese Archipelago, which occupied two years and four months.

A third period of four years which was devoted to the management of his Indian Missions, and to a voyage to Japan, a two years' residence there, and return to India.

The fourth, and remaining period of about one year, which was spent in India, and in an abortive attempt to enter China.

The first period will be comprised in the sections of the present chapter.

SECTION 1. *Xavier's arrival in India—Goa.*

Xavier left the shores of Europe for his Indian Mission, April 7, 1541, having just completed the thirty-fifth year of his age. The fleet comprised six vessels. The voyage was unusually lengthened, and they were compelled to winter in the island of Mozambique, where there was a Portuguese garrison. Here they were detained six months. The Viceroy's ship set sail for India before the rest of the fleet, and visited Melinda on the coast of Africa, where there was another Portuguese garrison, adjoining a large Mohammedan city. Xavier had here a conversation with an intelligent Mohammedan, who deplored, even then, the retrograde condition of their religion: out of seventeen mosques in the city, which were once all well attended, only five were now used. From thence they visited the island of Socotra, at the entrance of the Red Sea. Many of the inhabitants were, by profession, Christians, tracing their descent from the labours of St. Thomas the Apostle.* When Albuquerque first took possession of Socotra, early in the sixteenth century, he placed there Antonius Laurentius, a Franciscan, "who discharged Apostolic functions" for many years. (Maff. Hist. Ind. Lib. III.) Xavier, however, represents the inhabitants as sunk in ignorance, unable to read or write, knowing nothing of Christian doctrine, and not even keeping up the form of baptism; performing divine service in an unknown tongue, which he supposes to be Chaldee (Syriac), using

---

* Neander thinks that such legends are not deserving of much confidence; and that there is no earlier mention of India Proper than in the time of the Emperor Constantine, "when there was a Missionary, Theophilus, with the surname of Indicus, who came from the island Diu, by which is to be understood the island of Sokotra. He found in his native land, and in other districts of India which he visited from there, Christianity planted already, and had only many things to correct."—*Neander's Church History*, Section I. 2.

incense, and very strict in fasting. Xavier strove to benefit these ignorant Christians, and baptized many of their children. His zeal in baptizing children led him into a ludicrous predicament. Meeting on the road with a mother and two children, he seized upon the children to administer baptism. They fled to the mother's protection, complaining that they were to be baptized. The mother advanced to Xavier, denouncing his baptism of her children as she was a Saracen, and did not wish her sons to become Christians. The Socotrians raised a cry on their part that the woman and her children were unworthy of the benefit of Christian baptism, and that they would not allow any Saracens, however much they might wish it, to become Christians.

The Socotrians were very anxious to detain Xavier amongst them, promising that, if he remained, the whole island would receive baptism. Xavier requested the Viceroy to allow him to remain for so great a harvest; but the Viceroy assured him that he would find other Christians in a more advantageous position, and where he would have better fruit of his labours.

Xavier arrived at Goa, May 6, 1542. His first impressions of Goa must have been very different from his anticipations, when he looked forward to India as a country altogether heathen, which he was to envangelize. He found Goa a fair and flourishing city, situated on an island, the inhabitants, native and European, all Christians. It had a magnificent cathedral, a resident bishop, a chapter of canons, a large convent of Franciscans, and other religious houses. But as it contained a large body of Portuguese troops, and was a seaport, the European population bore the godless character which has too often belonged to such localities. The natives who lived in the Portuguese settlements were required, as a matter of course, to be baptized: many of them were employed as slaves. There was also a large number of a mixed race; for it was a part of the Portuguese policy to encourage marriages between the European and the native races, with the view of providing a nursery for their army and navy. When Albuquerque first took Goa he caused a number of heathen women to be seized and baptized, and married to his soldiers. (Maffeus, Lib. IV.) The neighbourhood of Goa had been frequently the battle-field between the Portuguese and the warlike natives; and from this circumstance, as well as from its insular position, it presented few facilities for direct Missionary work among the heathen.

Xavier would soon learn that Goa was only a type of other Portuguese settlements in the East. They were all upon the coast, and consisted of a factory for trade with the natives, a garrison of Portuguese soldiers, the baptized heathen, and a progeny of a mixed race. The communication between the settlements was kept up by a fleet of armed ships to protect the commerce against a Saracen fleet on the coast of Arabia, which was always ready to dart upon any weak settlement or any rich prize. Everywhere there was occasional warfare between the warlike native tribes and the garrisons or the fleet. Such settlements were little calculated to diffuse the light of Christianity.

Xavier gives an animated description of his labours during his five months' residence at Goa. He took up his abode at a hospital. His whole day was spent in receiving confessions, in preaching, in catechizing the young, and in visiting the asylum for lepers.

There was at Goa a spacious college in the course of erection by public funds, which was endowed for the support of a hundred native youths; who were to be gathered from different parts of India, and, after learning Christian truth and receiving baptism, were to be sent back to their countrymen to impart to them the knowledge of Christianity. This college was named the College of the Faith, and, afterwards, St. Paul's College. It owed its wealth, like the Escurial and many other splendid institutions of the Church of Rome, to the union of war and superstition. "The Viceroy, Martin de Soza" (writes Xavier) "has gained many signal victories over the heathen, with whom he is continually at war. He attributes his success to his having founded many religious houses. He therefore designs to make this college more magnificent than all other religious buildings in India, in the hope that his army will gain still more brilliant victories than ever over the natives." A Franciscan, James Borbon, was to be Principal of the college, and he had already collected together sixty children of different countries, and had instructed them in

Portuguese, with a view to their transfer into the college as soon as it should be completed.

It is important to notice these facts, which show how far the Missions had advanced in India before Xavier's arrival, and which dispel the very common error that he was in any sense the originator, or chief promoter, of the South-Indian Mission with which his name is generally associated.

Xavier at once set his heart upon making this college a Jesuit establishment; and by the authority of the Viceroy he wrote to Ignatius to send him over three or four able associates, to be placed at the head of it. The idea of such a Missionary college, where youths may be removed to a distance from their heathen relatives and associations, and may receive an European education, has always been a favourite "first thought" of zealous Missionaries. But experience has shown that the advantages gained by such a system of isolation are counterbalanced by the severance of the tie of sympathy between the native pupils and their countrymen. They return to native society as trained teachers, indeed, but with European habits and tastes; and are, for the most part, unfitted for the work for which they have been trained. It is clear, from Xavier's letters, that his experience of the Goa native priests was very unsatisfactory. The only one of the class singled out for a special mention was one whom he cited to appear before the Bishop of Goa to answer for his conduct as a "hinderer of the Gospel." A more effectual way of raising up native teachers is that of establishing a theological seminary in the midst of a Mission, selecting for it men of mature and settled Christian character, who have proved their "aptness to teach" as catechists and schoolmasters, who, living with their families while under instruction, may retain their native tastes. In this way, also, the wives receive instruction at the same time; and the native teacher exhibits before his countrymen the example of a Christian family, which is as important a testimony to the truth as the profession of the lips. The celibacy of the priesthood deprives the Romish Church of this powerful aid.

The Viceroy took advantage of Xavier's influence with Ignatius to supplicate from the Pope a variety of superstitious favours, such as privileged altars, and Indulgences for the Viceroy himself and his wife, together with some favours of a more practical kind, which none but Popes could grant, namely, that the season of Lent should be transferred from its present position in the Calendar, which was inconvenient for that climate, to the months of June or July, and that the Bishop of Goa should be spared the trouble of taking long voyages to administer confirmation, by enabling him to confer the benefits of that rite at distant settlements through the imposition of the hands of his vicars.

One fine passage occurs in Xavier's letters, written at this time from Goa. "The miseries of a long voyage; the dealing with the sins of other people, while you are oppressed by your own; a permanent abode among the heathen, and this in a land which is scorched by the rays of the sun;—all these things are indeed trials. But if they be endured for the cause of God, they become great comforts, and the sources of many heavenly pleasures. I am persuaded that those who truly love the cross of Christ esteem a life thus passed in affliction to be a happy one, and regard an avoidance of the cross, or an exemption from it, as a kind of death. For what death is more bitter than to live without Christ, when once we have tasted His preciousness; or to desert Him, that we may follow our own desires? Believe me, no cross is to be compared with this cross. On the other hand, how happy it is to live in dying daily, and in mortifying our own will, and in seeking, not our own, but the things that are Jesus Christ's!" "I trust that, through the merits and prayers of our holy mother the Church, in which is my chief confidence, and through the prayers of its living members, to which you belong, our Lord Jesus Christ will sow the Gospel seed in this heathen land by my instrumentality, though a worthless servant. Especially, if He shall be pleased to use such a poor creature as I am for so great a work, it may shame the men who were born for great achievements; and it may stir up the courage of the timid, when, forsooth, they see me, who am but dust and ashes, and the most abject of men, a visible witness of the great want of labourers. I will, indeed, cheerfully devote myself to be the constant servant of any who will come over here, and devote themselves to work in the vineyard of our common Lord." (I. 10. Fr. 10.)

SECTION 2. *Xavier's Missionary labours on the Fishery Coast.*

Goa was the centre of government, and of commercial intercourse with all other parts of the East. Xavier was able to survey from thence the vast expanse of heathen and Mohammedan nations which encircled him, and over which he had received a special commission, from the highest spiritual and temporal authorities claiming jurisdiction in those parts, to plant the Christian faith. On the west there was the coast of Africa, with Ethiopia in the interior; to the north there lay Arabia and Persia; to the east the region of Hindostan; to the south, round Cape Comorin, a still more extended range of unconverted nations, stretching through the Indian Ocean and the Straits of Malacca, to the Islands of the Pacific in the far East. Where shall Xavier turn to make his first aggression upon the kingdoms of darkness? The suburbs of factories and garrisons could scarcely, as we have remarked, present to him an attractive field of Missionary enterprise. To visit the courts of some of the powerful Kings in amity with the Crown of Portugal would be an appropriate sphere for the personal friend and commissioner of John III.; or to have visited some of the cities and seats of learning in the interior of India would have been a fitting enterprise for a late professor of the most celebrated university of Europe. But no such employment was before Xavier. He had allied himself with Kings and Viceroys in his Missionary character, and now he must suffer the penalty, by becoming an agent in a pet scheme of Don Alphonso Soza. This scheme was of a very uncertain, not to say visionary kind, and utterly inappropriate to the peculiar qualifications of Xavier. His first mention of the scheme, in his letter to the Roman Society, is the following curt description:—" I am now going, by the commission of the Viceroy, to a certain region where there is hope of making many Christians." That region was the pearl fisheries east of Cape Comorin. Xavier, after his arrival at the scene of labour, gives this more precise information of the circumstances.

"The Viceroy marvellously supports and cherishes these neophytes. A short time since he gave them help when they were oppressed by the Saracens. They are for the most part fishermen, and reside on the sea shore, and support themselves and their families by their occupation, chiefly in pearl fishing. The Saracens had lately deprived them of the boats which they used in fishing. As soon as the Viceroy of India heard of this, he went himself, with a powerful force, against the Saracens, and made a great slaughter of them, and seized all their ships. He restored to the richer neophytes their own vessels, and gave to the poorer amongst them the Saracens' boats. Thus he enhanced a signal victory by an act of large liberality; for as he had received Divine aid in his victory, so he wished the Christians to share with him its happy fruit. The Saracens are utterly prostrate and broken: not a man of them dares to lift up his eyes. Their chiefs, and all amongst them capable of resistance, are slain. Hence the neophytes love the Viceroy like a father, and he considers them as his children. I cannot describe the earnestness with which he commended to me this new vineyard of Christ. He has now a great enterprise in hand, which will find a place in history, and be greatly to the advantage of the Christian religion. He meditates collecting together in one island all these Christians, now separated from each other by long intervals, and giving them a King to administer justice, and to watch over their interests and security." (I. 11. Fr. 13.) It appears from subsequent letters that these neophytes had been converted some years before the arrival of Xavier in India by a Vicar-General named Michael Vass. Xavier bears high testimony to the eminently Christian character of this dignitary and to the success of his labours. Writing to the King of Portugal (Jan. 26, 1549,) after the death of Michael Vass, Xavier uses these remarkable words:—" Let compassion for the poor Christians of the Comorin coast touch your Majesty. Do not disdain to be their Father, for they are become orphans by the recent death of Michael Vass, having lost in him their most true and excellent Father." (III. 3. Fr. 69.)*

---

* Tursellinus gives this account of the conversion of these Paravars :—Being oppressed by the Mohammedans they sent a deputation of their tribe to Cochin, with an offer to turn Christians if the Portugese would deliver them from the oppression of the Mohammedans. The offer was accepted by the Governor of Cochin and by the Viceroy, who undertook

Such was the sphere of labour to which Xavier was destined to devote his first energies. In a Missionary point of view, he was set to build upon another man's foundation. In a political view, he was set to secure to the King of Portugal the monopoly of a lucrative pearl fishery.

Xavier arrived on the Fishery Coast towards the close of the year 1542. He took with him some young natives trained at Goa, who were able to speak Portuguese as well as Tamil, their own tongue. Francis Mansilla soon afterwards joined him as his companion.* After labouring for one year on the Fishery Coast, Xavier returned for a short visit to Goa. Our knowledge of Xavier's labours during this first year is derived from two copious letters, in which he gives the account. One is to Ignatius Loyola, the other to the Jesuit Society at Rome: they were written at the close of 1543 and beginning of 1544. From these we learn that Xavier, immediately upon his arrival, set to work to have the Creed, the Lord's Prayer, the Ave Maria,

the secular part of the agreement, while Michael Vass, the Vicar-General residing at Cochin, managed the spiritual part of the affair by baptizing the members of the deputation, and sending priests to the Fishery Coast, who, he says, baptized 20,000, and then left the coast.

* This appears from the dates of the Bologna edition. The biographers state that Mansilla did not join Xavier till the second year.

and the Decalogue, translated into the vernacular. He then committed the translations to memory. Four months were occupied in this work, during which time he resided in one of the Christian villages. Thus furnished, and with his youthful interpreters, he commenced his Missionary labours. The letter written to the Jesuit Society at Rome contains a well known and often quoted description of Xavier's proceedings.

"I have begun to go through all the villages of this coast, with bell in hand, collecting together a large concourse both of boys and men. Bringing them twice a-day into a convenient place, I gave them Christian instruction. The boys, in the space of a month, have committed all to memory beautifully. Then I told them to teach what they had learned to their parents, household, and neighbours. On Sundays I called together the men and women, boys and girls, into a sacred edifice. They came together with great alacrity, and with an ardent desire to hear. Then I began with the Confession of the Holy Trinity, the Lord's Prayer, the Angelic Salutation, the Apostles' Creed, pronouncing them in their own language with a clear voice. All followed me in the repetition, in which they take an uncommon pleasure. Then I went through the Creed alone, pausing upon each article, asking whether they believed without any doubt. All, in an equally confident tone, with their hands in the form of the cross over their breasts, affirmed that they truly believed it. I direct them to repeat the Creed oftener than the other prayers, and teach them, at the same time, that those who believe the things contained in the Creed are called Christians. I inculcate the Decalogue in similar manner, that I may show that the Christian law is contained in those ten precepts, and that whoever keeps all these as he should do is a good Christian, and attains to eternal salvation. On the other hand, that whoever neglects one of these is a bad Christian, and will be thrust into hell, unless he truly repents of his sin. At these things both the neophytes and the heathen are astonished, as soon as they perceive how holy is the Christian law, how consistent, how agreeable to reason. After this I am accustomed to pronounce the Lord's Prayer and Ave Maria, they following me. Then, in the same way, we say over again the articles of the Creed, that we may, after each article, recite a Pater and Ave together, with a certain versicle; namely, when they have chanted the first article of the Belief, I say before them this versicle in their native tongue — 'Jesus, Son of the living God, grant us that we may fully believe this first article of the Christian faith, to obtain which from Thee we offer to Thee this prayer which Thou hast appointed.' Then to the other we add this versicle—'Holy Mary, the mother of our Lord Jesus Christ, obtain for us from your most precious Son that we may believe, without any doubt, this article of the Christian faith.' We pursue the same method in the other eleven articles of the Creed.

"We then inculcate the precepts of the Decalogue, chiefly in this method; when we have chanted the first commandment upon the love of God, we pray together, 'O Jesus Christ, Son of the living God, grant that we may love Thee above all.' Then we say the Lord's Prayer. Afterwards we all chant together, 'Holy Mary, mother of Jesus Christ, obtain from thy Son that we may diligently keep his first commandment.' Then we add the Angelic Salutation. The same method is followed in the other nine commandments, the versicles being varied according to the matter. These are the things which I accustom them to ask of God in their prayers; and I assure them, that if they shall have obtained these things, other blessings will follow in greater abundance than they can ask. I then command all, as well as those to be baptized, to recite the form of general confession; and, as they repeat the Creed, I ask them at each article whether they believe without doubting. Upon their assent, I add an exhortation, composed in their own tongue, in which the sum of the Christian religion, and of the discipline necessary to salvation, is briefly explained. Afterwards I baptize those who have been instructed. The close of the ceremony is a Salve Regina, by which we implore the help and assistance of the Blessed Virgin.

"How great is the multitude of those who are gathered into the fold of Christ you may learn from this, that it often happens to me, that my hands fail through the fatigue of baptizing; for I have baptized a whole village in a single day: and often, by repeating so frequently the Creed and other things, my voice and strength have failed me." (I. 14. Fr. 14.)

This passage has been given in full, because the last clause is often quoted as a proof of Xavier's extraordinary influence over men, and of his success in preaching the Gospel to the heathen. But if an ordinary degree of attention be paid to the narrative, as contained in Xavier's letters, a very different conclusion will follow.

First, let it be noticed that Xavier is speaking of certain villages inhabited by those who had entered into a profitable alliance with the Portuguese, on condition of embracing Christianity, but who had been left for some time without Christian teachers or ordinances. The number of these villages he tells us was thirty. He says that when he had sufficiently accomplished his work in one village he removed to another, till all these thirty villages had been visited; and then adds, " All being thus surveyed, my labour comes over again in the same order. In each village I leave one copy of the Christian Instruction. I appoint all to assemble on festival days, and to chant the rudiments of the Christian faith; and in each of the villages I appoint a fit person to preside. For their wages the Viceroy, at my request, has assigned 4000 gold fanams.* Multitudes in these parts are only not Christians because none are found to make them Christians." The expenditure of 4000 rupees in thirty vil-

---

* Of about two shillings value.

lages would easily secure the attendance of the inhabitants to go through their recitations at the sound of Xavier's bell.

Again, let it be considered that Xavier could not speak the native language. Long after the date of these numerous baptisms, and after he had been nearly two years in India, he writes from the midst of the Tamil population, in a letter dated Punicael, August 21, 1544:—
"Here I am, almost alone from the time that Anthony remained sick at Manapar; and I find it a most inconvenient position to be in the midst of a people of an unknown tongue, without the assistance of an interpreter. Roderick, indeed, who is now here, acts as an interpreter in the place of Anthony; but you know well how much they know of Portuguese. Conceive, therefore, what kind of life I live in this place, what kind of sermons I am able to address to the assemblies, when they who should repeat my address to the people do not understand me, nor I them. I ought to be an adept in dumb show. Yet I am not without work, for I want no interpreter to baptize infants just born, or those which their parents bring; nor to relieve the famished and the naked who come in my way. So I devote myself to these two kinds of good works, and do not regard my time as lost." (I. 32. Fr. 32.) Such was Xavier's own account of his dependence upon native interpreters. In Xavier's examinations for baptism, therefore, there was no questioning to ascertain whether the words were understood—no spontaneous inquiry of the converts—nothing beyond the

Missionary's imperfect utterance of an unknown tongue and the response in a prescribed form.

There is reason to doubt whether Xavier's catechumens understood so much as the meaning of the words put into their lips; for after all the baptisms recounted above, Xavier informed Mansilla that they had mistranslated the very first word of the Creed, and that, instead of the word "I believe," (*credo,*) they had been using the expression, "I will," (*volo!*) (I. 19. Fr. 19.)

When all these circumstances are taken into consideration, the position of Xavier, in the midst of a crowd of natives, with his failing arms and voice, through the multitude of his baptisms, sinks from something which sounded very grand to that which is very small.

It will not escape the notice of an intelligent Christian, that, in the elaborate description which Xavier gives of his conversions, there is no reference to the divine power on the hearts of individuals. Xavier's favourite expression is, "I have made so many Christians," (Feci Christianos,) when he had baptized infants, or taught adults to repeat the prescribed formulas. Even when he introduces a notice of the divine power it is often in a way which exalts human agency, rather than the work of the Holy Spirit. Thus he writes to Mansilla:—"That you may not regard with complacency any present fruit of your labours, think within yourself if fine flour is elaborated by the cornmill, it is to the high praise of the great Lord and Master of the mill, who turns upon it the stream of water by which the mill is moved, and so the whole machine is set in motion and performs its work." (I. 20. Fr. 20.) The illustration is suggestive of Xavier's notions of religion— "grinding" men into good Christians. All his hopes of success rested upon the incessant inculcation of dry formularies, and in the strictness and severity of external discipline. This was the whole of the work, according to his limited views of true religion. But such nominal and deficient Christianity can never bring men out of heathenism, or, at least, enable them to stand in the day of trial. Xavier had light enough to see this. His early acquaintance with Protestants seems to have left on his mind traces of spiritual truth which soon dissatisfied him with the results of his own teaching, and made him tremble with apprehension for the house he had "built on the sand."

Only one instance of Missionary aggression upon the heathen villages, is given in these letters:—" I turned out of my road into a heathen village, where there was not a single person willing to become a Christian, although they had before their eyes several neighbouring villages which had embraced Christianity. The reason they gave was that they were in the power of heathen rulers, who forbade the common people to embrace the Christian faith. Here there was a woman who had been three days in her confinement, and her life was despaired of by many. Since the prayers of unbelievers are offensive in the sight of God—for 'the gods of the nations are devils'—they were unanswered. I went with one of my companions to the house of the woman. I immediately began to call upon the name of the Lord with faith, forgetting that I was in a foreign land. I thought upon the text, 'The earth is the Lord's, and the fulness thereof; the round world, and they that dwell therein.' Therefore I determined to explain to the woman the articles of our faith through an interpreter; and she, through the mercy of God, believed what was said to her. Being then asked whether she wished to be a Christian, she answered that she freely and truly desired it. Then, reciting the Gospel which had never been before heard in that place, I baptized the woman with due formality. What followed? Under baptism she gave birth to the child, because she hoped and believed in Christ. Then I, through baptism, gave a new birth in Christ, to her husband, her children, and the infant born on that day. Immediately the report of the divine miracle performed in that house spread through the whole village. I went to the headmen, and, in the name of the Lord, I adjured them to acknowledge His Son Jesus Christ, in whom alone is salvation for all men. They declared that they would not dare to change their old religion, unless they received the permission of their ruler. I therefore went to the steward of the ruler, who happened to be present collecting his lord's rents. After he had heard me discourse upon the Christian religion, he acknowledged that Christianity seemed a good thing, and that there was liberty for himself, and all who wished it, to embrace the faith of Christ. Yet the man who gave good counsel to others, did not himself take it. But the headmen of the village, each with his family, first joined the worship of Christ, the rest followed their example, and all, of every condition and age, were baptized." (I. 11. Fr. 13.)

It will be seen, from this extract, that Xavier had no hesitation in claiming the power of working a miracle, when there was any ground for the assumption. His reputation for healing the sick brought him such numerous applications for aid, that, being unable to attend personally, he selected a number of quick boys, and taught them to repeat the Creed, &c., and then to go to sick persons with a crucifix, and pray for their recovery, which, he reports, generally succeeded in restoring the sick to health. He then turned the same boys into Evangelists, and sent them out into the villages to convert their countrymen.

Xavier adopted the plan on the Fishery Coast which he had pursued at Socotra, of baptizing infants, even though their parents were heathen. In the course of twelve months, he tells us that he had managed to baptize more than 1000 infants, who had died before they could commit sin, and who, therefore, had gone up to heaven as intercessors on his behalf. It is a sad proof of the intellectual debasement of the Romish system that such a man as Xavier should descend to write such words as these:—" To obtain these blessings we may reckon as our intercessors, besides others, the souls of the infants and children whom I have baptized with my own hand, and whom God called away from these parts to his heavenly mansion before they had lost the robe of innocence. I estimate the number of such above 1000. Again and again I ask and entreat them to obtain from God this mercy for us, that for the rest of our life, or rather of our term of exile, He may teach us to do His will so entirely, that whatsoever he requires of us we may execute in the very way in which He wills it to be done." (I. 14. Fr. 14.)

This way of "making Christians" has prevailed in Romish Missions from Xavier's day to the present. Such statistics largely swell their number of converts. Take, for instance, the following extract from a volume of the Romish " Annals of the Faith," " published by authority, 1845," showing that, in this practice at least, Rome remains no wiser after the lapse of three centuries.

" The Mission of Su-Tchuen continues its work of baptizing children in danger of death, and the Lord continues to bless it. Each year the number of those whom they regenerate goes on increasing. It was in 1839 (12,483); in 1840 (15,766); in 1841 (17,825); in 1842 (20,068); in 1843 (22,292); this year it amounts to (24,381).

" We have remarked that about two-thirds of the number of these children died in the year in which they were baptized. Thus, out of the number of 1844, sixteen thousand seven hundred and sixty-three winged their flight, a short time afterwards, to everlasting bliss. These happy souls, thus regenerated by us in the saving waters of baptism, can they forget us? Can they lose the remembrance of that generous Association which, under God, has opened to them the gates of heaven?

"We pay some Christians, men and women, who are acquainted with the complaints of infants, to go seek out and baptize those whom they shall find to be in danger. It is easy for them to meet them, particularly in the towns and large villages, where, on fair-days, there is to be seen a crowd of poor people reduced to the greatest poverty, who come to ask for alms. It is in winter especially that the number is highest, because want is more pinching at that time. You see then on the roads, at the gates of the towns and villages, or crowded together in the streets, poor people without number, with hardly any clothing, having neither fire nor lodging, sleeping in the open air, and so attenuated by the protracted torture of hunger, that they are nothing but skin and bone. The women, who are, in this case, the most to be pitied, carry on their back children reduced to the same extremity as themselves. Our baptizing men and baptizing women accost them in the gentle accents of compassion, offer them, gratis, pills for these little expiring creatures, give often to the parents a few farthings, always with great kindness of manner, and an expression of the liveliest interest in their situation. For these poor creatures it is a sight of transport almost unheard of. They willingly allow our people to examine into the state of the child, and spill on its forehead some drops of water, which they declare to be good for it, while, at the same time, they pronounce the sacramental words.

"Our Christian baptizers are divided into two classes. Some are travellers, and go to a great distance to look for dying children. Others, being attached to certain stations in the towns and large villages, devote themselves to the same occupation in their neighbourhood. I have just caused to be printed some explicit rules, to direct them, and stimulate them in the exercise of their noble functions." — *Extract from a letter from his Lordship Doctor Perochean, Vicar-Apostolic of Su-Tchuen.*

Who can read the solemn institution of Christian baptism by our blessed Saviour, (Matt. xxviii. 19,) "Go ye, therefore, and teach all nations, baptizing them in the name of the Father, and of the Son, and of the Holy Ghost, teaching them to observe all things whatsoever I have commanded you," and then imagine Xavier and his successors seeking out infants likely to die before they could learn good or evil, the children of heathen parents, and using over them the form of baptism—without pronouncing such work the perversion of a Christian ordinance? I am not able to say whether Xavier began this practice, or to what date in the dark ages it may be traced; but I find abundant proof that such a practice was not allowed in the Primitive Church. For the councils of the universal church debated the question whether infants of heathen parents might be baptized, even when one parent was Christian, or when the infant was given up to sponsors for Christian instruction. Such baptisms were allowed. This allowance is sufficient proof that such baptisms as Xavier's were not allowed; so that the practice of Rome is no less condemned by the judgment of the Primitive Church, than by the letter and spirit of the Gospel of Christ.

Xavier gives a lively description of the character of the Brahmins, only one of whom had embraced the Christian religion, and that one for the sake of obtaining the stipend of a teacher. Xavier expressed his conviction of the deceit, covetousness, oppression, and ignorance of the whole caste. He had only met with one Brahmin who exhibited a candid and intelligent mind. This man had been brought up at one of their chief seats of learning, and informed Xavier that their sacred books affirmed that there is only one God, and that the whole human race will one day be of the same religion. He would have been willing to receive Christian baptism if the fact might have been concealed; but Xavier very properly refused him. On one occasion Xavier visited a temple which supported 200 Brahmins, with whom he held a long discussion on the arcana of their religion, and upon the principal articles of the Christian faith. The Brahmins parted from Xavier with warm expressions of personal regard; but assured him that it was quite impossible for them to give up their maintenance to embrace Christianity.

The following eloquent and animated appeal of Xavier to his friends in Europe to join him in his Missionary labours may well serve to stir up the Missionary zeal of the Protestant Church at the present day:—

"Vast are the numbers in this country who do not become Christians, only because there are none here to bring them over to Christianity. Often does it come into my mind to make the circuit of the Universities of Europe, and especially to visit that of Paris, crying out, even at the risk of being taken for a madman, to those who have more learning than charity, 'Alas! what a great multitude of immortal souls are shut out from heaven and plunged into the depths of eternal misery through your neglect.' Would to God, I often say to myself, that learned men would apply that energy to the conversion of souls which they now apply to the acquisition of knowledge; so that they might be able to render to God a good account both of their learning, and of the talents entrusted to them. Would that many of them might be stirred up by this consideration to apply their minds to divine things, so as to hear what the Lord will say concerning them. Would that they might cast behind them their own inclinations, and the thought of earthly things, and entirely mould themselves to the promptings of the divine will, and say with all their heart and soul, 'Lord, here am I, send me withersoever thou wilt, even to India.' Good God! what a happier and safer life would they then lead; with how much greater confidence in the divine mercy would they in their last moments await the decision of that tribunal which none can escape. Then might they adopt the language of the servant in the Gospel, 'Lord, thou deliveredst unto me five talents; behold, I have gained beside them other five talents.' If only they would bestow the same labour which they now expend by day and night in acquiring knowledge upon turning that knowledge to profit, and if they would give as much attention as they now devote to the study of science to the teaching the ignorant the things necessary to salvation, would they not be far better prepared to answer the Lord when he shall say, 'Give an account of thy stewardship.' I sadly fear that those who apply themselves so long to the study of science in the Universities regard the vain distinctions of honours and of the priesthood apart from their duties and responsibilities. It seems to me that things have now come to such a pass, that men devoted to learning openly profess that they are seeking to procure, by their literary fame, some ecclesiastical preferment, rather than the consecration of talents to Christ and His Church. But how miserably will they deceive themselves who consult their private benefit rather than the public good, and refuse to resign themselves to the divine will, because they fear lest God should not comply with their desires. God is my witness that I have formed the design, since I am myself debarred from returning to Europe, of sending a letter to the University of Paris, and particularly to our Professors Corne and Picard, to show them how many millions of savages might be brought, without any trouble, to the knowledge of Christ, if only there were a sufficient number of men who would seek, not their own things, but the things which are Christ's. Dear brethren, pray the Lord of the harvest that He will send forth labourers into his harvest." (I. 14. Fr. 14.)

The following expressions occur in the conclusion of the same letter:—" I have nothing further to write upon these topics, except that such is the force and abundance of my joys, which God is wont to bestow upon the workers in this part of His vineyard, who diligently labour for the conversion of the heathen, that if there be in this life any solid and true happiness, it is here to be found. I often overhear one who is immersed in these labours exclaiming—O Lord, I beseech thee do not pour out upon me such joy in this life: rather, when it is thy good pleasure so to pour it out upon me, transfer me into the abodes of the blessed. For truly the man who has once tasted, by spiritual perception, the sweetness of thy gift, must find this life bitter without the light of thy countenance." (I. 14. Fr. 14.)

Such were the seraphic feelings expressed in Xavier's annual letters to friends in Europe. But what, it may be asked, were his everyday feelings in the midst of his work? We are furnished with a reply to this inquiry in a very remarkable series of letters written to a brother Missionary upon the same field of labour with himself, and under the varying circumstances of their common work. Twenty-six of these letters are preserved. They were written to Mansilla within ten months,—from February to December 1544,—when they were labouring together on the Fishery Coast. These letters contain the outpouring of Xavier's heart, and reveal thoughts and facts which find no place in his letters to his friends in Europe.

The first letter of this series contrasts strangely with those seraphic expressions of joy in his work which have been just quoted, though written only a few weeks later. He says to Mansilla:—

"God give you patience, which is the first requisite in dealing with this nation. Imagine to yourself that you are in purgatory, and that you are washing away the guilt of your evil deeds. Acknowledge the singular mercy of God in granting you the opportunity for expiating the sins of your youth while you live and breathe, which may now be accomplished by the merit of grace, and at a far less cost of suffering than in the world to come." (I. 15. Fr. 15.)

This idea of the efficacy of sufferings in this life, when endured for God's glory, to diminish the pains of purgatory in the next life, strange as it appears to any one who takes his religion from the Bible, is a favourite notion with Xavier, and with Romish writers of his class. It is an element of their joy in sufferings, which must greatly qualify our estimation of many a glowing page in their writings.*

In another letter to Mansilla, Xavier describes his own state of mind as one of disgust with India, and of earnest desire to get away into other countries. Writing from Manapar, March 21, 1544, he says:—

"I shall turn my thoughts into another direction, and seriously take in hand a design, which has long allured me like a charm, of abandoning India, where so many obstacles to the promulgation of the religion of Christ are raised from quarters where it was least to be expected, and to transfer myself to Ethiopia, where I am called to publish the Gospel by a hope and probability of signally advancing the glory of our Lord God; where there are no Europeans to resist us by overturning what we build up. I do not conceal from you how vehemently I am drawn towards those regions. It is not improbable that I shall soon embark in one of those country vessels called 'dhonies,' of which there are always a large num-

---

* "It is vain to look out for Missionaries for China or Africa, or evangelists for our great towns, or Christian attendants on the sick, or teachers of the ignorant, on such a scale of numbers as the need requires, without the doctrine of Purgatory. For thus the sins of youth are turned to account by the profitable penance of manhood; and terrors, which the philosopher scorns in the individual, become the benefactors and earn the gratitude of nations."— Dr. J. H. Newman's *Essay on the Development of Christian Doctrine.* p. 423.

ber here, and proceed without delay to Goa, to prepare for my journey to the lands of Prester John."* (I. 18. Fr. 18.)

Another letter shall be given in full as a specimen of this series. It not only exhibits a discontented state of mind, bordering upon exasperation, but gives Xavier's low estimate of the morals and habits of the native Christians, as well as of the Europeans, amongst whom he was living.

" *To F. Mansilla.*
" *Manapar, March* 14, 1544.

" MY DEAREST BROTHER IN JESUS CHRIST,—

" Your letters have greatly refreshed me. Again and again I beseech you to behave towards those men, who are the scum (*fæces*) of the human race, as good fathers are in the habit of doing towards their wicked children. Do not suffer yourself to be cast down, however enormous their wickedness may be; for God, whom they so grievously offend, does not exterminate them, as He might do, by His single word. On the contrary, He does not cease to supply their wants. If He were to withdraw

---

* When the Portuguese first became acquainted with the Christian Emperor of Abyssinia, they imagined that they had found the famous Prester John of Tartary! They still continued to call him by that name after the discovery of their mistake; some of the Jesuit Fathers, by way of compromise, calling him " Precious John." (See Geddes' Church History on Ethiopia.)

His merciful hand from them, we should soon see them languish and wither away in the destitution which they deserve. It is in this way that I wish you to maintain an equanimity of temper, and cast from yourself all needless uneasiness.

"In your present position your labours are more fruitful than you think; and although your progress does not come up to your wishes, you make enough, believe me, to have no cause to repent it. Moreover, whatever your success may be, you have this consolation, that you are not there by your own choice; and that, however events may turn out, no fault can be laid to your charge.

"To proceed to other matters. As both reason and precedent teach us that it is often useful to employ force, in order to crush the obstinacy of the more rebellious among these people, who are subjects of his Portuguese Majesty, I send you an apparitor, whom I have obtained from the Viceroy. I have ordered him to inflict a fine of two silver pence, which is the amount of the coin they call a fanam, upon any woman who, in defiance of the public regulations, shall drench herself with the intoxicating drink they call arack; besides which, he shall imprison for three days all who are found guilty of such intemperance. You must see to the rigorous execution of this law in all the villages, and have it published in all the assemblies, so that no drunken woman, when punished, may plead ignorance.

"You must inform the Patangats,* or village headmen, that if, in spite of this, any more arack is drunk, I shall hold them personally responsible.

"Persuade Matthew to behave like a good son towards me. He may be assured, that, if he thus behaves, he will receive more benefits and advantages from me than he could have hoped for from his own parents.

"I cannot yet say when I shall be able to come to you; but, till then, you must enjoin the Patangats to correct their wicked manners. Tell them, that if I find them still plunged in their old vices, I have made up my mind, in virtue of the power which I hold from the Viceroy, to have them apprehended, and carried in chains to Cochin; and they must not flatter themselves with the hope of being soon released with a slight punishment, for I am thoroughly resolved to employ every means in my power to prevent their ever returning to Punicael. It is quite evident that the fault and blame of all the crimes and villanies, of which there are too many which disgrace this country, rests with them alone.

"Take the greatest care to baptize the children immediately after their birth, and to instil the first principles of Christianity into those who begin to show signs of reason, as I have expressly enjoined you.

"You shall publicly catechize, every Sunday, persons of every age and both sexes, in one assembly, and teach

---

* By this term Xavier probably means the Panchayat, or Council of Five, an institution common throughout India.

them prayer and the need of good works, as I was in the habit of doing. It is very useful, also, to add some short moral exhortation.

"Take the greatest pains to discover the workshops where the idols are secretly made and carved.

"With regard to the letter which A. Fogaza has written and addressed to me, do not send it on here, but keep it till I come. May the Lord our God bountifully bestow upon you all the consolations which I ask for myself, both in this life and in the next!

"Your loving brother in Christ,
(I. 16. Fr. 16.) "FRANCIS."

The severe and magisterial threats contained in the foregoing letter were not unusual in Xavier's correspondence. In a subsequent letter the Portuguese Governor of Tuticorin, who had opposed Xavier himself, and oppressed the native Christians, is threatened with the Inquisition. "Tell him that I will write to Prince Henry, the President of the Inquisition at Lisbon, to put the utmost rigours of that ecclesiastical court in force against him as a hinderer of the Gospel." In the same letter he enjoins Mansilla to keep a sharp and careful watch over the native Malabar teachers (*clerici*) associated with him, saying, "If you detect any thing wrong in them, restrain them, for God's sake, and punish them instantly and severely; for we shall have to bear a dreadful load of guilt, which many stripes will hardly serve to expiate, if we neglect to use the plenary power committed to us, carrying it like a sword in a scabbard, instead of punishing offences against God, especially such as are a stumblingblock to the multitude." (II. 5. Fr. 46.)

In another of the letters now under review, Xavier reveals the estimate which he had formed of the character of the government officers in India. Writing to his friend Roderick Bobadilla, at Lisbon, he says, " Suffer no one of your friends to be sent to India in the government service, either for financial or other employments; for of all such it may be said, ' their names are blotted out from the book of life, and they shall not be written among the just.' Whatever confidence you may have in the virtue of any one whom you know and love, yet believe what I say, and resist, with all your might, his being cast upon that risk. For unless he be confirmed in grace, as the Apostles were, you must not hope that he will persevere in the line of duty, or retain his innocence." (II. 3. Fr. 44.)

It is impossible not to be startled at the inconsistency, to use no stronger term, between these letters to his fellow-labourer Mansilla and those which Xavier sent to his friends in Europe. There can, indeed, be little doubt which give the genuine and habitual impressions of Xavier's views and feelings, because the letters to friends in Europe were annual letters, drawn up with great care, as he tells us at a later period of his correspondence, so as to produce the most favourable impression at home, and they were written out by an amanuensis: while the twenty-six letters to Mansilla were spread over less than a year, are evidently the simple effusions of the heart, and reflect the realities of the passing scenes. But how, it will be asked, is Xavier to be acquitted of dishonesty? We are prepared to offer a solution of the difficulty, but we defer it till we are more fully acquainted with Xavier's character and cast of mind, as well as the circumstances of his position.

It is clear that when Xavier had completed his first year's Missionary labour, he had abandoned all idea of the Christian kingdom of pearl fishers, and that all his thoughts were turned from the conversion of poor fishermen into a new channel. His imagination was now filled with the idea of converting the rich and powerful, especially native kings and princes. If they could be induced to profess Christianity, or, at any rate, to countenance its progress, he hoped that the rest of the population would follow their leaders. To this object the second and subsequent years of his labours in India were devoted.

The first Potentate whom Xavier attempted to gain, is called in his letters to Mansilla "the great King of Travancore," named Iniquitribirimus. This King, he tells us, had authority over the whole district of South India. A near relative of that King resided at Tael, about two leagues from Manapar, on the coast. Xavier remained several months at Manapar, carrying on negotiations with the King, and in expectation of being allowed to visit him at his court. But he was suddenly cast down from the very height of his hopes of success by the arrival of three chief men from the King, to complain that certain Portuguese had seized a royal servant, put him into irons, and carried him to Punicael or Tuticorin. The indignation of Xavier was roused at this untoward event, which postponed indefinitely his visit to the King. He ordered Mansilla immediately to procure the instant release of the captive, or else to ascertain precisely the crime of which he was accused, and to remit the case to the King of Travancore for judgment. Xavier gives expression to noble sentiments of indignation at the too frequent violation of the just rights of the natives by the Europeans, who had merely dwelt in their territories for purposes of trade—" Would the Portuguese bear it, if an Indian, who had a quarrel with one of our countrymen, should seize him by force, and carry him away from our territory into the interior? Certainly not. And have not the Indians feelings like ourselves? Why, then, do we act towards them as we would not suffer them to act towards us? Why are we surprised if they resent an injury as we should? If they denied us justice there would be more excuse for an act of violence on our part. But now, whilst they profess themselves ready, with all good faith, to do right—when they observe the laws of society, and carry on trade with us to the utmost of our desires, in all fairness and amity—what plausible excuse can we allege for our violence? with what specious disguise can we cover the reproach of 'covenant-breaking?'" (I. 18. Fr. 18.)

Xavier informs us that he eventually succeeded in pacifying the great King, and in interesting him in the protection of his Christian subjects upon the Fishery Coast. There was already a large body of Syrian Christians living under his protection on the Western coast, who were in a high social position, so that he would not be indisposed to look with favour upon these neophytes. Besides using his influence to shield them from oppression, Xavier incidentally mentions, in one of his letters, that this King had placed 2000 gold fanams in his hands for building Christian churches on the coast.

Those who are acquainted only with the common histories of India, and of its geographical divisions, will be not a little puzzled at the mention of 'the great King of Travancore,' whose sovereignty extended from the West to the East coast, as the kingdom of Travancore, properly so called, was bounded by the ghauts, and the country between the ghauts and the East coast was at that time part of the kingdom of Madura. The best solution which I can offer is, that the whole of South India then formed part of the Hindoo kingdom of Bijanagur, or Bisnaghur, which exercised a general sovereignty over the kingdoms of Travancore, Madura, Tanjore, &c. &c. It appears, from a work published by the Rev. William Taylor, at Madras, 1835, entitled "Oriental Historical Manuscripts in the Tamil language," that the Rayer of Bisnaghur governed fifty-six kingdoms. At the time at which Xavier wrote, the Rayer had placed the southern part of the country under a powerful general named Nagama-Naicker, who had 6000 cavalry and 20,000 infantry to support his authority, and to collect the "peiscush," or royal tribute "from Arcot down to Travancore." This Naicker might have been called "the great King of Travancore." Some confirmation may be derived from D'Anville's maps, which, in some editions, write the name of Travancore across the continent from the West to the East coast. There was the utmost confusion, however, in the names of Indian persons and places by the Portuguese writers of this period, and the Rayer himself might have been Xavier's friend.

An interesting episode to this historical investigation may be inserted. It appears that about this time the King of Tanjore quarrelled with the King of Madura, and expelled him from his capital: the expelled king appealed to the Rayer, who directed Nagama-Naicker to restore the King of Madura. But instead of doing so, he himself seized the vacant throne, and held it till the Rayer sent an army against him. This army was led by Visanatha-Naicker, the son of Nagama-Naicker. The son encountered the father in battle, gained a signal victory, and in the most respectful manner took his father prisoner, and carried him, with all affectionate care, to the Rayer, and there pleaded for and obtained his free pardon.

The persecutions from which Xavier desired to defend the converts, by engaging the protection of the King of Travancore, were chiefly inflicted upon them by the incursions of an armed host, called, by Xavier, "Badages." A letter from Goa by one of the Jesuit Fathers, given by Maffeus (1568—Organtinus Brisciensis), informs us that the Badages were "the collectors of the royal tribute, a race of overbearing and insolent men, and commonly called Nairs," or soldiers. They were probably the 6000 horsemen and 20,000 infantry already mentioned. Xavier gives many very lively descriptions of the anxiety and alarms under which he was kept for many months through this cause.

The Badages had expressed their determination to expel the Christians, both native and foreigners, from the coast. News was brought to Xavier in the summer of 1544, that the Badages had made an incursion upon the Christians of Cape Comorin: some were killed, a large proportion taken away as captives, and the rest driven into caverns of the rocks overhanging the sea, where they were perishing by hunger and thirst. Instantly Xavier freighted twenty of the country boats, called dhonies, with provisions, and started with them himself to succour the distressed Christians; but adverse winds baffled all his attempts to reach the promontory of Cape Comorin. He remained eight days at sea, using every effort, but in vain, and was at last obliged to return to Manapur, to which place many of the wretched fugitives found their way. Xavier having waited in vain for a change of wind, went on foot to Cape Comorin, a distance of fifty miles, and thus describes the scene:— "Never did I witness a more wretched spectacle: at-

tenuated countenances, ghastly with famine; the foul
carnage throughout the country—here unburied corpses,
there the sick and wounded at the last gasp; decrepid
old men fainting through age and want; women giving
birth to children on the public roads, their husbands with
them, but unable to procure help; all in the extremity of
one common destitution;—if you could have looked upon
such a sight, as I did, your heart would also have been
pierced to the quick by pity. I have provided for the
transport of all the poor to Manapar, where already the
greater part of their deeply-afflicted people is receiving
from us the succour we can render. Pray our God that
He will touch the hearts of the rich with pity for
these most unfortunates, withering away in destitution."
(I. 28. Fr. 28.)

Xavier not only made collections in all the towns for
the relief of these victims, but took means to prevent
similar misfortunes falling upon other Christian villages,
first, by providing boats in which the people might embark, with their families and property, upon the alarm of
the Badages; then in organizing a line of watchmen to
give notice; further, by obtaining a gun-boat to protect
the embarkation if necessary; and, lastly, by interceding
with the King of Travancore to repress the violence of
the Badages. He received from his friends at the King's
court the promise that, if the violence of the tax-gatherers
could not be effectually restrained, at least Xavier
should be informed of their intended visits in time for
the flight of the Christians. Later in the year, however,

an attack was made by the Badages upon the Portuguese Governor of Tuticorin, which shall be described in Xavier's own words, as it exhibits a beautiful specimen of lively sympathy, and has been made the basis of a famous legend, to which we shall have occasion afterwards to refer.

" *To Francis Mansilla at Punicael.*
"*Alendaly,* 5 *Sept.* 1544.
" My very dear Brother in Christ,

" I have just received the most terrible news respecting the Governor (of Tuticorin), that his ship has been burnt, and his house on shore also destroyed by fire; that he has himself been robbed of every thing, and has retired to the islands in broken spirits and utter destitution. Fly to his relief, I conjure you in the name of Charity; carry with you as many as you can get together of your people at Punicael, and all the boats which are there filled with provisions, and especially with a supply of fresh water. Use the utmost despatch, for the extremity of the man's distress admits of no delay. I am writing to the (Patangats) Headmen, in the most urgent terms, to render you every possible assistance in discharge of their bounden duty to their Governor. Let them load as many boats as are fit for the service with provisions and fresh water, for it is well known that they are deficient in that necessary. I wish many boats to be sent, that these may be the means of carrying over to the mainland the crowd of all ages, who were driven to take refuge in these inhospitable rocks by the same incursion as drove the Governor thither.

"I would go myself, leaving you at Punicael, if I could believe that my arrival would be agreeable to the Governor; but he lately renounced my friendship, writing letters full of atrocious complaints, in which, among other things, he asserted that he could not even mention, without scandal, the wickedness which had been reported to him respecting me. God and men know whether I ever did him any evil, especially such as he cannot speak of without scandal. But this is not the time for vindicating myself, or complaining of his conduct. As to our present business, it is sufficient to know that he has such feelings towards me, that I ought, for his own sake, to avoid meeting him, lest I should add to the grief of a man in his misfortune, and, by the sight of one whom he hates, increase a calamity already sufficiently great. This fear principally keeps me from going there, although there are other causes to dissuade me from the journey. Do you, for God's sake, perform my part with the most earnest despatch.

"I enjoin the Patangats of Coimbatore and Bembar that they hasten to the place where the Governor is, with the vessels they can collect, laden with provisions and fresh water. And do you devote all your energy to this affair, as you desire to please God, so that you may not have to reproach yourself with any neglect in giving relief to the Governor in time, under calamities which demand the most zealous exertions of charity and compassion. The same calamity has overwhelmed very many Christians also, my solicitude for whom obliges me to entreat you, again and again, that you will omit nothing which may convey prompt and effectual relief to such a terrible catastrophe. May the Lord always be with you. Amen.

"Your very affectionate brother in Christ,

(I. 31. Fr. 34.) "FRANCIS."

At the close of the year 1544, as in the former year, Xavier visited Cochin and Goa, travelling by land to Cape Comorin, and so on to Travancore, from whence he wrote his annual letters to his friends in Europe. His letter to the Society at Rome gives the account of his Missionary journey and voyage from the Fishery Coast to Cochin. The passage is one often referred to, as recording a signal triumph of his Missionary labours, namely, 10,000 converts in a single month. These are the words of Xavier's letter. "In this kingdom of Travancore in which I now am (since I should write something about Indian affairs, of which I know you are most eager for information), God has brought very many (*plurimos*) to the faith of His Son Jesus Christ. In the space of a single month I have made more than 10,000 Christians. In which affair I thus proceeded," &c. (II. 4. Fr. 45.) The letter goes on to describe, in nearly identical terms, the method he had pursued on his first arrival upon the coast.*

* Vide p. 33, &c.

If Xavier really baptized 10,000 in one month, upon the plan explained in a former chapter, it would be a flagrant instance of the hasty and rash administration of a sacred ordinance; but there is reason to believe that the number 10,000 has been inserted by some dishonest copyist. The expression is very unlike Xavier's style. He very seldom gives statistics throughout his correspondence. Besides which, in three other letters written to Europe, at the same time—namely, to the King of Portugal, to Roderick, and to Ignatius Loyola—he makes no reference to the 10,000. Nor does he make any mention of the number, in a letter sent to Francis Mansilla of the same date, but writes thus—"The day before yesterday I landed at Cochin, after having baptized all the Machus, or fishermen, on the coast of Travancore, whom I could visit. . . . At the receipt of this letter, I entreat you, by your love to God, to hasten to Travancore, in order to visit the very many Christians I have just baptized (*quos nuper baptizavi plurimos*). Establish schools in each village for the daily instruction of the children. . . . Anthony Fernandez, a Malabar Christian, will shortly join you, going from hence in a light and expeditious vessel. He will accompany you throughout, and assist you in all your functions, until you have baptized all who remain. He is an excellent Christian, very zealous for the glory of God. He knows perfectly the manners of the people, the means and precautions which we must take with them. Do whatever he tells you. Follow his advice; and let him do whatever he judges to be expedient. He merits your entire confidence. *It is thus that I have acted*, and the event *has justified my course.* Therefore I not only direct and invite you to defer wholly to his counsels, but I beseech and conjure you to do so." (I. 41. Fr. 41.)

Here the matter comes out. All was done through a native interpreter. Writing to distant friends at Rome, Xavier is made boastfully to exclaim, " I have made in one month more than 10,000 Christians!" Writing to a brother Missionary on the spot to follow up the work, he says that all was done by and through Anthony Fernandez, a native interpreter; and with ominous earnestness of entreaty he conjures his brother not to trust to his own judgment, but to follow implicitly whatever the native should judge expedient.

The presumption, therefore, is strong that the original of Xavier's letter to the Jesuit Society contained only the first part of the sentence as it now stands, namely, "God has brought *very many (plurimos)* to the faith of Christ his Son," which is identical with the expression used in the letter to Mansilla, and that the boast, " I have made in one month 10,000 Christians," was a subsequent spurious addition.

But though Xavier's reputation may be relieved from the broad and boastful assertion of "ten thousand" baptisms in one month, in an unknown language, by the help of a native interpreter, yet there remains the most objectionable practice of receiving converts into the Church of Christ in groups and crowds, without any sufficient evidence of their understanding what they are about. This practice prevailed in the national conversions of the middle ages. Xavier revived it. It became the characteristic of Romish Missions. Hence the loose statements, and round numbers, and varying statistics, in which their successes are reported. Romish Missionary reports take no account of the work of God's Holy Spirit on individual souls, which is the chief aim and solace of the true Missionary, and forms the staple of Protestant Missionary Reports; and which has the far higher sanction of the great Apostle of the Gentiles, who, amidst his vast successes in establishing Christianity in new regions, and his overwhelming anxieties in "the care of all the Churches," yet watched and rejoiced over the work of God in the souls of individuals. We look in vain, in Xavier's correspondence, for any indication of that spirit which spoke out in the writings of St. Paul in such passages as these—"My little children, of whom I travail in birth till Christ be formed in you." "We live if ye stand fast in the Lord." "Whom we teach, warning every man, and teaching every man in all wisdom, that we may present every man perfect in Christ Jesus."

Xavier returned from Goa to the Fishery Coast early in 1545, but only to pass on to a more northerly seaport, for a purpose which belongs to the history of his abandonment of India, and which will be, therefore, related in the next section.

SECTION 3.—*Xavier's abandonment of India, inconsistencies of Xavier's character.*

Xavier's visit to Goa Dec. 1544 had important political objects in view, which formed the turning-point of his Indian career. He had to settle accounts with another royal personage. In the previous summer the fishermen of the Island of Manaar, adjacent to Ceylon, who were of the same caste as those upon the opposite coast of India, sent a deputation to invite him to visit them. The Island of Manaar was at that time under the rule of the King of Jaffnapatam, whose authority extended over the northern part of Ceylon. Xavier, not being able to go to Manaar himself, sent another priest, who baptized many of them; upon which the King cruelly put a large number to death. Upon this horrible occurrence Xavier had recourse at once to the sword of Portugal, to coerce the King of Jaffnapatam. He would have hastened to Goa, he tells us, as soon as he heard the news, if he had not been detained by the calamities caused by the Badages. But as soon as he could leave the coast he hastened to Cochin, from thence to Goa; and not finding the Viceroy there, he went on to Cambay, to lay the matter before him. The result of his interview shall be given in his own words :—

"The Viceroy received the intelligence of the lamentable slaughter of the neophytes with such indignation, that almost as soon as I had opened the subject to him, he gave orders for the arming of a strong fleet of ships for the destruction of that tyrant, so that I was myself obliged to moderate his anger. The King, who murdered the Christians, has an elder brother, the true heir to the crown, who is an exile through fear of his brother's cruelty. This man has promised that, if the Viceroy will place him on the throne, he and all his princes would turn Christians. The Viceroy has therefore given his generals commands to restore the elder brother to the throne of Jaffnapatam, on condition of his receiving baptism, and to put to death the King who slew the neophytes, or else to deal with him as I shall determine. Indeed, I confidently hope that, through the intercession of those whom he has made martyrs, he will be brought to acknowledge his crime and his blindness, and, by salutary penitence, will at length obtain pardon from God for his atrocious cruelty." (II. 4. Fr. 45.) Again, Xavier's sanguine temperament built up splendid triumphs upon the prospect of this hostile expedition to evangelize Jaffnapatam. He thus expresses his hopes to the King of Portugal :—" In Jaffnapatam and the opposite coast more than 100,000 will easily be added to the Church of Christ."

Notwithstanding, however, the prompt acquiescence of the Viceroy in Xavier's projects, it would seem that Xavier was far from being satisfied with the Viceroy's general administration; for he writes a very solemn letter to the King of Portugal upon His Majesty's responsibility before the bar of God's judgment for the atrocities committed by his representatives in India; and he refers His Majesty to the confidential information which he was sending through Michael Vaz, who was about to visit Portugal. This confidential mission of Michael Vaz to the King of Portugal is also referred to in Xavier's letters to Roderick. The biographies give the following account of the issue:—" Michael Vaz negotiated so well with John III., by following the instructions of the Father Xavier, that he obtained another Governor of India, who brought out orders almost such as the Father wished them to be, signed with the Prince's own hand. These orders were, that no pagan superstition would be tolerated in the island of Goa nor in that of Salsette; that they should break all the idols that were there; that they should search in the houses of the heathen for those that were concealed there; that they should punish the makers of them; that they should punish every Brahmin who would oppose the preaching of the Gospel; that they should comfort the poor infidels newly converted with an annual income of a thousand crowns, which should be paid out of the mosque of Bassein; that they should confer no more public offices on the pagans; that no exaction shall remain unpunished; that they should sell no more slaves to the Mohammedans or the heathen; that the pearl fishing should be entirely in the hands of Christians; that the pearls should be taken from them only at their first value; that the King of Cochin should not be suffered to ill-treat the baptized Indians; in short, that if Soza had not avenged the death of the Christians of Manaar, massacred by order of the King of Jaffnapatam, Castro, who succeeded Soza, would not fail to do it."

In the letter of Xavier, in which he speaks of the Island of Manaar, he also mentions a visit which he himself made to Ceylon. "I lately went to the island of Ceylon, with Mansilla as my companion. Here a prince, the son of the King, and the heir of the kingdom, had determined to become a Christian; which, as soon as the King knew, he commanded the prince to be put to death. Those who were present at the execution say that he saw in heaven a fiery cross, and that on the spot in which he was killed there appeared a fissure in the earth of the form of a cross; and that many of the inhabitants who witnessed these prodigies are inclined to Christianity. The brother of the prince of whom I have spoken, moved by these miracles, prevailed upon a certain priest to baptize him, and then fled to the Viceroy of India, to ask his help against the King, who had killed his brother. I met and spoke with this very prince in his journey; and from his conversation I have conceived a great hope that, in a little time, that kingdom will become Christian, for the people are greatly moved by those prodigies and signs; and the crown will descend to the prince who was lately baptized." (II. 4. Fr. 45.)

Xavier, filled with bright hopes of success to the cause of Christ from the hostile expedition against the King of Jaffnapatam, hastened through the Fishery Coast to Negapatam, the nearest port of India to Jaffnapatam, to await the result. But unhappily for Xavier's hopes, that arm of flesh on which he was leaning again deceived him, like a broken reed, "on which, if a man lean, it will go into his hand and pierce it." In the curt style which Xavier is accustomed to adopt when his temper is tried, he writes—" The Jaffnapatam expedition has come to nothing; therefore the King, who had promised to become a Christian, is not restored: an accident put an end to the affair. One of the King of Portugal's merchant vessels, laden with silks from Pegu, and bound to India, was driven ashore within the dominions of Jaffnapatam by a tempest. The King seized the silks. The Portuguese chose rather to recover what they had lost than to prosecute the war; but if it be the will of God, let it be done." (II. 6. Fr. 47.)

This disappointment dissolved the last links of Xavier's attachment to India. He could no longer remain in those parts. The prospects which he had once indulged respecting Ethiopia had given place to brighter prospects among the islands of the Indian Archipelago, where he had heard that Missionaries had made many converts, and that three princes had embraced the Christian faith. These inviting prospects he had expatiated upon, in his letters, at the commencement of the year (1545), to his friends in Portugal. They occupied his mind while he was waiting at Negapatam for the result of the expedition against the King of Jaffnapatam. Nothing, he assures Mansilla, but the Jaffnapatam affair detained him. As soon, therefore, as he heard of its failure, he turned his back on his former fields of labour, and made his way to St. Thomé, near the modern Madras, from whence he sought a ship to Malacca.

Xavier wrote to his friends at Goa justifying his leaving the Fishery Coast on the plea that he was no longer wanted there. Writing from Amboyna (May 1546), he thus describes the Missionary operations in South India as he had left them:—" Before I embarked I took special care that the Comorin Christians should have no lack of spiritual aid. I placed over them five Priests, namely Francis Mansilla of our order, three natives, and Francis Lisianus, a Spaniard. The Christian inhabitants of the island of Ceylon, which is not far from Cape Comorin, are admirably instructed by two Franciscans and as many Priests. The fact is, therefore, that neither Church needs my labour. Other native Christians, who are in the Portuguese cities, are instructed by the Vicars of the Bishops. As soon as I perceived that my labours were not at all needed in India, I went to St. Thomé, on my way to Macassar." (II. 17. Fr. 58.)

Xavier's labours not at all needed in India! What, then, was the meaning of his earnest appeal to the Universities of Europe to send fresh labourers to reap the fields white to harvest? It is clear that after the fishery villages under the suzereignty of Portugal, and the Portuguese settlements were provided for, Xavier despaired of further success in India, and therefore he caught at the shadow of a more hopeful triumph at Macassar: which, as we shall see in the sequel, melted away in its turn from his grasp.

Xavier explains in another letter, that while he was praying at the shrine of St. Thomas his mind had been filled with joy at the prospect of new fields of labour. He took these very natural sensations of a sanguine temperament as a token of the divine approbation of his departure from India. So fixed was his determination to depart, that he declares, that if no Portuguese ship would take him, he would sail in a heathen or Mohammedan ship, or even in an open boat: so determined was Francis Xavier to turn his back upon the unconverted millions of India.

Before closing this section it will be proper to advert to the numerical results of Xavier's Missionary labours in India. An indistinct impression universally prevails, that however hastily he administered baptism, a vast multitude voluntarily submitted themselves to the ordinance. The expressions in the letter to the Society at Rome, that his hand and his voice failed through fatigue in repeating the baptismal service, and that in one month he baptized 10,000, in Travancore, have passed from mouth to mouth and have been received as unquestionable facts. Certain other vague assertions have also been unhesitatingly admitted, that his converts were numbered by hundreds of thousands. Putting aside, however, uncertain tales, it is not difficult to form a pretty sure estimate of his actual success from contemporary authorities.

His letters distinctly define his fields of labour to have been on the east and west of Cape Comorin. He visited Ceylon, and attempted in vain to gain access to Jaffnapatam in the north of the island; but he never claimed any converts from this field: it had been cultivated by the Missionaries of a different order, namely, the Franciscans. The results of Xavier's labours must therefore consist simply of the additions which he made to the Comorin Christians, who had professed themselves Christians many years before his arrival, to the number, it is said, of 20,000. Xavier's letters give no statistics except the very questionable account of 10,000 baptisms in Travancore.

The earliest collection of original documents is a volume entitled Epistolæ Indicæ (Louvaine, 1566) which contains statements of the number of " Comorin Christians" in four separate letters of different dates. Father M. Gaspar, general superintendent of the Missions, in a letter dated January 1553, estimates the Christians at Cape Comorin, at 60,000. Father A. Brandonius (or Blandonius), writing from Goa, 1554, accurately distinguishes each station occupied by the Jesuit Missionaries by the latitude of the place; and after giving the latitude of Cape Comorin, says, that in the coast extending from that point there are, more or less, 12,500 Christians. Father A. Quadrus, writing from Goa immediately after his arrival in India, Dec. 1555, says he hears that the Comorin Christians are 300,000. Father P. L. Frois, writing from Goa, Dec. 1560, estimates the Comorin Christians at 80,000. These variations in the numbers will naturally excite the suspicion that they refer to different limits of the field of labour. This is made clear by the "Commentary" of Acosta, 1570, being a digest of the Epistolæ Indicæ, published up to that time, which states, "In 1565 the Christians of Cape Comorin, of Goa, and of the mountain regions of Cochin, were 300,000."

Here, then, is the solution of the wide varieties in the estimates of the different writers quoted above. Goa had a large nominally Christian population. The mountain regions of Cochin, included the Syrian Christians, who had been established there for ten centuries at least, and whom the Portuguese endeavoured to bring under the dominion of Rome, and numbered in their statistics of the native converts. The number of Syrian Christians was not known at that time, but was variously stated at 100,000 and 300,000. The accurate statement of Father A. Brandonius, therefore, shows that Xavier's neophytes to the east of Cape Comorin numbered 12,500. The number remarkably agrees with the number of villages mentioned by Xavier to be thirty. These villages mostly retain their names and character to the present day, and may be estimated to have contained, on an average, not more than 400 inhabitants each, which would give a total of 12,000. If to these be added a large allowance for the converts to the west of the Cape in Travancore, so hastily visited and baptized by Xavier in 1544, the whole number of Comorin Christians may be estimated at 20,000, which is the number, according to Tursellinus, of those who originally stipulated with the Viceroy to become Christians upon their receiving Portuguese protection in their craft.

The caste of fishermen on that coast retain their nominal Christianity to the present day. But they seem never to have spread, or to have exercised any influence upon the surrounding heathen. The Comorin Christians are to be distinguished from the converts who were afterwards made by the Jesuit Missionaries at Madura and in the Mysore, by a Mission first commenced by the famous Jesuit, Robert de Nobili in 1626, upon the principle of avoiding the error committed, as he asserted, by Francis Xavier, in addressing himself to low-caste natives. To this Xavier's failure was attributed. Robert de Nobili, therefore, practised the most unjustifiable deceptions, professing himself to be a Brahmin from the north, forging a Veda, and addressing himself only to high-caste natives. Upon this principle, considerable numbers were brought over to a nominal profession of spurious Christianity. These facts will be noticed in a subsequent part of this volume.

If we trace the history of the Comorin Christians we find them described by a Jesuit Father, Peter Martin, who resided amongst them in 1699, while studying the Tamil language and learning the habits and idolatrous practices of a native, that he might afterwards enter the Madura Mission under that deceptive character. He describes them as still confined to the fishing villages upon the coast. The Danish Missionaries who were stationed at Tranquebar about 1706, and who had many opportunities of ascertaining the state of these converts, represent them as little distinguished from the heathen around them, and as conforming to many of their customs. In this state they were found by the English Protestant Missionaries who have since occupied Tinnevelly, in which the fishery villages are for the most part situated; and by their labours some scriptural light has been diffused amongst the Romish native Christians. Many intelligent and serious native Romanists now annually join the Protestant Missions. The Romish Missionaries, after withholding the Scriptures from the people for three centuries, have been at last compelled to publish a Tamil version of the New Testament for the use of their congregations, to prevent their supplying themselves with Protestant versions.

We have thus brought to a close the first period of Xavier's labours in the East, namely, the three years spent in South India. This review cannot but leave upon the mind a strong conviction of Xavier's inconsistency of character. He was a man of strong impulses, of quick transitions of feeling, liable to pass from extravagant hope to unreasonable despair. This we conceive to be the solution of the contradictions in his letters. He probably wrote from the impulse of the moment. He lacked, in fact, that stable confidence in the enterprise he had taken in hand, which every true Missionary derives from a supreme regard to the word of God. It is impossible otherwise to reconcile his sudden abandonment of India, after so short and imperfect a trial, with his previous professions of spiritual comfort and success in his work,—or his sublime appeals to men of learning and science in the Universities of Europe to become his associates, with the fact that his chief comfort was the baptism of moribund infants, and the dumb show of a crowd of adult worshippers. It is impossible also to reconcile, on Christian principles, the various offices which he attempted to sustain. At one time he was the preacher of love and peace; at another the agent of the cruel and accursed Inquisition; at another the instigator of a crusade. Compare the two pictures— See Xavier on the Fishery Coast, toiling in the instruction of Christian neophytes, and professing to find his chief joy in divine consolations: he appears as an apostle. See Xavier at Negapatam, on the look out for the earliest intelligence of a hostile and murderous expedition, which he himself had instigated, for the advancement of true religion: in what did his spirit then differ from that of a Mussulman?

It will not, indeed, be fair to judge Xavier altogether by the standard of the Primitive Church, or of the Missionary spirit of the present day. We must not forget that he belonged to a Church which canonized Charlemagne, of whom a church historian writes, "He engaged in a sanguinary war against the Saxons for the purpose of converting them to the Christian religion. It seemed as if that zealous prince was, for a season, possessed by the spirit of the Arabian, and that he imitated the fury of his armed apostles; and as if Christianity had not already sufficiently suffered by adopting the vices of other systems, Charlemagne dragged into its service the most savage principle of Islamism. After eight years of resistance and misfortune, the Saxons were compelled to take refuge in the profession of the Gospel, and the Huns of Pannonia were soon afterwards driven, by the same victorious compulsion, to the same necessity." (Dean Waddington's History of the Church, Ch. x.) From the reign of Charlemagne till the times of Xavier, through eight centuries, the Church of Rome spread Christianity mainly by the sword, sometimes accompanying the evangelists, but far oftener preceding them. If we cast our eye over the first chapters of Mosheim's Church History of each of these centuries, in which the historian relates "the prosperous events which happened to the Church" in each century, we shall see that Christianity was introduced into Sweden and Denmark by a king placed on the throne by the sword of Lewis the Meek, and supported by his authority. In the tenth century, Otho the Great made the national profession of Christianity a condition of peace with conquered tribes. In the twelfth century, "no Prince appears with a more distinguished lustre than Waldemar I., King of Denmark, who acquired an immortal name by the glorious battles he fought against the pagan nations, such as the Sclavonians, Venedi, Vandals, and others, who, either by their incursions or revolt, drew upon them the weight of his victorious arm.

He unsheathed his sword, not only for the defence and happiness of his people, but also for the propagation and advancement of Christianity." (Mosheim, Cent. xii. Ch. 1.) The Augustinian Missionary, Mainard, having preached the Gospel with no effect in Livonia, as a Missionary, was consecrated a Bishop, and declared a "holy war" against that obstinate people. His successor, Bishop Berthold, marched into his see " at the head of a powerful army, which he had raised in Saxony, preached the Gospel sword in hand, and proved its truth by blows instead of arguments. Albert the Third, Bishop of Livonia, followed, with a barbarous enthusiasm, the same military methods of conversion that had been practised by his predecessors." In the thirteenth century the paganism of Prussia was subdued by "booted Apostles," in the persons of the Teutonic knights, settled there by Conrad, Duke of Massovia. (Mosheim.)

These are the principal so-called triumphs of the Church of Rome in the propagation of the Christian faith during the eight centuries preceding the age of Xavier. Such precedents may be fairly cited as some excuse for Xavier's military methods of conversion. But the portion of blame of which Xavier is thereby relieved falls back with increased weight upon the church to which he belonged.

It is to be feared that this sentiment of "military conversions" has not yet died out in the Romish Church. The sword of France has been in modern times, as of old, unsheathed to open the way for Romish Missionaries in the islands of the Pacific. Even while these sheets are passing through the press we read the speech of a French Minister of State, which declares, respecting the late military expedition to China—" We went into the extreme East, and shed the blood of France there, to represent the spirit of religion, and plant that cross which is the symbol of the empire and of civilization." (Speech of M. Billault in the Senate. *Times*, Feb. 27, 1862.) The story of Cochin-China adds another sad illustration of these anti-Christian proceedings.

CHAPTER III.

Legendary Life of Francis Xavier.

CONTRADICTIONS BETWEEN XAVIER'S LETTERS AND THE STATEMENTS OF HIS BIOGRAPHERS—THE STORY OF THE BADAGES — THE WORKING OF MIRACLES ATTRIBUTED TO XAVIER IN DEFIANCE OF THE CONTRARY EVIDENCE OF HIS OWN LETTERS—THE STEALTHY AND DELUSIVE INTRODUCTION OF ROMISH MIRACULOUS LEGENDS, CONTRASTED WITH THE CREDIBILITY OF THE MIRACLES OF THE NEW TESTAMENT.

WE have hitherto given the account of Xavier's labours in India from his own reports. We are therefore in possession of the truth of his history, as to all the events recorded in those reports. Let us proceed to inquire what additional information may be gleaned from his biographers.

A comparison of Xavier's own narrative, with the statements of his biographers, will at once show that all their main facts have been taken from his letters, but that these facts have been very clumsily put together; and that the truth of the history is often distorted, and often lost amidst a redundancy of detail, such as none but an eye-witness could have supplied; whilst the circumstances of the case, and the distance of time at which his biographers wrote, prove that they did not possess the advantage of eye-witnesses.

The additional facts supplied by the biographers, which are not found in the letters, are nearly all of a marvellous and miraculous character. Many of these marvellous stories have been manifestly fabricated by persons who had no just conception of Xavier's character. They fall far below the moral standard which justly belongs to him; and many are artful, though flimsy expansions of Xavier's own narrative into extravagant or miraculous romances. One example may be cited. A story is thus told by Bohours. The Badages entered the kingdom of Travancore with an army, to ravage the country, and to destroy the Christians. The King of Travancore collected an army to oppose them. As the two armies were marching to a bloody contest, Xavier, with a company of fervent Christians, and a crucifix in his hand, met the enemy, and forbade them, in the name of the living God, to pass further. These few words, and the sight of the saint, struck the enemy with amazement and terror; and all of them fled with a precipitate confusion.

Let us trace back this story to the pages of the first biographer, Tursellinus. The account there stands thus. A company of Badages made an irruption into Travancore, to lay waste the Christian villages. Xavier happened to be there at the time, and flew into the midst of them. The enemy were struck with astonishment at his boldness and his rebukes, but rushed on to the attack. Xavier threw himself into the front of the Christians, ready to protect his flock by his authority, or to die with them. "The Badages could not resist the fervid spirit which flashed from his eyes and countenance, and, out of reverence for Francis, spared the rest." From this version the opposing army of the King of Travancore, and the precipitate flight of the Badages at the sight of Xavier and his crucifix, have disappeared.

Let us go twenty-five years further back, to the "Commentary" of Acosta, which relates the circumstance thus:—" Xavier, resolutely and fervently denouncing the wickedness of the Badages, threw himself into the midst of the Christians, that they might spare the rest, out of respect for him." In this version the ravages of the Badages are only partially commenced when Xavier throws himself among the Christians.

In Xavier's own letters to Mansilla all the circumstances of the irruption of the Badages are vividly described. To these letters reference has already been made. It appears from them that Xavier visited the despoiled Christians; in one case after the affray was over; and in another case he would have gone and thrown himself into the midst of the victims for their relief, but he was restrained by a fear of wounding the morbid feelings of one of their number, and so he sent Mansilla in his stead. Acosta and Tursellinus had not the letters to Mansilla before them; for these were brought from Goa many years after their histories were published. They were misled, therefore, by some blind account of the affair; and the geographical blunder already noticed respecting the King of Travancore, and their ignorance that the Badages were the collectors of his tribute, led them to place the scene of the narrative in Travancore Proper. But Bohours, though he had in his hands the facts of the case, in the letters of Xavier to Mansilla, expands the story of Acosta and Tursellinus into the legend which has been given above, making the King of Travancore raise an army to oppose his own tax-gatherers! And this legend has served its purpose; for it has been often cited by Protestant eulogists as a proof of Xavier's Christian heroism, and of his commanding powers over the minds of savages.

This shameless fabrication by Xavier's biographers lies within a very small compass. Any one who will take the trouble of reading the letters to Mansilla, and compare them with the biographies, may satisfy himself upon the subject.

It would be easy to point out, even in the part of Xavier's history already given, numerous similar fabrications: but it will be unnecessary after this specimen. It is right, however, to except one of Xavier's biographers from these censures. John de Lucena, a Portuguese Jesuit, and Professor in the University of Evora, wrote a life of Xavier in Portuguese, in 1600, which appears to be far more sober and carefully considered than that of Tursellinus, published a few years earlier. I have no doubt that a comparison of Lucena with

Tursellinus and Bohours, would serve to dissipate far more than half of their legends. But I have thought it needless to enter upon this work, having taken the shorter method of bringing all legends to the test of Xavier's own letters.

It is more important to pass on to another point in which the biographers have the hardihood to contradict the positive assertions of their hero; namely, by ascribing to him the power of working miracles. In this case, also, we may trace back most of the miracles reported by the more modern biographers to their very diminutive proportions in the ealier record. In one respect, indeed, the analogy with the story of the Badages fails. Xavier's letters do not afford the slightest foundation for the alleged miracles; whilst it is manifest, from an incident already related, that he was not indisposed to claim the power of working miracles; for the birth of the child at the moment of the mother's baptism is termed by him "a miracle," though it is common to this day, in the same parts of India, for the women under such circumstances to send for a heathen priest to make a charm, or at times for a Missionary. In the same style Xavier speaks of heathen infants "miraculously" sustained in life till he had baptized them, and of their then dying that they might go to heaven as his intercessors. Things also marvellous in the natural world are noticed by Xavier in his letters; *e. g.* He saw in Malacca a he-goat suckling two kids, and advised the owner to send it to Portugal as a sight. His readiness to believe in the occurrence of miracles in that day appears further from his relation of the fissure of the earth, in the form of a cross, which had occurred in Ceylon, and of a fiery cross in the heavens at the grave of the murdered prince.

The omission, therefore, in Xavier's own letters, of any allusion to such miracles, as his biographers attribute to him, especially as those letters profess to describe all important occurrences, might well shake the belief of any candid Romanist in their truth. But this is not all. Xavier's own words, in many cases, distinctly negative the possibility of the alleged miracle having occurred. It is not merely that he makes no mention of having such a power, but that his statement of facts is at direct variance with his biographers. Yet the Church of Rome has had the hardihood to fix upon Francis Xavier, despite himself, the reputation of working miracles; to sacrifice his truthfulness, in order to maintain his miracles; and to convict him of systematic falsehood, in order to put his name in the calendar of Roman Saints.

One species of miracle may be taken as an example of palpable contradiction between Xavier and his biographers, namely, the gift of tongues. Bohours asserts, during Xavier's labours among the Travancore Fishermen—"It was at this time when God first communicated to Xavier the gift of tongues." Then follows the recital of the Badages. Yet a letter written to Mansilla, in the midst of these events, contains the confession, already quoted in a former chapter, of Xavier's total incapacity of making himself understood, and of his dependence upon his interpreter, Anthony. This interpreter, he also tells us, he took with him to Travancore, and acted through him in his baptisms on that coast, till their arrival at Cochin. In a letter written to Ignatius Loyola, immediately after his arrival at Cochin, January, 1554, giving an account of his labours for the last year, he says—" I have no news to tell you, except that we have so few labourers, that you should send us as many as possible." (II. 2.) No news! though, as his biographer asserts, he had then just received the gift of tongues! So shamelessly do the biographers of Xavier contradict Xavier's own narrative.

A matter of wider interest and importance than the truth of legends is involved in this subject. The reputed miracles of Xavier are referred to in Paley's invaluable work on the Evidences of Religion, as presenting an illustration of the contrast between false pretensions to miraculous powers and the truth of the Gospel History of our Lord and his Apostles. This subject has a special interest in the present day, and it will be well, therefore, to pursue the accounts of Xavier's miracles somewhat into detail, in order to expose the shifts to which the Church of Rome has been put in the maintenance of its pretensions to the divine sanction of miracles.

The strength of Paley's argument consists in the two following propositions:—

" I. That there is satisfactory evidence that many, professing to be original witnesses of the Christian miracles, passed their lives in labours, dangers, and sufferings, voluntarily undergone in attestation of the accounts which they delivered, and solely in consequence of their belief of those accounts; and that they also submitted, from the same motives, to new rules of conduct."

"II. That there is *not* satisfactory evidence, that persons professing to be original witnesses of other similar miracles, in their nature as certain as these are, have ever acted in the same manner, in attestation of the accounts which they delivered, and properly in consequence of their belief of those accounts."

Let us judge by these criteria of the authenticity of Xavier's alleged miracles. Where are original witnesses? His own letters negative the supposition of his performance of miracles. Many letters are in existence, written during Xavier's lifetime by his associates, none of which give any indication of Xavier's miracles.

The earliest reference to Xavier's miracles is found in a letter dated two years after his death, and recorded in a volume published in Europe a few years later. The precise nature of that reference shall be stated presently. But first let it be observed that the volume in which the account of miracles appears, is entitled "Epistolæ Indicæ de stupendis et præclaris rebus, quas Divina bonitas in India et variis insulis per societatem nominis Jesu operari dignatus est, in tam copiosa Gentium ad fidem conversione. Louvain, 1566." The book was compiled by a Jesuit Father, who states in his preface that he had put together, in a readable form, extracts from a multitude of letters, to prove against heretics the signs of Apostleship, and the stupendous miracles of the Church of Rome. So that the Jesuit Fathers who first promulgated Xavier's miracles, instead of sacrificing their personal interests, as in Paley's proposition, had the strongest motives for asserting and giving currency to the miracles. The establishment of Xavier's miracles served to strengthen the cause of their Church in a controversy with Protestantism, and especially to gain credit to the Jesuit order, which was, at that time, assailed and censured even within the Church of Rome. Compilations of "Letters from India," with these objects in view, soon became numerous and so full of palpable legends as to disgust Romanists themselves. Another Jesuit Father, John Hayes, a Scotchman, published a volume of Letters at Antwerp, 1605, in the Dedication of which he distinguishes the collection of Maffeus as "in the judgment of all learned men, pure both from all defilement of falsehoods and of barbarisms." This sufficiently indicates the character of the generality of such books.

Let us turn, however, to the particular consideration of the first published assertion of Xavier's miracles in the volume of Epistolæ Indicæ, 1566. There will be found in this volume two letters written from India to Europe, conveying the account of Xavier's death, and both, probably, sent by the same ships. The one is from the Rector of the Goa College, Melchior Nunez, who went to Malacca very soon after he had received the news, and wrote from thence to Ignatius Loyola.

The other letter is by Arius Brandonius, who remained at Goa, and was directed by Melchior to write to the Jesuit College at Coimbra the full account of Xavier's death and burial. Both letters are dated in 1554. Now one of these letters, that of A. Brandonius, makes no mention of Xavier's miracles, and uses language which goes far to negative his belief in them. The other timidly asserts that some persons reported that Xavier had wrought miracles.

The letter of Arius Brandonius is full of admiration and affection for Xavier, and says—" Truly, my very dear brethren, we owe him much, because he has left us the most illustrious pattern of patience under the endurance of labour, ignominy, and injury; through which he brought a multitude of souls into the path of truth; and he persevered in his course from first to last, with such energy of mind, and such alacrity, that the men of this present day will hardly believe the things told of him, as they seem to exceed human strength." It is pretty clear that the writer of such a sentence had no idea in his mind of Xavier's possession of miraculous powers.

The other letter from Melchior Nunez, uses these remarkable words—" Many persist in the affirmation that Xavier raised a dead person to life at Cape Comorin;" and adds two other reported miracles, viz. Xavier's knowledge of the secret thoughts of another person, which he gives upon the authority of John Durus or Deiro, who had been discarded by Xavier, as his biographers assert, for stealing and lying. The other reputed miracle was the restoration of sight to a blind man in Japan; this is given upon the authority of Paul, the Japanese, who had remained in Japan after Xavier's departure, and the story must therefore have reached Melchior by hearsay.

The bearing of the testimony of these two writers, Nunez and Brandonius, upon the credibility of Xavier's reputed miracles, is very remarkable. They had both been some years in India, both had resided at Goa, the centre of all information in the East. They were both writing officially to parties in Europe, and wrote under the strongest impulse to do justice to Xavier's reputation, and in the belief that a posthumous miracle had been wrought in respect of Xavier's corpse. Yet the one negatives the idea of Xavier's miracles; the other gives the rumour of miracles having been wrought in distant and obscure localities, and rests these rumours upon insufficient and delusive authorities.

Another letter in the same volume was written from Goa a year later, December 8, 1555, by Anthony Quadrus, to a provincial of the Jesuit Order in Portugal. The writer had but just arrived in India, and could not have had personal acquaintance with Xavier. He records the marvels he heard there of the success of the Jesuits in India; and gives, in the form of positive assertion, an extended list of Xavier's miracles, namely,—The healing of many sick,—The casting out devils from possessed persons in Comorin,—The gift of prophecy,—

The raising a dead man to life,—The curing of three men in Japan—a dumb man, a paralytic, and a deaf man.

The story of raising a dead man to life was published eighteen years after Xavier's death by Acosta, in his "Commentary," in the following terms:—" A young man had died who had a large circle of relatives. A number of the townspeople brought the corpse with great clamour to Xavier, who, taking him by the hand, raised him to life. The fact was constantly affirmed at Goa. Xavier returned to Goa not long afterwards, and resided with James Borbon at the College of the Faith. Borbon greatly desired to be certified of the matter from Xavier himself, and therefore invited Cosmus John, the King's Advocate (Procuratorem Regium) that they might both together inquire about it of Xavier. Cosmus, restrained by delicacy, left the matter to James Borbon. He, having undertaken it, a few days afterwards, addressing Xavier by name, said, 'For the praise and glory of the Lord, I beseech you, Master Francis, what was the fact respecting the young man whom you recovered from death at Cape Comorin?' At those words Xavier blushed, and, embracing his friend, said, with a smile, 'Good Jesus! could I raise the dead? O, wretch that I am! They brought to me a young man to all appearance dead. Being commanded by me, in the name of the Lord, he rose up. That appeared, indeed, to the people a new thing.' James Borbon, afterwards relating these things to Cosmus, said, 'I cannot doubt but that Xavier, through divine power, raised that young man from the dead. (Ad ea verba Xaverius nimirum erubiit, hominemque amplexatus, atque subridens, Jesu bone, ait egone ut mortuos excitaverim? O me nequam! Juvenem ad me, mortui specie, attulerant: jussus a me surgere nomine Dei surrexit: ea videlicet populo nova res visa). If the words of Xavier be correctly reported, it is to be regretted for his credit's sake that he did not say more or less. But the story must have come to Acosta through many hands.

It is not a little curious to notice how the more candid Lucena was puzzled by finding a report of Xavier's raising the dead in a letter of a Jesuit brother, Amador da Costa, dated from China, Nov. 23, 1567. The letter contained these words:—" I have seen a priest of our company, of the age of thirty years; when he was a child, his friends having already wept for him, and prepared him for burial, Father Francis, of blessed memory, took him by the hand, and said to him, 'Arise, in the name of Jesus:' and so he arose; and from that hour resolved to serve God as a Jesuit." Now, by the dates as they stand, the story may be the old one of the "young man" on the Fishery Coast, though this would make "the young man" about five years old. But Lucena, through some unaccountable mistake or miscalculation, makes the date of the child's birth 1547, which makes the reputed miracle fall in the year of Xavier's death, when the letters of Xavier negative any occurrence on which it could be grounded. Lucena does not attempt to solve the mystery, and confesses to the uncertain and weak reports on which the Romish miracles were founded in these remarkable words. "Brother Amador da Costa has shown himself so little inquisitive as not to particularize the part of India in which our Lord worked this miracle by His servant. We have already noticed that all our brethren act in the same way in their relations of marvellous works." (Lucena, B. x. Ch. 26.) This is the nearest approach to the evidence of an "original witness" which I have found; yet it completely breaks down upon investigation. Upon such flimsy foundations the Church of Rome builds her faith!

Four years after the death of Xavier, the King of Portugal wrote to the Viceroy of India to collect all the information attainable respecting Xavier. The letter is given in Acosta's "Commentary." It does not expressly name his miracles. The expression is, "all the illustrious acts of the man, and the things which the Lord has accomplished, beyond the powers of human nature, through his instrumentality, whether whilst he was alive, or after his death—"res quas per eum sive adhuc viventem, sive defunctum Dominus noster supra naturæ vires effecit." Again, all who could give information respecting Xavier's life, deeds, and behaviour—"de vita, factis, moribusque"—were to be interrogated upon oath. The information thus obtained was to be authenticated by the most rigid formalities, and to be transmitted in triplicate copies to Portugal.

It is easy to perceive that the responses to such a

King's letter would contain all the wonderful stories which were afloat. Here was an additional and strong motive supplied to all the official persons in India to report miracles of Xavier, in order to gratify their royal patron. Emmanuel Acosta states, in his Commentary, published eighteen years after Xavier's death, that he had seen the documents sent over from India in reply to the King's letter, and that he gives the chief particulars in that Commentary. His list of miracles is, nevertheless, but little extended or varied beyond those already noticed. He asserts the raising of *two* dead persons to life, together with the gift of prophecy, and the restoring speech to a dumb, and hearing to a deaf man.

At this point, eighteen years after his death, we might well conclude that all Xavier's reputed miracles, which had any shadow of credibility, must have been collected; and that the Jesuit Fathers, Acosta and Maffeus, writing under the motives we have already described, would present us with the strongest evidence which existed of their number and authenticity. Yet, forty-four years after Xavier's death, Tursellinus published his life of Xavier, in which he greatly enlarged the list of miracles, asserting the raising of *four* dead persons; and adding many miracles, which verge at least upon the humorous, in which mould many of the subsequent miraculous statements seem to have been cast. A mendicant sailor asked alms of Xavier, who put his hand into his pocket, but found it empty. Upon which he told the beggar not to despair, but to put his trust in God; and

F

casting his eyes upwards, he put his hand a second time into his pocket, and took out a handful of gold, and gave it to the beggar. A Portuguese soldier lost 600 pieces of gold by gambling, and came to tell his grief to Xavier, who desired him to bring his dice. Xavier turned the dice over in his hand, and then told the soldier to go back and try again. The soldier did so, and won all his former money back again, and then gave up gambling for ever afterwards.

Seventy years after Xavier's death his canonization took place (1622) under Gregory XV. Ten miracles, besides the gift of tongues and of prophecy, were then pronounced to be established beyond all dispute, in the process of canonization. The gift of tongues is thus described:—" When he visited people of various tongues, which he had never learnt, he was in the habit of speaking their language with as much elegance and fluency as if he had been born and educated in the countries: and it often happened that when men of different languages composed his audience, each heard him speak in his own tongue."

The list of miracles is the following:—

1. " Salt water turned sweet, upon making the sign of the cross":—while sailing to China in the " Sainte Croix".
2. " A dead child restored to life." (Mutano in oppido Indiæ Orientalis.)
3. " A dead body, which had been one day buried, restored to life." In Cape Comorin, when he could

not convert the people, he prayed that he might perform this miracle.

4. "Whilst he celebrated mass he was lifted a cubit from the ground."
5. "A boy drowned in a well restored to life;"—at Coimbatore, on the Fishery Coast.
6. "A blind man restored to sight;"—in Japan.
7. "A beggar, full of ulcers, miraculously cured;"—at Cape Comorin.
8. "A sea-crab miraculously brings Xavier a crucifix lost in the sea." He was sailing from Amboyna to Baranula, and in a storm he held his crucifix, the length of a finger, in the sea, and let it drop. On the following day he reached Baranula and went towards the city Tamalo. After 500 paces, a crab jumped out of the sea upon the shore, and ran (festinus accurrit) with the crucifix in his claws to Xavier, and stood before him, and waited till Xavier took the crucifix, and then went back into the sea.
9. "A boat separated in a storm miraculously returns to the ship."
10. "He rains ashes upon the city of Tolo."

(Relatio facta in Consistorio secreto coram S. D. N. Gregorio Papa XV. a Francisco Maria Episcopo Portuensi S. R. E. Card. A Monte, Super vita, sanctitate, actis canonizationis et Miraculis Beati Francisci Xavier. Romæ, 1622.)

From this date the floodgates of miraculous fictions

appear to have been opened, and the result may be read in the life by Père Bohours, where miracles of all kinds are multiplied beyond calculation, many of them being palpable and impudent parodies upon the miracles of our Lord and his apostles; *e. g.* Xavier comes to the sea shore and finds fishermen who had toiled all night and taken nothing. He told them again to cast their nets into the sea, and they enclosed an immense multitude of fishes. But the miracle did not stop here. Whoever, since that day, has cast a net into the sea at that spot, calling on the name of Xavier, encloses a multitude of fishes. Xavier listened in silence for a whole day to a multitude of questions upon a diversity of subjects—religion, science, medicine, literature. At the close of the day he opened his lips in a few words, which proved to be a full answer to every question which had been asked.

We have thus traced the account of Xavier's miracles from their origin, resting not on the testimony of original witnesses, and persisted in amidst dangers and sufferings even to death, but on the mere breath of vague and uncertain rumours,—rumours discredited and refuted by Xavier's own letters, and by those written during his life by his immediate associates. We have also marked how gradually a belief in their truth crept in amongst a community, which had the strongest possible temporal motives for admitting and maintaining their authenticity. We have shown the expansion of their number and dimensions as they receded into the regions of the past; till at length the Pope of Rome and his associates palmed upon their votaries the most palpable fictions. Let us bring these reputed miracles to the criteria of Paley, and their authenticity vanishes. Let us look back upon the miracles of the New Testament, and thank God for the broad, firm, and unassailable foundation upon which the authenticity of these repose.

Having devoted this chapter to the legendary life of Xavier, it will not be necessary, in the further prosecution of our narrative, to do more than offer passing observations upon the legends which have obtained notoriety. Enough has also been stated to show that no dependence can be placed upon the biographies even in statements where nothing marvellous occurs; so that it must be a vain attempt to pick out a true life of Xavier from the biographies which have been published of him. The course, therefore, will be pursued which was proposed in the first instance, of drawing our narrative from what may be fitly termed Xavier's Autobiography.

CHAPTER IV.

Xavier's visit to the Spice Islands of the Indian Archipelago.

XAVIER'S ARRIVAL IN MALACCA—EXTRAVAGANT ACCOUNTS OF CONVERSIONS IN MACASSAR—XAVIER'S VISIT TO AMBOYNA—MOLUCCAS, ANTONIO GALVAN, MOHAMMEDAN KING—TERNATE—MAURICÆ, EARTHQUAKES—LEGENDARY STORIES—STORM AT SEA—RETURN TO INDIA.

THE period of Xavier's history on which we now enter extends from the summer of the year 1545, when he left India in hopes of a more fruitful Missionary field at Macassar, till his return to India in the early part of 1548. The account of his proceedings is contained in twelve copious letters, four written from Malacca in 1545; four from Amboyna, written in May 1546; and four from Cochin, after his return to India in January 1548.

The exciting news from Malacca and Macassar, which Xavier received while yet in India, it will be remembered, drew his heart towards those countries. A Portuguese historian has preserved an account of the matter, which is thus recorded in Millar's history of the propagation of Christianity.

"Manuel di Faria says, that about the year 1544, in the government of Martin Alfonso de Sousa, one Anthony de Payva, who went as a merchant, but proved more preacher than merchant, had some conference with the King of Supa, who was seventy years of age, and was very near being converted. Payva, sailing thence, went to the port of Siam, where he explained the articles of religion to the King, and urged the absurdity of the adoration of idols, pressing him to embrace the Christian faith; but the King desired time to consider. Meantime the King of Supa arrived at Siam, and hearing what had passed, said, 'a work so good ought rather to be put in execution than delayed.' He was only sorry for the time he himself had lost, and would atone by being the first convert, and desired immediately to be baptized. All stood amazed, and there being no priest, the ancientest of the Portuguese performed the function, and he was christened Lewis. Then the Queen, and many who came with him, were baptized also, which solemnity was celebrated by the guns and warlike instruments in the place. The King of Siam, moved by this example, was baptized, with his whole family. I relate the story as I find it." (Millar's History of Christianity, Vol. II. p. 234.)

Xavier was supplied with a passage to Malacca, and with a companion, in a remarkable way. While waiting at Madras, a merchant, John Durus, or Deyro, thirty-five years of age, came to him for confession: and was so wrought upon "by divine influence," as Xavier represents, as to decide the next day upon selling his ship and his merchandize, and distributing the proceeds to the poor, and upon becoming the companion of Xavier in his expedition to Macassar. Another friend, named Simon Bolettus, supplied him with an outfit and a free passage to Malacca. In the course of the summer he sailed from Madras, and arrived at Malacca at the end of October 1545.

John Deyro accompanied Xavier to Malacca, and is mentioned in a letter from Amboyna a few months afterwards, and then all mention of him in the letters ceases. The biographers report that he turned out a rogue, and embezzled some money given for the poor; that Xavier sent him to do penance upon an uninhabited island; that, while there, it was revealed to Xavier that Deyro had had a vision of the Virgin and Child, but that Deyro positively declared he had no such vision; upon which Xavier dismissed him as a liar as well as a rogue.

Xavier had requested, before he left India, from the Viceroy at Goa, a commission to the naval commander at Malacca to provide a ship for him upon his arrival there, to take him at once to Macassar. Upon reaching Malacca his heart was rejoiced by fresh tidings of the readiness of the inhabitants of Macassar to embrace Christianity: they had no temples and no priests, and only worshipped the rising sun as a god. But the governor of Malacca prudently suggested, that as he had sent, only a short time previously to Xavier's arrival, a pious and very able Missionary to Macassar, with a band of Portuguese soldiers to protect the neophytes in case of persecution, it would be well for Xavier to wait for the return of the ship which had conveyed the Missionary party to Macassar. This advice he complied with, and immediately began with zeal and diligence to labour for the spiritual good of the people around him.

"I had no lack," he says, "of opportunity for meritorious acts. On the festivals and Sundays I preached to the people. Nearly all the rest of my time was occupied by hearing the confessions of the sick and relieving their distresses, for I lodged in a hospital. I also instructed in the elements of the Christian doctrine the neophytes, chiefly the boys. I adjusted quarrels among citizens and soldiers. Each day, after sunset, I went round the city with a bell, admonishing the inhabitants, who were attracted by the sound, to pray for mercy upon the souls tormented in the fire of purgatory. A crowd of boys, chiefly from the Catechetical School, joined in repeating the words after me, and a great impression was made upon the city." (II. 17. Fr. 58.)

Upon a subsequent visit to Malacca, two years later, Xavier provided a deputy bellman, persuading the town council to hire a man and a boy to perform that office.

After waiting three months at Malacca, either the patience of Xavier failed, or he feared to lose an opportunity of visiting more remote regions. His account of his abandonment of Macassar, on which his heart had been fixed for many months, is thus given in his letters:—

"When I perceived that the wind had been favourable for ships from Macassar, yet no intelligence arrived from the priest and the soldiers, I determined not to delay longer, but to sail for the Moluccas." In another letter he gives an additional inducement for this sudden change of his plans. "Later intelligence from Macassar has informed me that affairs are not in so good a position as was first represented to me, therefore I shall not go there, but think of going to Amboyna, where there are many Christians, and where the teachableness of the rest of the people is so highly spoken of, that the accession of great numbers to the Church will be easily accomplished." (II. 10. Fr. 51.)

It is imposible not to refer back to the passage in which Xavier describes the divine impulse which moved him, at the shrine of St. Thomas, to undertake the mission to Macassar, and to contrast it with the slight grounds for changing his destination. Whether the change arose from impatience, or disappointment, or the tidings of a more hopeful field of labour, it is another proof of the inconstancy which marks the career of Francis Xavier.

Xavier, in his future course, followed the usual track of the Portuguese merchants, and of preceding Missionaries, in their visits to the Spice Islands; namely, to Amboyna, from thence to the Moluccas, then to Mauricæ, returning by the same route to the Moluccas, Amboyna, and Malacca. Three months he spent at Amboyna on his first visit, and one month on his second. Three months each time at the Moluccas, and three months at the Mauricæ, which, apparently, was the time spent by the annual ships which visited those settlements.

It is clear that the object of these flying visits was not to commence or organize Missionary operations, but rather to see and judge of the state of things, and to provide for the introduction of Jesuits into important positions; and especially to get into their hands the educational establishments.

Of Amboyna Xavier reports, that it was an island well peopled, both by natives and by settlers. He notices the departure of two Spanish Augustin Friars to Goa, who had been residing in the island, and were holy and excellent men. There were six or seven towns or villages inhabited by Christians. A priest who had ministered to them had lately died. Xavier, therefore, immediately visited these Christians, and describes, with great satisfaction, his baptizing children and infants, many of whom died immediately afterwards, from which he inferred that they had been kept alive by a divine interposition until the entrance to eternal life had been thus opened to them. (II. 17. Fr. 58.) As soon as he had made the circuit of these Christian villages, a Spanish fleet of seven or eight vessels arrived at the island, and Xavier's time was wholly occupied in ministering to his countrymen. He expresses his conviction that the whole island of Amboyna might be easily brought over to Christianity, because the people had been unsettled by a Mohammedan invasion about seventy years previously, by which multitudes of the inhabitants were allured to become nominal followers of the False Prophet, but the majority still remained heathen, and entertained a greater hatred for Mohammedanism than for Christianity.

The hope of the island's conversion was also greatly strengthened by the fact that the King of Portugal had given the sovereignty of the island to Jordan Freita, a Portuguese nobleman, now governor of the Moluccas, who was a pious man, most zealous for the propagation of the faith, and who, in the course of two years, was to come to reside upon the island as "Dynasta" of Amboyna, with his wife, children, and a large company of emigrants. Here we have an anticipation, by three centuries, of the Rajahship of Sarawak in an adjoining island.

The islands next visited by Xavier were the Moluccas. This group was peculiarly valuable to the Portuguese commerce as being the only mart for cloves. "Of all useful plants (writes Crawford) the clove has, perhaps, the most limited geographical distribution. It was originally confined to the five Molucca islands, and chiefly to Marchian. From these it was conveyed to Amboyna a very short time only before the arrival of the Portuguese." Hence the Moluccas were much resorted to by the Portuguese ships; and there was a large Portuguese population settled upon them.

There was also another and higher interest attached to the Moluccas. We read in the pages of Crawford's History that — "Of all the Portuguese names connected with the Indian Archipelago incomparably the greatest, except of Magellan, is that of the virtuous, the pious, the discreet, and heroic Antonio Galvan. He composed the odious dissensions of his countrymen in the Moluccas, introduced order and tranquillity into those oppressed islands, purity into the European administration, and instituted seminaries for education of such approved wisdom, that they afterwards became the models for similar ones established on the continent of India, and in Europe. The high and heroic enthusiasm of his character is displayed in his successively challenging to single combat the two principal Kings of the Moluccas to save the effusion of blood, and put a speedy end to the horrors of war. This great man, whose high endowments were not in request with his countrymen in the East, and were not appreciated in the West, was, after a short administration of two years, removed from his trust, and, on his return to Portugal, permitted to die from want, in prison." (Crawford's History of the Indian Archipelago.) These events are repeated somewhat more in detail by Crawford, in his "Chronological Table:"—"(A. D. 1537.) Tabarija, King of Ternate (the capital of the Moluccas), sent by Ataida (a Portuguese governor) to India, is there converted to Christianity, and sent back to be reinstated in his kingdom, but dies at Malacca on his way to the Moluccas." "Galvan employs himself zealously in the task of converting the islanders of Ternate, (the capital of the Moluccas) to Christianity: he institutes a seminary for religious education, afterwards approved of by the Council of Trent; and Christianity not only makes rapid progress in the Moluccas, but is spread to Celebes and Mindanes." Under the date 1544, the same author states, "George de Castro renews the scenes of iniquity transacted by the Portuguese in the Moluccas, and sends another King of Ternate prisoner to Goa."

At the Moluccas, therefore, as at Amboyna, Missionary efforts had been in progress long before the arrival of Xavier. But he makes no reference to these interesting particulars, or to the previous government of the pious Galvan. All his hopes were fixed upon a certain Mohammedan King of the islands, who owed the maintenance of his sovereignty to the King of Portugal, and therefore naturally enough received Xavier with open arms, to the great disgust of his chief men. This King assiduously cultivated the friendship of Xavier, and held out a hope of some day becoming a Christian. "He is withheld (says Xavier) from embracing our religion, not by the Mohammedan faith, but by his own lusts; for he has 200 wives and an incredible number of courtesans. He speaks Portuguese tolerably, and he entreats me not to hold myself aloof from him on account of his external profession of Mohammedanism, because both Mohammedans and Christians worship the same God, and the time will come when they will unite together in the same faith. But I never could induce him actually to become a Christian. This promise alone I could extract from him, that he would give up one of his sons, of which he has many, to be baptized, upon the condition of that son's being hereafter made King of the Mauricæ Islands. (II. 21. Fr. 62.)

Xavier had, however, some royal converts during his stay in the Moluccas. A former Queen, the mother of the present King's predecessor, whom he styles the Lady Isabella, was, through his ministry, admitted into the Christian Church; and Xavier applied to the King of Portugal for a pension for this lady as soon as she had been baptized. He mentions, also, that Balthazar Velozo, the brother-in-law of the reigning King, was very partial to the Jesuits, and very zealous for the cause of Christ. For him, also, Xavier applied to the King to bestow some honour or immunity. Xavier expresses a particular anxiety that the letters patent should be transmitted through the hands of the Jesuits, that it might be seen what influence they possessed to reward the favours which they received from persons in those countries. (III. 10. Fr. 76.)

In the large Portuguese garrison at Ternate, in the Moluccas, Xavier found full occupation during his residence there in preaching and ministering to the Europeans, and the neophytes, having also a special class of the native wives of the Portuguese. The only notice taken of the seminary, already established for Christian instruction, is an intimation that it was to be transferred to the Jesuit Society; and he at once issued his command to two of the brethren at Cape Comorin to come to the Moluccas by the next ship that sailed, to establish themselves in so promising a position.

Xavier gives the following account of his departure from these islands, which exhibits a trait of natural character eminently calculated to have made him a successful Missionary, if he had possessed the essential foundation of Missionary success:—" That I might escape the tears of my friends and of the neophytes in our parting, I went on board the ship suddenly in the night. But that device did not effectually conceal my departure, no, not from many. I was discovered by them. Then I was so deeply affected by the thought of my nocturnal flight from those children whom I had begotten to Christ, that I began greatly to fear lest my departure might imperil their salvation. I enjoined them, therefore, to meet daily in a certain church, to go through the catechism. A pious priest and friend of mine undertook to see to this, and to devote to them two hours daily." (II. 21. Fr. 62.)

From the Moluccas, Xavier visited the islands which he terms the Mauricæ, or the country of the Moor (Mauri Regio). He describes the locality of these islands as 400 miles from Amboyna, and sixty leagues from the Moluccas. The name of "Mauricæ" has slipped out of modern Gazetteers and maps; but the Bolognese editor uses the terms " Isla del Moro, Morolay, ad boream Giloli." This notice seems to fix the locality to Mortay, and other islands in that position. While yet at Amboyna, Xavier had heard of these islands that they were in a state of the utmost lawlessness, and that the inhabitants were famous for poisoning each other; that a priest had formerly visited them, and died upon their islands after making numerous converts; that no Christian teacher had subsequently dared to visit them on account of the risk of life. Xavier, however, now expressed his determination to go there. His friends tried their utmost to dissuade him, but he was firm in his resolution. They then brought him all manner of antidotes against poison, all which he rejected, determined to trust only in the help of God, and to obey the Gospel maxim, "He that will save his life shall lose it, and he that will lose his life for my sake shall find it." In writing to his friends in Europe in the prospect of his voyage, he adds the following wise and candid remark:—"Believe me, my very dear brethren, although the sense of this precept is daily apprehended by the generality of Christians; yet, when the hour arrives to make the critical decision to lose your life for God, and to submit to the fatal stroke, the sentence, hitherto most clear, is apt at that hour to become obscure, so that no man can then understand it but he to whom the Lord himself reveals it. In such an hour as that it is seen how weak and infirm is human nature. The Lord, out of his infinite mercy, so confirms and strengthens us in such circumstances by his might, that we may in all things bravely endure and persevere, according to his will." (II. 14. Fr. 55.)

After such pious and magnanimous resolutions we might expect to hear that Xavier fixed his abode amongst these neglected savages. We might be prepared to read of his labours among the people in letters written in the vivid style in which he described his labours among the Comorin Christians. But his good resolutions were fulfilled by a transient visit to the islands. His stay there was only three months. He describes the islands as a volcanic formation, very sterile, and having no sheep or cattle, only pigs and wild boars. The inhabitants were utterly uncivilized, and lived in constant jealousies and wars. Great numbers were destroyed by poison. They had no written language, and nearly every island had a different dialect. Their trees furnished them with bread and wine, and from the bark of another kind of tree they made their clothing. There was a race of people called Javars or Tabars, who thought that they acquired immortality by killing as many persons as came within their reach; and when there was a lack of other victims, they even killed their own wives and children. This tribe had made a great slaughter of the Christians. One of the islands was perpetually shaken by earthquakes, and the volcano, when the wind was high, covered every thing with poisonous ashes: even the fishes were poisoned in the sea, and the wild boars upon the land. Xavier adds that he saw nothing of this kind during his stay, but he felt the earthquakes. When the inhabitants inquired of Xavier what caused the volcanoes, he replied, as he tells us, "That they were the infernal regions, where all who worship idols will be thrust down." This was not said merely to terrify the natives, but represents his own belief, for he writes—"How severe were the shocks, may be gathered from this fact, that on the Feast of St. Michael the Archangel, while I was celebrating mass, the earth shook to such an extent that I feared the altar itself would be overturned. Perhaps St. Michael, armed with divine power, was chasing all the evil spirits of that region, who opposed the true worship, into hell." (II. 21. Fr. 62.)

Xavier closes his account of these islands with a sentiment, which might have come with a better grace from a Missionary residing there for a more lengthened period, mingling among the unconverted natives, and able to preach and minister to them in their own tongue:—"My very dear brethren, I write these things that you may know how greatly these islands abound in spiritual joys. Truly, all these perils and discomforts, encountered for the sake of our Lord, are treasuries filled with heavenly consolations, so that you may believe these islands to have been pre-ordained to destroy the sight of the eyes, in a few years, by weeping tears of joy. I never, indeed, remember myself to have been so penetrated by a flow of perpetual happiness, nor to have borne labour and bodily trials so lightly. Although I traversed islands in the midst of enemies and of faithless friends, although they be destitute of all remedies for disease, and even of all safeguards for life itself, yet they appear to me to deserve the name of 'the Isles of divine hope,' rather than the region of the Moor." (*Ib.*)

What explanation can be given of the excessive emotions which Xavier here describes, as having caused such floods of tears during his three months' stay in the Mauricæ? Such rapturous expressions of joy in suffering are not uncommon in Xavier's letters. Had Xavier been a nervous and timid, as well as a pious man, the explanation would have been obvious. But he was, in his general temperament, bold, calm, and fearless of death. His emotional joy is not accompanied by the exercise of a lively faith in the divine presence, or of anticipations of future glory, such as we meet with in the writings of St. Paul, and of many eminent saints of later times. The prospect of a speedy admittance into the Saviour's presence has ever inspired a more calm and dignified joy, far removed from animal excitement. It is impossible not to revert for an explanation to Xavier's endeavour to comfort Mansilla under trials, by thoughts of the merit of suffering, and the pre-payment of the penalties of purgatory. Such notions would naturally inspire joy in the mere act of suffering.

In reviewing Xavier's account of his voyage among the Spice Islands, we meet with no report of Missionary success beyond the royal converts who have been referred to. We must remember, however, that he had no means of communication with the common people, as the languages of the different islands, he says, were various, and his whole Missionary furniture consisted of a few scraps of Malay translations. In each place he could do no more than visit the people already baptized, and admit infants to baptism. This is all he claims, and all that was in his power to do, in his ignorance of the language, and during the extremely short period of his residence. But if we turn to the biographies of Xavier we meet with abundance of legendary tales, such as that of the crab and the crucifix, and general statements of great success among the heathen. The value of such vague statements of multitudes brought to embrace Christianity may be judged of by one specimen.

Xavier's own account of his employments in the islands of Mauricæ is in these precise words:—" In these islands I baptized very many infants; and in the space of three months—for that was the time I staid there—I searched through all the localities of the Christians, and bound them anew to Christ and to myself. .... All the Christian villages being thus examined, I returned to the Moluccas."

Père Bohours' account is in these exaggerated terms:— " He restored those Christians to the faith who had before forsaken it, and brought into it those idolaters who had refused to embrace it when it was preached to them by Simon Vaz and Francis Alvarez. There was neither town nor village which the Father did not visit, and where those new converts did not set up crosses and build churches. Tolo, the chief town of the island, inhabited by 25,000 souls, was entirely converted, together with Momoya."

Another legendary tale is told with great pomp by the biographers as having occurred at Malacca, while Xavier was waiting for a ship to convey him to India. Xavier's own account of the employment of this interval is given again in few and simple words:—"This time was not without spiritual occupations; but as I could not, single handed, satisfy all applications, I encountered the displeasure of some. Such displeasure did not offend me, but rather gratified me, as it sprang from their anxiety about their souls, and bespoke pious resolutions for the future. I also spent much time in composing dissensions and quarrels, which easily arise amongst the warlike Portuguese. I also catechized the children, &c."

The biographers assert that, during this interval, an attack was made upon the Portuguese vessels lying in the harbour of Malacca by a formidable armament from the opposite island of Sumatra. The enemy destroyed a multitude of ships by a night attack, and retired. The Governor of Malacca and the military officers were hesitating whether to attack the enemy. But Xavier came forward and forcibly represented the necessity of revenging the insult and retrieving the honour of the Portuguese name and of the cause of Christ; and then incited seven sea captains to fit out and arm a galley each, which were filled with soldiers, who pursued the enemy, and slaughtered thousands. Xavier purposed to go with the expedition, but yielded to their entreaties that he should remain at Malacca. But, though absent, he was cognisant of what passed at the distance of many hundred miles, and described the scenes which were passing, and the victory gained, five days before the news arrived. Such legends not only contravene Xavier's own letters, but are very alien from the character of Xavier, and had, probably, their origin in the guard-room gossip of the next generation, when Xavier's name became a household word, and the soldiers of a superstitious age delighted to justify their slaughter of the natives by the sanction of so great a name.

On Xavier's return from the Spice Islands to India the ship encountered a violent storm, of which he gives a graphic description. He also reveals the state of his feelings, and the grounds of his confidence in an hour of danger.

"On my return from Malacca to India I passed through the utmost perils, for the ship was driven for three days and nights before such a tempest as I never remember to have seen. Many of the passengers lamented their approaching death, and vowed that if, through divine aid, they should be delivered from this peril, they would never again trust themselves to the sea. The merchants were forced to redeem their lives by casting their goods overboard. As to myself, when the tempest was at the highest, in my supplications to God I availed myself of intercessors,—first out of those upon earth, the men of our Society and those who are friendly to us; afterwards, the whole company of Christians, hoping that I was being most fervently commended to the King of heaven by the spouse of Christ, whose prayers are heard in heaven though she dwells upon earth. Then I supplicated all those in the world above, and especially Peter Le Fevre of our order, that I might employ departed as well as living intercessors to appease the divine wrath. Afterwards I went through all the orders of angels and saints, naming each, that I might more surely obtain pardon for my innumerable sins. I took for my Patroness the most holy mother of God, the Queen of heaven, who obtains, without difficulty, whatever she asks of her Son. Lastly, all my hope being placed in the infinite merits of our Lord and Saviour Christ, while fortified with so many and such powerful safeguards, I enjoyed far more pleasure in the midst of that horrible tempest than afterwards when I was delivered from the danger. Truly I am ashamed that, being as I am the vilest of mortals, I could shed a flood of tears through heavenly joy in the hour of greatest danger; and I humbly besought the Lord Christ not to snatch me from that danger, unless He would preserve me to encounter equal or greater dangers for the sake of his glory, and in accordance with his will. Very often has God showed me, by a certain internal instinct, out of what great perils of body and soul I have been preserved by the intercessions of my associates, part of them being below and part above." (II. 21. Fr. 62.)

We have here the same emotional joy in the hour of suffering and of imminent death as in the visit to the islands of Mauricæ. But how far removed was his confidence from the "faith and hope"—"which is in God," whilst he taxed his memory to supply a list of fellow-creatures as his patrons and intercessors! How debased by superstition and "creature" dependence were his sentiments; how opposite from those of a saint of old— "Whom have I in heaven but thee, and there is none upon earth whom I desire besides thee!"

CHAPTER V.

Xabier a Director of Jesuit Missions in the East, and a Royal Commissioner from the King of Portugal.

SECTION 1. *Xavier's direction and management of the Jesuit Missions in the East.*—EXTENSION OF JESUIT MISSIONS—PEREMPTORY TONE OF XAVIER'S INSTRUCTIONS—HIS DIRECTIONS FOR LEADING A HOLY LIFE—HIS CATECHISMS, MIXTURE OF ROMISH FABLES—SPECIMENS OF INSTRUCTIONS TO MISSIONARIES, ADJUSTING QUARRELS AMONG THE CONVERTS, PROPER BEHAVIOUR OF MISSIONARIES TO ALL CLASSES, EXCELLENT PRACTICAL DIRECTIONS ON MAKING SERMONS AND WRITING LETTERS.

SECTION 2. *Xavier's conduct as a Royal Commissioner of the King of Portugal to his dominions in the East.*—XAVIER'S AUTHORITY OVER THE PEARL FISHERIES—HIS PATRONAGE OF PIOUS GOVERNORS—EFFORTS TO COERCE THE SYRIAN CHRISTIANS OF TRAVANCORE INTO SUBMISSION TO ROME, JACOB ABUNA.

SECTION 3. *Xavier's Confession, after seven years' labour, of the failure of Romish Missions.*—NO TRUE CHRISTIANS IN INDIA—PROPOSAL TO THE KING OF PORTUGAL TO TRANSFER TO THE CIVIL AND MILITARY GOVERNORS THE DUTY OF CONVERTING THE HEATHEN—ROMISH CONFESSION OF THE FAILURE OF XAVIER'S MISSIONS.

Section 1. *Xavier's direction and management of the Jesuit Missions in the East.*

XAVIER, upon his return from the Spice Islands, remained fifteen months in India. His time was occupied by the direction of a numerous body of Jesuit Missionaries who had followed him to India, and over whom he was invested with supreme authority. He spent some time at Goa; he visited the new Viceroy at Bassein; he went, probably twice, to inspect the work amongst the Comorin Christians. His correspondence during this period consists of six long letters to friends in Europe, and four letters to friends in India, together with five elaborate letters of instructions to brother Missionaries. To these may be added several letters to Europe, written subsequently from Malacca, respecting the events and employments of this visit to India.

Xavier had at this time under his direction more than twenty Jesuit Associates, whom he placed out in the various stations which he had selected for them. The stations were the most important Portuguese settlements in the sea route from the Cape of Good Hope to the Spice Islands, namely, Socotra, at the entrance of the Red Sea; Ormuz, in the Persian Gulf; Goa, the capital of the Indian empire; Cape Comorin; Malacca; and the Moluccas. He secured to the Jesuits the direction of the great Missionary College at Goa, with its provision for one hundred native students in divinity: more Missionaries were on their way to India, and he had the prospect of soon acquiring possession of the Missionary colleges at Cranganore, in Western India, and Ternate, in the Moluccas. Xavier had little hesitation in superseding the Missions of other orders, by introducing his own Society, and by gaining possession of their educational establishments. He aimed at a large scheme of Jesuit Missions for all India. Writing to Ignatius Loyola, he says, " In these parts of India there are fifteen Portuguese cities, in which many houses of the Society might be raised up, if the King would contribute an annual sum to begin them out of the public revenue. I have, by letter, submitted this matter to the King. I have also fully informed Simon Roderick of the whole affair, and have assured him that it would be greatly for the advantage of the Christian cause if he would obtain your permission, and transfer himself here with as many Associates as possible, especially with a large band of preachers: with such an arrival, and the royal patronage, several colleges of the Society might be raised up." (III. 1. Fr. 67.) This project was gradually, and, to a great extent, carried out, and Jesuit Missions took the lead of all other efforts of the Church of Rome for evangelizing the heathen world. It is a question whether the earlier Franciscan and Augustinian Missions which were thus superseded had not been conducted upon more scriptural principles; whether their Missionaries had not been more careful respecting the administration of baptism; and whether they did not impart more of scriptural instruction to their converts. In the latter years of Xavier's labours he became more respectful towards the Missions of other orders; and, in the prospect of opening China, expressed the hope that other Missionaries would enter in together with the Jesuits.

In reviewing the instructions which Xavier gave to his brethren as their director, the most striking feature is their precise and peremptory tone. He gives directions respecting their private religious exercises, their preaching, their course of catechetical instruction for the children. He commands all the Missionaries of his order, whatever their employments or engagements may be, or whatever the entreaties of the people amongst whom they labour, to hold themselves in readiness to leave at an hour's notice upon receiving his directions, and to go wherever he shall appoint. He enjoins upon them the transmission to himself of their daily journals of all their employments; appoints one at each station in authority over the rest, who was to be Xavier's special correspondent on all matters relating to the Missions. He constitutes one of the Missionaries at Goa superior, in Xavier's absence, over the whole Jesuit body in India. He appoints another at Goa to collect all the news which might arrive by ships from Europe, and to digest it under proper heads, both political and ecclesiastical, especially information respecting other Missionary fields, and to transmit the same to him by the earliest possible opportunities.

Xavier frequently points out to his brother Missionaries the merit before God, as well as the comfort, of implicit obedience to the will of a superior; even as he was himself in subjection to Ignatius Loyola. He does not, however, anticipate a retort which might be made, that his own subjection to Ignatius was purely ideal; for it is clear, from Xavier's letters, that the distant General of the Jesuit order favoured him with very few communications or counsels.

Yet this peremptory and absolute authority which Xavier assumed was never pressed in a way to offend the feelings of his brethren. Its exercise is blended with so much tenderness of affection, and with such expressions of personal humility and Christian courtesy, as cannot but excite our admiration at the natural magnanimity of the man. The sequel of this history will, however, show how little success attended the exercise of such peremptory authority in the midst of a Mission.

The documents now under consideration give a full view of Xavier's plans and methods in conducting his Mission. They contain, first, general Directions suitable for all Christians; secondly, a Manual of instruction for native neophytes; thirdly, Letters of instruction to Missionaries.

1. Xavier's *Directions for leading a holy life* contain a short course of religious meditation, self-examination, and prayers. In these prayers, petitions to the Virgin, to Michael the Archangel, and to "the Saint Guardian Angel," are strangely mixed up with divine worship: for instance, a petition to the latter imaginary being runs thus, " Bear my prayers before the Lord our God,

and whisper in His holy ears that He may grant me pardon for all my past sins, through his mercy and your intercession," &c. (II. 11. III. 17. Fr. 58, 83.)

2. *A Manual of instruction for neophytes* was drawn up by Xavier, and translated into several languages, and he enjoined its use upon all the Missionaries and catechists. It might have been hoped that a man of Xavier's sagacity would, in such a document at least, have presented only the leading truths of revelation in a simple form, and that, though upon the Romish system, many essential truths would have been withheld, yet that the grosser fables of Roman Catholicism would have been omitted. But how little such a hope has been realized one specimen may show. The doctrine of man's recovery after the fall is to be taught in the following form :—

"There was no hope of escaping damnation till the holy Michael, our true friend, and, with him, the angels who had persevered in obedience, and received, as a reward of their constancy, the fruition of eternal glory in heaven, all united in compassion for the calamity of human nature, fell down as suppliants before God, and endeavoured to obtain some remedy from Him of the great evils which had so widely overspread the progeny of Adam and Eve. This was the form of their prayer: 'Oh, gracious God, most merciful Lord and Father of all men; the time is at length arrived, and the long-expected day from the beginning of ages dawns, which, in Thy eternal purpose, thou hast appointed for the exercise of mercy towards miserable mortals. Behold, we see the morn of the day in which the gates of heaven are about to open to the sons of Adam restored to favour through divine adoption, since the Virgin has been born of holy Anna and Joseph, without the original sin of Adam, the most blessed of all women, Mary by name, whose virtue and holiness infinitely excels all which is beneath God. Since there is now such a pure and illustrious Virgin, it seems a work not unworthy of Thy infinite wisdom and omnipotence, to deign to form a human body from her virgin substance, which Thou canst easily effect, as formerly, O Lord, Thou didst form the body of Adam,'" &c. &c. (II. 13. Fr. 54.) An apology must be made to any Protestant reader for recording such blasphemous fables; but the mistaken veneration which has been attached to the name of Xavier as a teacher of Christianity in the East requires such a revelation.

Throughout the Manual thus prepared for the use of neophytes, the reference made to the Bible, to the need of repentance, or to faith in the atonement of Christ, is the slightest possible. It contains a dry statement of certain abstract truths, and of the facts of Scripture history, mingled with fables, and concludes with a sweeping affirmation of implicit faith in the canons of the holy fathers, the decrees of councils, the edicts of the Popes, propounded by cardinals, patriarchs, archbishops, bishops, and other prelates of the church, all to be dutifully received with deep veneration, sure faith, and prompt obedience, &c. &c. This mixture of truth and fable was taught to Xavier's converts: can we call them converts to the Christian faith?

3. We have also several specimens of Xavier's *Letters of instructions to Missionaries*. One letter is to the Fathers labouring on the Fishery Coast. As he had himself formerly laboured in that field, and it was the furthest removed from the Portuguese population, it would be here, if anywhere, that we should look for Missionary principles, and the pouring forth of Missionary yearnings for the conversion of the heathen. But we find nothing of the kind. Xavier had evidently given up all hope of benefiting the adult heathen. In these instructions he says emphatically—"Believe me, trust my experience, all our ministry to this nation reduces itself to two capital points—the baptism of children, and their instruction as soon as they are capable of it." His directions are wholly confined to the labours of the fathers amongst the population nominally Christian, and living under the protection of the Portuguese governors. Xavier alludes to the authority which had been obtained from the King of Portugal to put to death any converts who were discovered making idols, but he advises the Missionaries rather to procure their imprisonment or banishment. The advice which these instructions contain for the treatment of native converts is, however, as far as it goes, very wise and useful, and may well serve for the direction of Missionaries of the Protestant church.

"As soon as you have arrived in a village, inquire whether there are any quarrels or animosities between individuals. Endeavour not only to reconcile them by making them abjure all rancour, but also let the reconciliation be made in the churches as a reparation for the scandal. The men shall make their's on the Sunday, the day of their meeting; the women, on the Saturday, on which day their meetings are held. These reconciliations shall be made aloud in your presence. They shall declare that they repent of the insults they have given, and forget those they have received, and promise to render to each other all the services required by Christian love." " Put an end to all law-suits which arise between Christians, using all possible gentleness in order to bring the parties to an agreement, and to settle the matter *ex æquo et bono.* If you cannot succeed, and if the affair is not of great importance, put it off till Sunday, and, after divine service, try to have it concluded by the headmen and the principal people of the place. Do not give too much time to affairs of this sort, in order not to lessen the estimation which is necessary for your ministry. Prudently refer important matters to the Portuguese authorities."

" In the presence of a Portuguese, take good care not to reprove or condemn the native Christians. On the contrary, defend them, praise them, apologise for them on every occasion. Point out to their detractors how short a time it is since they embraced the faith; that they are still in infancy; that if one considers how many helps to a Christian life are wanting to them, how many obstacles are opposed to their Christian advancement, by the penury of the priests, by the incursions of the barbarians, by their terror of the Badages—far from being surprised at the defects of so rude a nation, one can only wonder that they are not worse.

"Render to the native priests all possible services, especially in what concerns religion. Take care that they confess, that they celebrate mass often and decently, and that they set the people a good example. Be careful not to write any thing against them to any person whatever: do not keep by you the vestige of any writing which may injure their reputation. Use every means to live on good terms with the Portuguese governors. Manage so that it may never be perceived that there is the slightest misunderstanding between you and them. Be equally careful to conciliate the goodwill of all the Portuguese, by avoiding every collision. Repay by kindness, by prudence, and by love, those who appear incensed against you. Make them feel, in spite of themselves, that you love them. By this means you will restrain them, and they will not dare to make an open rupture with you. But you must not carry this condescension so far as to allow them to illtreat the neophytes. Oppose that, but gently. If you see that your representations are of no avail, carry your complaints to the governor. Plead the cause of the innocent and oppressed with modesty, and without bitterness towards those whom you accuse.

"As for the governor, I repeat what I have already said to you. Apply yourself to maintain a good understanding with him. Have nothing more at heart than to avoid any thing which may deprive you of his friendship.

"Let your conversation with the Portuguese turn upon spiritual subjects, on death, on judgment, on purgatory, on hell, on the use of the Sacraments, on the exact keeping of the commandments of God. If you speak to them of nothing but these matters, one of two things will happen; either they will court your society because it interests them, and so they will profit by it; or they will avoid it because it wearies them, and so they will not rob you of the hours set apart for your spiritual duties.

"I enjoin upon you, above all things,—and I cannot often enough repeat it to you,—that wherever you bend your steps, or wherever you may be called, you should try to make yourself beloved by every one, by rendering to them kind services, by good manners, and by seasoning your reproofs with gentleness and modesty. This kindness in words and actions will conciliate the affection of every one, will open their hearts to you, and will give you the power of labouring with great success in the winning of souls." (II. 22. Fr. 63.)

Another letter of instructions is addressed to Father Michael Gaspar Barzeus. This Missionary appears to have been a man of a very superior stamp. He was a Belgian by birth, and had served in the army with the Emperor Charles V. He had afterwards studied at Coimbra, and arrived in India at the close of the year 1548. He was appointed by Xavier to labour at Ormuz, a Portuguese settlement in the Persian Gulf of great importance as a commercial dépôt, with a large

European population and a concourse of various other nations. The place was already supplied with a vicar-general and five priests, besides religious fraternities. Xavier, however, appointed Gaspar to that place, upon the principle of occupying every important post by Jesuits; and he expressly forbade him to leave the city for three years, unless at his own call. It was clear, therefore, that the appointment had no view to the work of Missions. Several letters of Gaspar are preserved in the Epistolæ Indicæ, in one of which Gaspar complains that he was prevented by Xavier's injunctions from making Missionary tours into the neighbourhood, though the openings in Persia and Arabia were most inviting.

Xavier's letter of instructions to Gaspar is a remarkable document, entering fully and minutely into all particulars respecting his public ministrations, and especially his management of the confessional. It occupies thirty-four pages of the octavo edition of Xavier's letters, but it contains only one paragraph relating to the heathen, namely—

"Spend all the time which can be spared from necessary daily duties on the conversion of the heathen. Always prefer, in the choice of ministerial duties, those which are most extensively profitable. This rule will teach you never to allow the confessional to interfere with preaching to a congregation, or to give up the Catechetical School at the appointed day and hour to visit an individual. An hour before the catechetical lecture,

go yourself, or send your associate to the bazaar and to
the main streets of the city, and with a loud voice invite
all to come and hear the explanation of divine doctrine."
(III. 7. Fr. 73.)

In relation to the general duties of the ministry
amongst Europeans, the letter contains much excellent
practical advice, mingled, however, with some very
questionable suggestions, and grounded upon motives
far inferior to, if not at variance with, the Christian
standard.

Gaspar is enjoined to be punctual and constant in
catechizing, in visiting the hospitals and prisons, and in
other humble employments, since he will thus acquire
the reputation of modesty and lowliness which will in-
sure his future influence. A variety of expedients are
suggested for gaining influence over men, such as ascertaining their private history, and their besetting sins.
Gaspar was also advised to regulate his intercourse with
others upon the principle that they may one day become
his enemies, and turn to his disadvantage what may have
passed between them. This odious principle was afterwards embodied in the "maxims" of the Duke de Roche-
foucault, as a part of a system which, Voltaire had the
sagacity to discover, rests upon the foundation of self-
love as the spring of all our actions. (Siècle de Louis
XIV. Tom. 2. Ch. 29.)

Gaspar was enjoined to exhibit the utmost deference
to the bishop's vicar. As soon as he arrived he was to
kneel before him and kiss his hand, and ask his permis-

sion to exercise his ministry. He was on no account to dissent from him. It was also added, "Strive to win over all the other priests by kind offices. If any occasion of dissension arises, shun controversy as you would a mad dog or a viper. Treat them with the utmost respect, and with a delicate attention to their feelings, that you may conciliate their love to you, and draw them over to adopt our spiritual exercises."

Upon no one point is Xavier more urgent than upon the importance of aiming at an effective style of preaching. His remarks are—" Men will only listen attentively to that which responds to their internal consciousness. Sublime speculations, perplexed questions, and scholastic controversies overshoot the capacity and the interest of men who grovel upon the earth: they make a vain sound, and pass away without effect. You must show men to themselves, if you wish to hold them enchained by your words. But before you can express what they feel in the depths of their heart, you must know it; and there is only one way of knowing it,—to be much amongst them, to test them, to observe them. Take in hand these living books: hence derive your rules for teaching with effect: hence obtain your ability of dealing with sinners, of bearing with them, and, for the sake of saving their souls, of moving and bending their wills in the right direction.

"I do not, indeed, forbid the reading of lifeless books. Let the holy Scriptures, the Fathers of the church, the sacred canons, the books of devotion, and those which treat of the rules and qualifications of the moral law, be diligently consulted at proper times. From the lives of the saints you may derive most profitable remedies against temptation, arguments of persuasion, stimulants to heroic zeal, examples of all that is praiseworthy: but these appliances are cold, and effect little, until the minds of the auditors are opened by things which reach the bottom of their hearts. There is but one key which will unlock those hearts; namely, the presentation to them, as I have said, of their interior convictions, skilfully pourtrayed by a preacher well versed in human affairs, and brought home clearly to the apprehension of each individual."

Xavier reminds Gaspar of the prevailing character of a commercial population, and of the need of acquiring a knowledge of the artifices of trade, and of the matters with which such people are most conversant, in order to maintain his influence amongst them.

"The men of the world are apt to despise the admonitions of the religious orders, because they think them ignorant of life. But as soon as they perceive such an one not less versed than themselves in secular matters, they admire him, they give themselves up to him: with such a guide they will not doubt their power to accomplish the things, however arduous, which he advises them to attempt. See, therefore, the great fruit of such knowledge. For obtaining it, believe me you must labour as you did formerly in the schools to acquire philosophical and theological lore. But you must seek it, not in lifeless books, whether written on paper or vellum, but from living books, that is, from men of business and men of the world. From this kind of converse you will profit more than if you tumble over a whole library of speculative authors."

Xavier instructs Gaspar upon the style of letters which it was incumbent upon him to write to his superiors and to friends of the Mission.

" Write from time to time to the College at Goa, how you exercise your ministry to advance the glory of God; in what order you take your various employments, what spiritual fruit, God prospering your weak endeavours. Let your letters be written with great exactness, such as our friends at Goa may send to Europe, that they may afford there a testimony to our diligence in these parts, and of the favour of God who deigns to give some success to the poor efforts of so small a company of labourers. Let nothing slip into these letters at which any one may justly take offence—nothing which shall not approve itself, at first sight, as truthful, and such as excites readers to praise God, and to fulfil His will. Send, also, upon the same subject, special letters to the bishop and Cosmus Agnesius, writing with due regard to their position; so that each may be made aware of the welcome tidings of fruit abounding, by the divine blessing, from your cure of souls." (III. 7. Fr. 73.)

Xavier frequently enjoins upon the Missionaries great care in the letters they wrote respecting their labours. His advice is sometimes admirable, but too often alloyed by Jesuitical suggestions. One other specimen may be added from his instructions to Father John Beira at the Moluccas.

"In writing your letters there must be a choice of topics, omitting whatever may seem to convey insinuations against others, or be otherwise offensive; and let the method and style be such as becomes the gravity of a clergyman, so that your narratives may be transmitted to Europe, dispersed through the Society, and communicated by publication to the world at large. Do not forget that Missionary journals from distant countries are eagerly read in Spain, Italy, and elsewhere. Hence it is specially desirable, that whatever we send from hence should be written with great accuracy and caution, as they may not only fall into the hands of friends, but of very different characters, sometimes of invidious opponents. Let them, therefore, if possible, satisfy all parties, and incite all to the praise of God and of His holy Church. Above all, let your letters never present a fair ground of offence, or be capable of a sinister interpretation. Upon the same principles I wish you to send encyclical letters to our brethren throughout India, to convey to them the welcome intelligence of your labours for the glory of God." (III. 11. Fr. 77.)

A third specimen of Xavier's Missionary instructions must be given. It is a letter addressed to Father Paul Camerti, rector of the College of Goa, constituting him and Father Antony Gomez to the supreme direction of the Missions during Xavier's absence in Japan. This letter contains admirable advice respecting the tender treatment of Missionaries: in this particular it will form a useful guide for Secretaries and Committees having the responsible office of directing the labours and supplying the wants of Missionaries abroad. The letter is given in full.

" *To Father Paul Camerti,*
 " *Rector of the College at Goa.*
          " *April* 1549.

" On my departure for Japan, I earnestly beseech and entreat you, as the head of the college at Goa, by your zeal for our Lord God, by your love for our Father Ignatius, and for the Society of Jesus, to live in love and harmony with Antonio Gomez, and with all our brethren dispersed throughout India. You must strive to do this with the utmost humility and circumspection; exercising upon all questions a ripe and sound judgment. From my intimate acquaintance with all the labourers of the Society of Jesus who serve God and the Church in these regions, I am of opinion that they do not need any ruler to guide them in the ways of God; nevertheless, in order that they may not lose the opportunity of gaining additional merit by obedience, and since strict discipline requires it, I think it expedient that they should have some one to whom they may pay obedience. Wherefore, relying on your humility, prudence, and learning, I have thought it best to appoint you their Director and Leader, to whose authority all (with certain restrictions, to be mentioned presently,) are to be subject. It matters not whether they be Associates or novices, at Goa or elsewhere, they are to obey the rules of the Rector of the College of the Holy Faith, and to follow his guidance as they have been accustomed to do. You are to exercise this authority over them till the revocation of it be duly signified to you.

"I now state the restrictions, which, for certain good reasons, I lay upon your authority. First of all, I reserve for Antonio Gomez full and absolute power over the novices of the seminary, whether they be Portuguese or natives. I entrust to him the entire management of the revenue and property of the college: he is to exact the payment of all debts, and apply the proceeds to the general purposes of the establishment as he shall think fit: you must not, therefore, interfere with his conduct in these matters, or require him to state his reasons. You must, therefore, leave to his will and judgment all that relates to the admission, or to the sending forth of pupils, whether they be of Portuguese or Indian birth; regarding as right whatever he orders, and not interposing your authority in any of these matters. If your opinion should differ from his, arrange the matter by consultation or by earnest entreaty, but never exercise authority in such cases. I commit entirely to his management, without any interruption or opposition on your part, or on that of any one else, the punishment of the children of both nations, their domestic arrangements and discipline, as well as the appointment or dismissal of the college servants, and the assigning to each their duties.

"And here again, on account of the importance of the matter I request, and by the obedience which you of your own accord have promised to our Father Ignatius, (in whose name I give you this commission,) I enjoin, adjure, and entreat, with all the earnestness in my power, that there may be no dissension, no altercation, not even the beginning or appearance of a quarrel between yourself and Antonio Gomez. Rather let your fraternal relation be manifest to all by the exhibition, on both sides, of oneness of purpose, of mutual affection, and of hearty co-operation in promoting the common good of the whole college. If this be clearly displayed, all possible occasion for offence or murmuring, either in doors or out of doors, will be cut off.

"Whenever those brothers of our Society who itinerate among the villages on Cape Comorin, or Nicholas at Quilon, or Cyprian at Madras, or Melchior Gonzalez at Bassein, or Francis Perez at Malacca, or John Beira and the Associates at Moluccas, write to you, you must immediately set about their business with all diligence, and at any inconvenience, whether it be to request your interest with the Viceroy or the Bishop, whose assistance may possibly be necessary to them, or any other spiritual or temporal aid or relief which they may stand in need of. You must also confer with Antonio Gomez, that he may promptly and fully transact those matters which belong to his department. In writing to those who, amidst sufferings and exhaustion, are bearing the heat and burden of the day, be careful that you never blot the page with the smallest drop of bitterness. Let the accents of authority be expressed only in love and tenderness. Let no tinge or shadow of scolding, of bad feeling, or of any thing which might wound or grieve them, ever enter your mind. Supply promptly, kindly, and liberally, whatever they require, whether it be food, clothing, or any thing for retaining or restoring health. For you must compassionate their great and continual labours both day and night in the service of God, unmitigated by earthly consolation. I now speak more especially of those who have the care of the churches at Moluccas and Comorin, for they are weighed down by a most heavy cross. Beware, in the name of God, of letting them remain in need, or of forcing them to ask twice for what you know they require for the solace of their minds, or for the support of their bodies. By the failure of such supplies their spirits will infallibly sink and faint. It is such a just and all-important duty in those who guard the camp to assist their brethren who are fighting, that I should not hesitate to charge you, in the name of God and of our Father Ignatius, to discharge this duty with the utmost diligence, cheerfulness, and completeness, so that nothing may be left to be done under the pressure of the last moment.

"To come to that which more immediately concerns yourself. I earnestly entreat you, my brother, to aim at continual progress in all virtuous attainments. Be a bright example to all, as, indeed, you have always been; let slip no opportunity of writing to me. I look for long letters, full of good news of your welfare—accounts of the whole household—of your mutual agreement—of the unbroken love between you and Antonio Gomez—of each one of those who are working at Cape Comorin—how Cyprian is going on at Madras—about the Associates whom the ships from Portugal have brought this year—their number, and what signs they give of possessing the gift of speaking to the people—the number of priests and of laymen;—distinguish between these two orders, explain at large their number and character, the name, talents, powers, and virtues of each one.

"There are only two certain opportunities in the year of communicating with each other by letter. A king's ship sails twice every year from Goa, in September going to Banda, in April to the Moluccas. Both, however, touch at Malacca on their route, where our Brother Francis Perez will receive letters addressed to me, and will not fail to forward them to me in Japan. Do, I beseech you, read over once a week the paper which I left with you on my departure, so that you may recall to your memory not only my commands, but also my person. I desire by this means to prompt you to procure for me the favour of God by your prayers, and by those of our Associates at Goa, both men and women.

"I have desired Antonio Gomez, if any good preachers should come from Portugal, to send some of them into the surrounding districts; as, for example, to Cochin, where a good ecclesiastic of our Society is needed; also to the district of Cambay, as, for instance, to Diu. This I recommend to you also. If, therefore, the ships which arrive this year should bring any fair number of our Associates who are well trained in preaching, you had better agree with Gomez as to the proper disposing of them, that they may be sent to the places which I have pointed out, by one or other of you. Since, however, I fear, that in the numerous occupations of your position you may not have leisure to write so often, and with all the minuteness and care that I desire, I think you had better entrust that duty to our Brother Dominic, or to any other Portuguese of the household. You must desire him to collect carefully, and write down a narrative of, all that transpires at Goa worthy of note respecting any of our brethren scattered throughout our Missions and stations, especially about Gaspar, who is living at Ormuz. These writings you shall make up into a packet, and send them, addressed to me, by the regular ships which touch at Malacca: if you have any thing private to inform me of, write it yourself, and add it to the others.

" Since you have not yet personally visited the various establishments connected with the college, and cannot, therefore, know by experience what is their condition, and the mode of life on the Comorin Coast, at Madras, Quilon, Moluccas, Malacca, or Ormuz, you must not, by an absolute summons, send for any one who is labouring in those parts. It might happen that, through your ignorance of their affairs, you may be cutting short a good beginning of an important work; and you might, by inopportunely calling away the labourers, check the work when things are taking a long-wished-for turn: this may create an irreparable hindrance to the salvation of souls and to the glory of God. This is the cause of my writing (as I am now doing) to Father Antonio Criminalis, to tell him on no account to move from his position at anybody's summons, or to allow any one of his Christian pupils at Comorin to do so, unless he thinks, on consideration, that it can be done without hindering the work. I give the same orders to those who are occupying other stations, that they are not to neglect the work they undertake, or to permit any of their associates, who are necessary to the carrying on that work, to be withdrawn from it, lest brilliant hopes be destroyed and precious opportunities be lost of extending the kingdom of Christ. The withdrawal of a brother from his post of labour may often prove both inopportune and especially hurtful to the interests of a divine work. It will be better, therefore, for you not to interpose your authority, or to command any thing positively, without having clearly ascertained that it is expedient.

"Further, whilst I forbid you to summon to Goa any of our distant labourers without first ascertaining the concurrence of their judgment and their full consent; yet if any of them, for urgent reasons, should, without your direction, come to you, I would have you receive them kindly, and treat them with the utmost affection, attending to them with all care, whether they need the strengthening and support of their physical or mental constitution; whether they have come of their own accord and upon their own responsibility, or by the persuasion of their companions, to seek the spiritual medicine of penance and correction, or of temporary retreat: whatever offices you can perform for them, see that you behave yourself with parental tenderness, lest they fall away or suffer some serious ill.

"I charge you, most earnestly, my beloved brother Paul, to observe carefully what I have said."

"Wholly your's,

"(III. 8. Fr. 74.)" "FRANCIS."

Upon reviewing Xavier's character it will appear that he possessed in a very high degree some of the essential qualities of the leader of a great enterprise. He was of a generous, noble, and loving disposition, calculated to gather followers, and to attach them firmly to his leadership. But in respect of Missions Xavier was little fitted to direct others. Of the peculiar duties of an evangelist to the heathen he had no conception. His directions to his Missionaries are wholly addressed to their conduct as pastors of Christian communities. In his voluminous "Instructions," all that can be gathered of Missionary directions amounts to little beyond the general relations of the clergy with their flocks, with each other, and with their ecclesiastical superiors.

Even if Xavier had better understood the work of

Missions, there was one great fault in his system which would have proved fatal to success. He attempted to carry every thing by authority. He constantly inculcated the supreme merit and advantage of implicit obedience to himself. The sequel of his history will show how completely this system failed to form an efficient body of coadjutors. Xavier's history will, therefore, afford a useful caution against a notion, too much countenanced at the present day, that an ecclesiastical head of a Mission is needed to secure efficiency by uniformity of action, and to counteract the evils which may arise within a Mission from the contrariety of individual opinions. Such absolute power may consist with the government of a settled Christian Church, where the relation between ecclesiastical authority and the pastoral function has been defined by canons, and by experience. But no canons or regulations have been yet laid down for Missions to the heathen. That work is so varied, and its emergencies so sudden, that the evangelist must be left to act mainly on his own responsibility and judgment. It pre-eminently requires independence of mind, fertility of resource, a quick observance of the footsteps of Divine Providence, a readiness to push forward in that direction, an abiding sense in the mind of the Missionary of personal responsiblity to extend the kingdom of Christ, and a lively conviction that the Lord is at his "right hand." These qualifications are, like all the finer sentiments of Christianity, of delicate texture; they are often united with a natural sensitiveness; they are to be cherished and counselled rather than ruled; they are easily checked and discouraged if "headed" by authority. Yet these are the qualities which have ever distinguished the Missionaries who win the richest trophies, and advance the borders of the Redeemer's kingdom. Among such a body of workmen no formidable difficulties will arise from the contrariety of individual opinions; and such as do arise will be easily composed by affectionate, Christian, and wise counsels, whether offered on the spot, or transmitted from Europe.

Section 2.—*Xavier the Royal Commissioner of King John III. of Portugal.*

In the preceding pages many indications have appeared that Xavier was mindful of the extraordinary powers conferred upon him, upon his departure from Europe, by the King of Portugal, for the support and encouragement of religion in the East. When the interests of religion appeared to him at stake, he did not hesitate to employ mysterious threats of the possible result of his displeasure. It was not personal ambition which induced Xavier to assume a position far above that of ordinary Missionaries. In him every personal consideration was absorbed in the ecclesiastical sentiment; and he thought that the royal authority was at that time more necessary for the propagation of the faith than the preaching of the Gospel. He had no hope of the conversion of the natives to Christianity while they had before them the scandalous examples of European Christians, and while they smarted under the oppression and persecution of Portuguese officials.

In his capacity of a Royal Commissioner he encouraged the officers of Government favourable to religion by assurances of the royal favour; and, on the other hand, he compassed the degradation or removal of those whom he regarded as "hinderers of the word." He also used his influence with the King of Portugal to send to India a large body of Jesuits, and to provide for their maintenance, and especially to select powerful preachers, who might be placed in the different Portuguese garrisons and towns, to reform the European society.

The present section will contain a few specimens of Xavier's letters, in which he assumes the tone of special authority in these respects.

In a letter to Mansilla, before he left the Fishery Coast (8th Nov. 1544), Xavier thus exercises his authority in respect of the pearl fisheries:—

"Tell N. Barbosa from me not to employ any in the pearl fisheries at Tuticorin who have taken possession of the houses of the Christian exiles. As the King and the Viceroy have given me authority in this matter, I positively forbid it. It will greatly displease me if those who bear the Christian name, but are both contumacious and disobedient, or, to speak more correctly, downright apostates, should have the advantage of our sea fisheries.

Let the privilege be granted to the inhabitants of Punicael. If any one of that party wishes to dive round the Islands of Tuticorin to dig up mother-of-pearl shells, he has my licence to do so. Therefore Barbosa can hire their services; but if he is too hard with them, warn the man seriously from me: let him be very careful on his own account not to heap up fresh vengeance, for he is not the only person who knows that he has quite enough to answer for on other grounds." (I. 40. Fr. 40.)

In a letter to the King of Portugal (23rd June, 1849), Xavier enumerates the supplies which he had received from Peter Sylva, the Governor of Malacca, and adds: "I describe all these particulars to your Majesty, that you may know with what benefits and with what honour your faithful subjects in India treat me. Indeed, Sire, I may truly say that no one ever came to India who received from the Portuguese living here so much favour and respect. I owe all this to your Majesty, and to the repeated and powerful commendations of me to the Governors of your Indian dominions; amongst whom, as Peter Sylva, the Governor of Malacca, has excelled others in the signal help, courtesy, and honourable distinctions he has bestowed upon me; so he has bound me to him by these favours, though my poverty and weakness prevent me from making any equal return. I petition your Majesty, therefore, to allow me to supplement my poverty by your liberality towards him. I shall be able to do this if your Majesty will deign to recompense this and other benefactors, who have large claims upon my gratitude, for the favours I owe but cannot repay." (III. 9. Fr. 79.)

In other recommendations of friends to the royal patronage, Xavier is more particular in the favours he asks, and more amusing in the reasons he assigns. He tells Simon Roderick—"I have besought the King in my letters to appoint Stephen Louis Buranus one of his chaplains. I have done so, not so much for his sake, as because he has sisters who have neither home nor means of support. The brother, if he obtain the honour of being a member of the royal establishment, would easily place out his sisters in marriage; for in these parts there is a wonderful desire to be connected by matrimonial ties with honourable men, especially with those in royal favour. If you can aid the accomplishment of this affair, you will place three destitute young ladies in safety." (III. 4. Fr. 72.) In another letter to the King he highly commends Edward Barret, who had lately been the King's Advocate at Malacca, for his uprightness and fidelity to the King's interests, adding—"The governorship of Malacca must not be thought a sufficient reward for so many years of faithful service; first, because accidental circumstances have prevented its being sufficiently lucrative to him; and, secondly, because he has not enjoyed it for the full time, so that he leaves it a poor man. Deign, Sire, to consult for his interests, as for one who has greatly deserved your Majesty's favour." (III. 16. Fr. 82.)

Another instance of the exercise of Xavier's influence

with the King of Portugal is of a less creditable kind. It was in connection with a scheme for bringing an independent Christian Church under the yoke of Rome.

The existence of an ancient Christian Church in Travancore, on the Malabar coast, has been well known in England since the popular accounts of it by Dr. Claudius Buchanan, and the labours in that country of the Church Missionary Society. There is a legend that the Gospel was preached there by the Apostle St. Thomas. But the first authentic mention of this Church is placed by Neander in the middle of the sixth century. There is very little evidence of any Christian life in the Church during the ten succeeding centuries; nevertheless it maintained its Christian ordinances in the midst of a heathen population, and under heathen sovereigns. It was under the government of a single Bishop or Abuna, who received his consecration from the Syrian Patriarch at Mardin. Dr. Geddes, in his history of this Church, states, that "In the year 1545, Don Joan d'Albuquerque, the first Archbishop of Goa, being ashamed, it is like, of their talking so much in Europe, and doing so little in India, in the matters of religion, sends one Vincent, a Franciscan Friar, of which order the Archbishop himself was, to Cranganore, to try what he could do towards the reducing of those Christians to the obedience of the Roman Church. He erected a College at Cranganore, in 1546, to instruct their sons in the learning and usages of the Latin Church."

Dr. Geddes is mistaken in speaking of the Archbishop

of Goa, as the head of the Romanists in the East was at that time only designated Bishop of Goa. It appears from Xavier's letters that he had himself a chief hand in this scheme for enlarging the apparent success of the Romish Mission in India. In a letter to the King of Portugal (25th Jan. 1545), he strongly recommends the College to his Majesty for a fixed endowment, intimating that it would be the means of a great increase of the number of Christians. In another letter to the King, three years later, he endeavours to secure a higher salary to the Syrian Abuna than the Franciscans could obtain for him from the local Governors. It would appear that an intrigue to deprive the Syrian Church of its independence was going on through the Abuna, or Bishop, of the Syrian Church, as well as through the operation of the College at Cranganore. Xavier had met this Bishop at Cochin, and describes him to the King as most laborious in visiting and instructing all the Christians of St. Thomas residing in his diocese, but who only received from the men in power in those parts " such wages as saints generally receive from the men of the world." He entreats the King not to believe, as it had been insinuated through a sinister channel, that this excellent Bishop had had any hand in the death of the Portuguese Chaplain, Michael Vaz. Xavier had certain proof that it was not so, though he could not commit the proof to writing.

In another letter to the King, written a year later (26th January 1549), Xavier breaks out into indignation at the treatment of this bishop, and supplies the following particulars:—" For forty-five years a certain Armenian bishop, Jacob Abuna by name, has served God and your Majesty. He is a man equally dear to God on account of his virtue and his sanctity, yet despised and neglected by your Majesty, and by all who have any power in India. God has himself provided for his welfare. He regards us as unworthy of the honour of being employed as instruments for the consolation of his servant. The Fathers of the order of St. Francis alone take care of him, and surround him with benevolent attentions which leave nothing wanting. Without such care the good old man would have been overwhelmed by his misfortunes, and have lost his life. I must open my mind. I earnestly prompt your Majesty to write to that excellent prelate, in your own name, a letter of respect and benevolence. Insert in the same letters what he may show to the governors and officers, especially to the Commandant of Cochin, so that they may honour him, show him hospitality, and treat him with favour, especially when he petitions for any thing, or is in want. In writing thus I do not reckon myself to do a service to that prelate, but to your Majesty; for, through the fervour and love of the Franciscans, he is in want of nothing at present. Your Majesty is greatly in want of the favour and intercession of a man who is beloved of God, which you may earn by the measure I suggest. This man is most worthy of the character I give him, because he spares no labour in ministering to the Christians of St. Thomas, and now, in his decrepid age, *he most obediently accommodates himself to all the rites and customs of the holy mother Church of Rome.* I know that your Majesty is in the habit of writing to the Franciscan fathers. The letter to the Armenian bishop can be enclosed in their packet. Such a letter I entreat you to send, full of all expressions of favour, respect, and affection." (III. 3. Fr. 69.)

It would seem from this letter that the King of Portugal and his officers refused sufficiently to remunerate, and support the bishop in his intrigues against the ancient privileges of his Church, and the universal wishes of the Syrian Christians.

Xavier wrote at the same time to Ignatius Loyola at Rome, and to Simon Roderick at Portugal, describing the college at Cranganore and its objects; and adding that the Franciscan friar intended, at his death, to make it over to the Jesuit Fathers, and entreating both his correspondents to procure indulgences from the Pope for the Syrian Church, and to send a powerful Jesuit preacher to perambulate the sixty villages of the Syrian Churches.

These events were the beginning of a long course of oppression exercised by the Portuguese civil and ecclesiastical authorities against the liberties and independence of the Syrian Christians. In the sequel, bloody feuds arose. The Syrian bishops were imprisoned; the churches were wrested from the people; and divisions introduced which have produced baneful results to the present day.

It is easy to perceive how disadvantageous to Xavier's Missionary character his royal commission must have proved. It not only led his own mind into schemes of a politico-religious character, but it surrounded him with flatterers who desired to use his influence with the King for their own purposes, and raised up many bitter enemies who were jealous of his interference. It cherished the great fault of Xavier's character, viewed from a Missionary point of view, namely, his trust in an arm of flesh, rather than in the power of divine truth. Had he been a mere Missionary he might have been led to a blessed discovery of the truth of the Gospel, and that it is the power of God unto salvation. The arm of flesh on which he leaned was a snare and a weakness to all his Missionary enterprises.

SECTION 3. *Xavier's confession, after seven years' labour, of the failure of his endeavours to convert the heathen.*

The foregoing narrative contains many indications of the disappointment of Xavier's hopes of converting the adult heathen to the Christian faith. In our summary of the results of his labours on the Fishery Coast, we have shown that it is doubtful whether he made any addition to the number of nominal Christians which he found there. His avowed reason for seeking distant fields of labour was the failure of his first hopes. Such confessions become more numerous and distinct as his correspondence advances.

In a letter to a brother Missionary in Travancore, he writes, December 1548:—" If you will, in imagination, search through India, you will find that few will reach heaven, either of whites or blacks, except those who depart this life under fourteen years of age, with their baptismal innocence still upon them." (II. 24. Fr. 65.)

In a letter, dated January 14th, 1549, he writes to Ignatius Loyola:—" The Portuguese in this country only rule the sea and the coast. They have no footing in the interior, except in the cities where they have established themselves. The natives, on account of the enormity of their wickedness, are as little as possible fitted to embrace the Christian religion. They so abhor it, that they have no patience to listen to us if we introduce the subject. To ask them to become Christians is like asking them to submit to death. Hence all our labour is at present to guard those who are now Christians. And yet, if there were more manifest interest taken by the Portuguese in the converts, many more might follow Christ. But when the heathen see Christian converts treated with contempt and oppression, they are not likely themselves to become Christians. Hence, since there is not the least need of my labours in these parts, and as I have also learnt, from sufficient testimony, of

Japan, a region adjacent to China, that its inhabitants are heathen, untouched as yet by Mahometans or Jews, and are most eager in listening to news, whether of matters of religion or of science, I have determined to start for that country as soon as possible." (III. 1. Fr. 67.)

It must be borne in mind, that Xavier is not only speaking of the failure of his own efforts to convert the natives, but that he had now visited the most important places in the East, and had therefore witnessed the results of Romish Missionary labours in India,—the labours of nearly half a century before his time, and which had been conducted, at some periods, under enlightened rulers, such as Albuquerque and Galvan.

The confession of the failure of the work of Romish Missionaries in India is rendered still more manifest by a proposal which Xavier made to the King of Portugal. He solemnly proposed that the conversion of India should be taken out of the hands of Missionaries, and put into the hands of the civil authorities! The scheme was elaborately drawn out, in a letter from Cochin (Jan. 20th, 1548). These are Xavier's words:—

"To come to a matter which concerns myself indidually, I have often pondered in my own mind, after carefully considering the question on every side, what I could write to your Majesty, as to the best means of spreading, and of firmly establishing, the Christian faith in this country. I am impelled to this course, on the one hand, from my desire to obey God and to promote his glory. I am deterred from doing it, on the other hand, because I despair of ever seeing my proposal carried into effect. Yet it has not appeared possible for me to be silent with a safe conscience, especially as it is evident to me that the thought has been put into my mind from above, for some special purpose; and I cannot devise any more probable reason for God having thus revealed the matter to me, than that I might make it known to your Majesty. And yet, again I tremble, lest, while I thus relieve my mind of its burden, my very letter may prove a testimony against your Majesty before God in your last hour, and aggravate your doom in the day of judgment, by depriving you of the plea of ignorance. I beseech your Majesty to believe that this fear greatly distresses me, since I am deeply conscious that I have no wish or intention, beyond finishing my labours and spending my life here in India, in working for the salvation of souls. I trust that, by so doing, I may, to the best of my ability, relieve you of the weighty duties resting upon you, and, by discharging a part of your proper function, may lighten the burden of your Majesty's conscience, and enable you to await with greater safety the terrible decision of the last day. Your great love for our Society is such, that I ought to think this benefit cheaply purchased for you at the cost of any labour or troubles of my own. These conflicting anxieties, Sire, between my duty and your danger, have, I confess, caused me extreme agitation and distress, but at last I have made up my mind, once for all, to relieve my conscience of the burden which I have long concealed.

"Here, then, is the discovery which I have made during my long experience in India, Malacca, and the Moluccas, and which makes me sick at heart. Your Majesty must receive it as a certain truth, that much is neglected which God requires to be done in this country and elsewhere, through the hurtful and disgraceful rivalries which, under the mask of sanctity, prevail amongst your officers, arising out of trivial and concealed causes of offence. One declares—'It is my duty to do this, and I will suffer no one else to usurp the honour of it;' another says—'If I am not the doer of it, I have no wish to see others do it;' whilst a third complains—'I am bearing the burden and heat of the day, whilst others receive all the profits and thanks.' With their passions heated by these altercations, they each strive, both by correspondence and manœuvres, to further their own interests. Thus, time is consumed, opportunities are lost, and no place is found for the things which relate to the cause of God. In the same way it often happens that the honour of your Majesty, and the interests of your empire in India, are neglected.

"I have discovered one only remedy for this evil, the adoption of which, if I mistake not, would both increase the number of Christians in these parts, and protect those amongst them who now suffer injuries from the want of powerful patrons; so that no one, either of the Portuguese or Indians, would dare to molest or despoil them. That remedy is, that your Majesty should signify and clearly explain your intention, both by letter to the Viceroy and magistrates now in India, and verbally to those whom you may hereafter send here, that you confide that which is your principal care—namely, the spreading of our holy faith—to the Viceroy and Governor of each province, more even than to all the ecclesiastics and priests who are in India; that you will call each of them strictly to account; and that you will impute to them every success or failure in this respect, and reward or punish them accordingly.

"In order that there may be no mistake about this declaration, I should wish you to mention each of us who are in these parts by name, declaring that you do not lay upon *us*, either individually or collectively, the duty which conscience demands of you; but that, wherever there is any opportunity of spreading Christianity, it rests upon the Viceroy or Governor of the place, and upon him alone. That, since God has imposed upon your Majesty the weighty duty of watching over the salvation of the souls of your subjects, you can only demand the fulfilment of this duty from those to whom you have delegated your authority, and the honour of the magistracy, and who therefore represent the person of your Majesty in this country. And if you find that, owing to the negligence of any one of them, few have embraced the faith of Christ within the limits of his jurisdiction, you will devolve upon *him* the punishments which, otherwise, such neglect would call down upon your own head;—you having already given them full warning, that you have committed to your chief officers here the weighty charge of imbuing the souls of your heathen subjects with the faith of Christ.

"Whenever, therefore, the Viceroy or Governors write to you, let them describe the state of Christianity; the number and quality of the converts from heathenism; what hopes, what means there are of adding to their number; that for information upon these points you will trust only to their letters, passing over without notice all other reports, from whomsoever they come. Your Majesty should solemnly pledge your word, in the diplomas by which you institute and confer power on any one, that you will severely punish the Governor of any town or province in which few neophytes are added to our Holy Church, when it seems plain that, if it had been the wish of those in authority, many converts might have been secured. I very earnestly desire that you should take an oath, invoking most solemnly the name of God, that in case any Governor thus neglects to spread the faith, he shall, on his return to Portugal, be punished by close imprisonment for many years, and all his goods and possessions shall be sold, and devoted to works of charity. In order that none may flatter themselves that this is but an idle threat, you must declare, as plainly as possible, that you will accept no excuses that may be offered; but that the only way of escaping your wrath, and obtaining your favour, is to make as many Christians as possible in the countries over which they rule.

"I could give many instances to prove the necessity of this, but I will not weary your Majesty by what would only be the recital of my past and present anxieties, undergone without any hope of reward. I will only assert this much: if every Viceroy and Governor be fully persuaded that you have bound yourself by oath to do this, and that you will perform all that you have threatened, the whole island of Ceylon, many kings of the Malabar Coast, and the whole promontory of Comorin, will embrace the religion of Christ in a single year. But so long as the Viceroys and Governors are not urged by the fear of disgrace and fine to make many Christians, your Majesty must not hope that the preaching of the Gospel will meet with great success in India; or that many will be brought to baptism, or make any progress in religion. The only reason why every man in India does not acknowledge the Divinity of Christ, and profess His holy doctrine, is the fact that the Viceroy or Governor who neglects to make this his care receives no punishment from your Majesty.

"But as I can scarcely hope that this will ever be done, I almost regret having written it, for fear lest these warnings may add to your condemnation at the last day. I do not know whether the excuse will then be admitted which you allege, namely, that you were not bound to give credence to my letters. But I can from the bottom of my heart assure your Majesty that I should never have written this about the Viceroy and Governors of this country, if I could in any way have reconciled it to my conscience to keep silence." (II. 18. Fr. 59.)

We pause upon this revelation of Xavier's notions of evangelizing a heathen country; and while we give him credit for a noble intrepidity in thus addressing his royal master and patron, we are constrained to ask, What was his notion of the genius or worth of a religion propagated by the means which he recommends? Had he ever meditated upon the genius of Christianity, as exhibited in the Scriptures of the New Testament, or even in the early records of the Church,—upon its perfect adaptation to the social condition of mankind, under every variety of external circumstances, so that it has often thriven most when under the sharpest pressure of persecution? Had he actually thought out the scheme he enjoined upon the King of Portugal, and its results; when every Governor was to give up the tale of the Native Christians he had made, under the penalty of confiscation if the numbers were not sufficient? Had he reflected upon the system of bribes, threats, artifices, which must have been put into exercise for making up the number of converts? Place Xavier's letter to the King of Portugal in the hands of any one, suppressing the author's name, and saying only that it was from a Missionary, and would not the author be at once pronounced to be a mere enthusiast who knew as little of Christianity as of politics? How, then, are these sentiments to be reconciled with the sound penetrating judgment of Xavier upon common subjects? Are we to sacrifice his good sense or his Christianity, or are we to take refuge in a confession of the glaring inconsistencies which mark his character?

It is scarcely possible to conceive a more pointed contrast than between the letters of Xavier and the letters of the great Apostle of the Gentiles, in which he declares—"We preach Christ crucified, unto the Jews a stumblingblock, and unto the Greeks foolishness; but unto them which are called, both Jews and Greeks, Christ the power of God, and the wisdom of God." "God hath chosen the foolish things of the world to confound the wise; and God hath chosen the weak things of the world to confound the things which are mighty; and base things of the world, and things which are despised, hath God chosen, *yea*, and things which are not, to bring to nought things that are: that no flesh should glory in his presence."

The utter failure of Xavier's attempts to convert the heathen in India is a fact admitted by Romanist and Jesuit writers who have had any true knowledge of the subject. The Abbé Dubois, who went to India in 1790, and laboured as a Jesuit Missionary for twenty-five years in the South of India, afterwards published a volume entitled, "Letters on the state of Christianity in India; in which the conversion of the Hindoos is considered as impracticable. 1823." In this volume the Abbé states:—

"Francis Xavier, entirely disheartened by the invincible obstacles he everywhere met in his Apostolic career, and by the apparent impossibility of making real converts, left the country in disgust, after a stay in it of only two or three years. The disappointment and want of success of Xavier ought to have been sufficient to damp the most fervent zeal of the persons disposed to enter the same career. When a man of his temper, talents, and virtues, had been baffled in all his endeavours to introduce Christianity in India, his successors could scarcely flatter themselves with the hope of being more fortunate."

CHAPTER VI.

Xabier's Labours in Japan.

SECTION 1. *Xavier's preparations for his visit to Japan.*—FIRST DISCOVERY OF JAPAN—HISTORY OF PAUL ANGER AND OF COSMO TURRIANUS—GROUNDS OF HOPE IN JAPAN—VOYAGE TO MALACCA—TO JAPAN.

SECTION 2. *Xavier's arrival in Japan, and first account of its people.*—RECEPTION AT CANGOXIMA BY PAUL'S RELATIVES—THE GOVERNOR OF THE PROVINCE—MARIOLATRY OF THE FIRST MISSIONARY EFFORTS—MORAL CHARACTER OF THE JAPANESE—JAPANESE RELIGIONS—IMMORALITY OF MONASTIC INSTITUTIONS.

SECTION 3. *Conclusion of Xavier's labours in Japan.*—PERSECUTION OF CONVERTS—REMOVAL TO AMANGUCHI—FIRANDO—JOURNEY TO MIAKO AND RETURN TO AMANGUCHI—REMARKABLE CONVERSIONS—POLITICAL COMMOTIONS—XAVIER INVITED TO BUNGO—SAILS WITH AN AMBASSADOR TO INDIA—EXPENSES OF THE MISSION—TRANSIENT GLIMPSE OF XAVIER'S PERSONAL RELIGIOUS EXPERIENCE—SENTIMENTS IN THE PROSPECT OF SUCCESS—SUBSEQUENT HISTORY, AND FINAL EXTINCTION OF THE JAPANESE MISSION.

SECTION 4. *Legends of Xavier's labours in Japan.*—REPUTED MIRACLE—LEGENDS OF SUCCESS—STORM AT SEA.

Section 1. *Xavier's preparations for his visit to Japan.*

The next portion of Xavier's history which comes under review is his Mission to Japan. India had lost its charm as a Mission field. The Spice Islands presented but a limited sphere. Japan was unexplored. No Portuguese officials were there to discredit the Christian name, or to impede the progress of the Gospel. The intelligence which Xavier received from merchants, respecting the character of the Japanese, was most encouraging. The providence of God, also, had brought to Xavier a native of Japan, whose story presents one of the most remarkable illustrations which the history of Missions affords of a *living* "man of Macedonia," and his invitation, "Come over, and help us."

Xavier's first mention of Japan occurs in his letters from Cochin, after his voyage to the Spice Islands, January 1548. He says, "I met in those islands a Portuguese merchant, a man of deep religious feelings and strong faith, who spoke much about certain very large islands, lately discovered, called Japan, and assured me that much more success would attend the propagation of the Christian religion there, than in any part of India, because the whole race inhabiting those islands were eager for knowledge beyond all other people. With this merchant, a native of Japan arrived, named Anger, who had determined to seek an interview with me; for he had opened to the Portuguese traders the grief of a wounded conscience, and had besought them for some remedy, and means of appeasing the wrath of God: upon which they proposed that he should come to me at Malacca. He consented, and sailed with them in their ship."

"I inquired of Anger whether, if I should go to Japan, he thought that the inhabitants would embrace Christianity. He replied that his people would not immediately assent to what might be said to them; but they would investigate what I might affirm respecting religion, by a multitude of questions, and, above all, by observing whether my conduct agreed with my words. But if I should satisfy them on these two points,—by my suitable replies to their inquiries, and by a conduct above all reproach, that then, as soon as the matter was known and reflected upon, the King, and all the nobility and the adult population, would flock to Christ, being a nation which always follows reason as their guide.

"The Portuguese merchant, an intimate friend of mine, having had much intercourse with Japan, has left with me a treatise, carefully written out, containing a description of the country, the manners of the people, and other particulars, which he had partly himself witnessed, and partly ascertained from authentic sources. This treatise I send you, with this letter. All the Portuguese merchants who return from Japan confirm me in the assurance that, if I should go there, my labour would be better applied than in India; for in that case I should have to do with a nation which obeys reason. I have a presentiment that, within two years, I or some other brother of our Society will go to Japan. Although the voyage is full of perils, on account of the terrible storms in that sea, and the atrocities of the Chinese pirates, and many vessels are lost, either by the sea or by the pirates." (II. 21. Fr. 62.)

Anger had been placed by Xavier, after his arrival in India, in the College of Goa, and two other youths, the one a Chinese and the other a Japanese, servants of Anger, whose previous histories are not given, were associated with him.

After the lapse of another year, in January 1549, when the annual letters to Europe were despatched, Xavier wrote to his friends, giving further and very interesting accounts of the Japanese youths, and of their progress in general knowledge, and in Christian attainments. In nine months they had learned to read, write, and converse fluently, in Portuguese. They had also translated into Japanese the Creed and Xavier's explanation of Christian doctrine. Anger had learned by heart the whole Gospel of St. Matthew before he had been six months at Goa. At their baptism, Anger took the name of Paul. A letter has been preserved, written by him from Goa to Ignatius Loyola, which is here introduced as giving a view of the character of this interesting Japanese youth.

"*Letter of Paul Anger to the Society of Jesus.*
"*Goa, 29th November* 1548.

"It hath pleased Him, who took me out from my mother's womb, to seek me when I was lost and wandering, like a lamb from the flock, and not to leave me when I was far off, but to bring me from darkness to light, and from death to life. His many and great mercies to me testify to His infinite goodness and bounty. I have therefore thought it a religious duty to give you a full account by letter of the means of my conversion.

In my native country, Japan, while I was lying buried in the thick darkness of superstition, a fear of the rage of my enemies induced me to flee for refuge to a monastery of bonzes. Whilst there a Portuguese trading vessel arrived. One Alvarus Vaz, whom I had formerly known, happening to be on board, invited me, as soon as he learnt the situation in which I was, to leave Japan with him. His departure was however delayed, and fearing lest I should incur any further risk, he gave me letters of recommendation to a friend who was staying in the same port. In the darkness of the night I mistook the vessel, and gave the letter to Ferdinand Alvarus instead of George, to whom it was addressed. He received me, however, in the kindest manner, and took me away with him, desiring to present me to Francis Xavier, who was an intimate friend of his. In the mean time, in order to inspire me with due esteem for the man, he gave me much information about him and his doings, and began himself to instruct me in the rudiments of the Christian faith. Through this means the desire was kindled of knowing more of Xavier and of the Christian religion. When we had arrived at Malacca I should have been immediately washed in the sacred font, had not the bishop's vicar, on becoming acquainted with my circumstances, forbidden it: his main reason was the undesirableness of my return to my heathen wife after undergoing the sacred rite. My object, therefore, having failed, and Xavier not having arrived as I had hoped, I thought it time to return to my own country. Accordingly, I went to China, which is not more than about 200 leagues from Japan, (a voyage of six or seven days), in order that I might go to Japan by the first ship which offered itself. When the opportunity of sailing from China occurred, I embarked, and reached within sight of Japan, not more than twenty leagues from land, when the ship was suddenly overtaken by a most terrible storm, which lasted during four days, and drove us back to the same port in China from which we had started. Still terrified by the fear of shipwreck, and agitated by the deepest feelings of religion, I was in great doubt what to do, when I suddenly met the Portuguese, Alvarus Vaz, by whose kindness, as I have already said, I first escaped from Japan. He was surprised at my having left Malacca; and after he had heard of my dangerous voyage towards Japan, he persuaded me to return with him to Malacca. To his invitation was joined that of Lawrence Botellius, an honourable man, who assured me that he had no doubt but that Xavier would have returned to Malacca by this time; adding that he would take me to the college of St. Paul at Goa, instruct me in the Christian religion there, and afterwards provide some one of the members of the Society who should accompany me to my own country.

I accepted his proposal, and therefore returned to Malacca. As I disembarked from the vessel I fell in with George Alvarus, who had brought me from Japan: he took me at once to Xavier, who was then engaged in celebrating a marriage; told him who I was and why I had come. He showed such signs of joy, both in his countenance and by his words, (I was just beginning to understand Portuguese,) received me so kindly, and showed me, subsequently, such signs of friendship, that I have ever since borne in mind his appearance and the way in which he welcomed me. I see very plainly from this that my whole journey was ordered by the providence of God. As Xavier intended to visit the Christian neophytes at Cape Comorin, on his way to Goa, he sent me on at once with George Alvarus, by a shorter way. We reached Goa in the month of March 1548; he himself arriving not more than four or five days after us. I was exceedingly glad to see him, as I had been wonderfully taken by his wisdom and kindness. When I, and a servant whom I had brought with me from Japan, were sufficiently instructed, we were baptized by the hands of the bishop, in the cathedral, on the day of Pentecost. Now that God, the Creator of all things, and Jesus Christ, who died on the cross for our salvation, have thus furthered our undertaking, we trust that all may turn out to His glory, and for the propagation of the Catholic faith. I am every day more and more convinced of the truth of the Christian religion, both by the many mercies which God has lately granted me, and by the deep peace which I experience through my whole soul. I have learnt to read and write well in a very short time. I have learnt the Gospel of St. Matthew by heart, and I am now translating it into Japanese. Xavier is turning his thoughts to the province of Japan, and will take me with him. Offer up your earnest prayer to God for both of us, that our affairs there may prosper according to our hopes: do so by all means for me, that I may show that the grace of God has not been bestowed upon me in vain; but that, should death be encountered a hundred times, I may willingly meet it for the sake of the truth. I am full of hope, and feel confident, that before I die I shall see much spiritual fruit among my countrymen, and a college of our Society founded in Japan for making known the name of Christ." (Maffeus, Epistolæ de Japonicis rebus.)

Xavier has recorded other interesting particulars respecting Paul and his companions. "When I asked them (writes Xavier) what part of the sacred books they read with most delight, they answered, the sufferings and death of Christ." He also states, "I overheard Paul sighing deeply and exclaiming—'Oh, unhappy people of Japan, who adore the creatures which God has made, as if they could save you!' then I asked him, 'Why do you speak thus, Paul?' To which he answered, 'I pity my people who pay divine honour to the sun and moon, when those luminaries are for the service of those who acknowledge the Lord Jesus; for by His command they afford light by day and by night, which light the servants of Jesus Christ, the Son of God, employ for searching out His glory.'" (III. 13. Fr. 79.)

It is impossible to contemplate the story of Paul Anger, without recognising in it a signal instance of the providence of God, which has often thus facilitated the entrance of His gospel into a dark region. We look forward with high expectations to the results of a work so auspiciously commenced.

But amidst many solid grounds of hope for a favourable entrance into Japan, Xavier alleges one of a more questionable kind. He states that Portuguese merchants had written to tell him that, upon their arrival at a city of Japan, the governor had assigned them a deserted house, which was haunted by demons. In the middle of the night one of their servants uttered loud screams. The Portuguese within, and the Japanese without the house, ran to ascertain the cause. The lad declared he had seen a terrific spectre, which vanished upon his making the sign of the cross. The next day the lad made a great number of crosses, and put them in all parts of the house, and no more alarms occurred. When the Japanese had observed for some time that the inhabitants of the house were protected from all future disturbances, they eagerly adopted the cross in their own houses and places of public resort, where they had been accustomed to be annoyed by demons, and thus, writes Xavier, they have already conceived a veneration for that symbol of Christianity.

In addition to his encouragements, Xavier does not hesitate to tell the King of Portugal, in a letter from Malacca, on his way to Japan, that he had sought direction in earnest prayer that God would deign to signify His will whether he should go by sending into his mind a clear and internal persuasion of his duty, and would, at the same time, give him strength to perform all His will. "God," he adds, "has granted my petition. I feel, and am thoroughly persuaded in my mind, that I go to Japan in obedience to the will of God. Therefore, putting on a cheerful courage, breaking off all delays in India, I follow God, who has assuredly called me to the enterprise, and invited me to it by impulses, both frequent and vehement." That Xavier was perfectly sincere in his determination to follow the call of God had been evidenced before he set out from India, by his conduct upon receiving intelligence that Japan had closed its ports against the Portuguese. "By God's help," he wrote, "I will go; for there is no better enjoyment in this miserable world than to live in peril of death, when death is encountered from the sole motive of His love, and a desire of pleasing Him, and of spreading His holy religion. Believe me, it is sweeter to live in the midst of such peril, than to be free from it and at ease." (II. 6. Fr. 47.)

Xavier had now to select his companion for this most promising Mission to Japan. He had twenty Jesuit Missionaries at his absolute command, and others were expected soon to arrive from India; but he passed them all over, and chose one who had not been regularly trained for the ministry, but who had lived many years a seafaring life, and had only lately taken orders, whose name was Cosmo Turrianus, and of whom an interesting history is given, in a letter written by himself, to the Jesuit Society at Rome, dated from Goa, March 25th, 1549, which is preserved by Maffeus. In this letter he states that he left Spain eleven years previously, with no plan before him; and, after visiting various countries, spent four years in New Spain, where he had witnessed the fruit of the labours of the Dominicans and Franciscans. That though he there enjoyed all secular advantages, even to satiety, his mind was not at rest, but yearned after something more solid and excellent: that having met with a fleet of six ships, he sailed on the 1st January 1542, from New Spain, towards the west, and visited several islands, in one of which they lost 400 of their men. They were therefore driven to make for the Moluccas, where they were detained for two years, being unable to return to New Spain. At the advice of certain priests, and of some of the most considerable men of his company, he negotiated with the Portuguese governor to convoy them to India. In this voyage they touched at Amboyna, where he found Xavier: that at his first interview with him he was seized with a vehement desire to imitate his course of life: that he would, therefore, have instantly followed his steps, if he had not made a previous determination to visit the bishop of Goa; on which account he did not then open his mind to Xavier, but proceeded to Goa; where he afterwards entered the College of the Faith, and joined the Society of Jesus. Xavier soon arrived, and proposed that Cosmo should go with him to Japan, to which he cordially assented, and availed himself of the aid of Paul Anger to prepare for the Japanese Mission.

Such a companion as Cosmo, with his long and varied experience of life in those climates, and his natural love of enterprise, after a training of one or two years in a Jesuit College, would certainly appear to be admirably fitted for the Mission to which Xavier believed himself to be called.

The party therefore consisted of Xavier, Cosmo Turrianus, Fernandez, a lay-assistant or servant, Paul, his Japanese servant Manuel, and another youth, a Chinese, named Amator. They sailed from Cochin on the 25th April 1549, and arrived at Malacca after a pleasant voyage of forty days. Here they were received by the governor and citizens with every demonstration of respect, and a liberal supply was given them for all their necessities.

In a letter to the King of Portugal, Xavier gives a full account of the munificent liberality of the governor of Malacca, who had taken the utmost pains to procure a ship, but had been obliged at last to engage a Chinese junk for the voyage. He had procured for them abundant supplies for their accommodation, for their provisions, and for their celebration of the holy sacrifice; and, at his own cost, he had supplied them with thirty bushels of the best pepper, selected out of the stores of Malacca. He had added many splendid and costly presents for the King of Japan, that he might be conciliated, and grant Xavier a free entrance into his dominions, and a full tolerance of the Christian religion.

The voyage from Malacca to Japan was a very trying one to Xavier and his companions. Like the Chinese junks of the present day, Xavier's ship carried its idol, before which the sailors burnt scented wood, and which they consulted, by lots, as to the course they should pursue at different points in the voyage. It was with great difficulty, and only after many threats, that the captain was persuaded to fulfil his engagement to carry the Missionaries to Japan, instead of wintering in China. Xavier's spirit was stirred within him at the sight of these idolatrous rites, and at being compelled to shape his course (to use his own expression) "by an appeal to the Devil." He speaks of the prayers which he offered up for the conversion of the captain and crew; but he cannot record any beneficial influence over their minds, and he afterwards reports that the captain died a heathen in Japan.

SECTION 2. *Xavier's arrival in Japan, and first account of the people.*

Xavier arrived at Cangoxima in Japan, August 15, 1549. That port is situated at the extreme south-east point of Kew Sew, the most southern of the Japanese group of islands. It was the place to which Paul belonged, and all his relatives welcomed him upon his return. In the early part of November an opportunity occurred of sending letters to India and to Europe. Six letters are preserved which Xavier wrote on this occasion, giving full and minute accounts of the commencement of his labours, and of his observations upon the people. They occupy nearly seventy pages of the octavo edition. (III. 18—23. Fr. 84—89.)

The arrival of the Missionary party at Cangoxima was auspicious. Xavier writes—" The chief magistrate of the city, the principal inhabitants, and the whole community, received us with the greatest kindness. They greatly admired 'the new priests' who had arrived from Portugal. No offence was taken at Paul's having become a Christian: they rather respected him the more on that account. His relatives, and all who had been formerly acquainted with him, presented their congratulations on his having visited India, and seen things which no one of his countrymen besides himself had ever witnessed."

" The zeal of Paul for the religion he had embraced proved itself to be eminently sincere. He devoted whole days and nights to the instruction in Christian doctrine of his parents, relatives, and friends of every age and rank, and he exhorted them with such success, that within three months he brought over to Christianity his mother, his wife, his male and female relatives, and no small number of his other friends and former intimates."

"The governor of the province resided between five and six leagues from Cangoxima. Paul went to pay his respects to him. The governor was greatly rejoiced at his return, and paid him much respect. He inquired minutely respecting the manners, virtues, and wealth of the Portuguese. When Paul had satisfied his curiosity, he appeared to be highly gratified by the recital. Paul had carried with him a beautiful picture, which he had brought from India, of the blessed Mary and the child Jesus sitting in his mother's lap. When the governor had looked upon this picture he was overwhelmed with emotion. Immediately falling upon his knees, he very devoutly worshipped it, and commanded all who were present to do the same. Afterwards, the mother of the governor, having contemplated the picture, was seized with the highest delight and admiration, and sent a few days later, when Paul had returned to Cangoxima, a very respectable person to procure, by some means, a copy of it. But there were no means of accomplishing this in Cangoxima. The lady also made a request, by the same person, that we should commit to writing, for her use, the chief articles of the Christian religion. Paul devoted some days to this work, and prepared a treatise in the native language upon the chief mysteries and institutions of Christianity.

"In reviewing these events, believe me, when I say, and, at the same time thank God for it, that a very wide field is opened before you, which your pious zeal should occupy. (Xavier is writing to his Jesuit Associates.)

Had we been acquainted with the Japanese, we should long since have reaped in this vast province a large harvest of souls. Paul diligently preaches the Gospel day and night to his neighbours and friends, by which he has brought over his wife, daughter, and many friends and relatives to the faith of Christ. The decision of those who become Christians is not, to this time, disapproved of by the people. And as the Japanese, for the most part, can read, they quickly learn our prayers. May God grant that we may soon acquire the Japanese language, that we may explain the divine doctrine. Then at last we shall be able to effect something for Christianity; for now we are in the midst of the people as mute as statues. They are all engaged in discourse and action about us. We are dumb through ignorance of their language. For the present we are going back, as it were, to childhood in studying the elements of the language. Would that we could imitate also the simplicity and candour of children."

But again Xavier's better sentiments are debased by the alloy of Romish superstition. "I am full of hope," he writes, "that divine assistance will be granted to us, because, distrusting our own strength, we put all our confidence upon the strength and power of the Lord Christ, and of his most holy mother, and of all the angels, especially the Archangel Michael, the patron of the Church militant. We place much hope in that Archangel, because Japan is under his patronage, and we daily commend our cause to him, and to the other guardian angels." (III. 18. Fr. 84.) How, we may well inquire, did Xavier ascertain that this newly-discovered country was specially under the patronage of Michael the Archangel?

A desire soon sprung up in the minds of several of the Japanese to visit the Portuguese settlements in India. Xavier took advantage of this natural curiosity, by commending two Bonzes, or Japanese priests, to the college authorities at Goa. His advice was excellent:—"Be careful to treat them kindly and courteously, as I treated Paul when I was with you."

To an intelligent Christian, much will have already appeared to excite apprehension, that, notwithstanding all these providential and external advantages, there were serious defects at the root of this Jesuit Mission to Japan. The exhibition of the picture of the Virgin Mother, and the child Jesus in her lap, and the worship which was paid to it, cannot be regarded as an isolated circumstance, but a significant mark of a system fatally erroneous. Here the first public exhibition of Christianity was an act of Mariolatry. The Saviour is, indeed, exhibited, but as inferior to the mother. The mind is involuntarily carried forward to the issue of the Mission, when the religion thus introduced was barbarously expelled from Japan; and a festival was instituted to commemorate that event, in which a ceremony is annually performed of casting on the ground the representations of the cross, and the Virgin Mother and child, and all the inhabitants stamp upon them: rich and poor, old and young. Even mothers bring their children in arms and place their little feet upon the execrated symbols.

Very few matters of any present interest can be gathered from Xavier's first letters from Japan. His sanguine temperament, and his ignorance of the language, led him to record his first impressions at great length; many of which were afterwards modified, or proved incorrect. Yet the following notices may be given as presenting the earliest extant account of the state of Japan, upon its first introduction into the comity of Western nations.

"The Japanese excel all other nations yet discovered in honesty; so that I believe no uncivilized nation can be compared with them in natural goodness of disposition. They are ingenious, yet not in the least given to fraud. They are wonderfully ambitious of honour and dignity, for they regard honour as the greatest good. Many of them are poor, but poverty is no discredit. We witness among them what, as far as I am aware, is not met with amongst any Christian nation. Even an indigent nobleman is treated by all others with as much respect as if he were wealthy; and no person of rank, however poor and needy, can be induced by any consideration to join in marriage with a plebeian, however rich. This arises from the conviction that they will lose in dignity and general estimation by a plebeian alliance, and wealth is despised in comparison with honour. They are very respectful to each other. They have the highest delight in arms, which is their only security: all, from highest to lowest, wear in public a sword and dagger, even boys of fourteen. They never submit to an insulting word or deed. As the common people hold the nobility in great honour, so the nobles are most submissive to their kings and rulers, and esteem it a distinction to obey their commands. They appear to me to act thus rather out of zeal for honour, than out of the fear of their power. They seem to feel that if they should act otherwise, they would lower their own dignity. They are spare and frugal in diet, but not in drink. They use a wine made from rice. No other wine is made in the country. They abhor gambling as most disgraceful, because they say gamblers must be covetous of the wealth of others, and will be tempted to steal for the sake of gain. If they employ an oath, which is very rare, they swear by the sun. The people are generally instructed in reading, which will be a great advantage for comprehending our forms of prayer and the articles of our faith. A man has only one wife. There are very few thieves amongst them on account of the severity with which theft is visited, being invariably punished by death. Every kind of theft is therefore held in detestation. They are naturally inclined to honesty, and most eager in the acquisition of knowledge.

" They eagerly listen to discourses about God and divine things, especially when they sufficiently understand the speaker. Out of the many races I have seen, I remember none, either Christian or barbarians, so averse to every kind of theft." (III. 18. Fr. 84.)

Xavier reports that there was an almost universal belief in the immortality of the soul; and that the learned amongst them indulged in deep speculations upon such questions as these:—" When death has silenced the voice of the body, has the soul, at the moment of its departure, the power of utterance ?" "If a departed soul were to return to the world, what would be his chief address to the living ?"

Xavier states that several religions were equally tolerated and protected, and that the freedom of religious profession was so great, that often a husband and wife, or parents and children, followed different religions, without creating any inconvenience. The different religions which he describes may be classed under the ancient form of demon worship, or the Sinto religion; and the Buddhist and Philosophical systems introduced from China. He long and diligently searched, but in vain, for any vestige of Christianity. He once discovered, in the armorial bearings of a family, a white cross; but he could gain no hint which could identify it with the emblem of the Christian religion.

Xavier was evidently not acquainted with the Buddhist religion, and therefore he does not identify that system among the religions of Japan, though probably it was at that time the most prevalent. His descriptions of the religions of Japan are very vague. " None amongst the Japanese worship gods under the form of animals. Multitudes pay divine honours to certain men, who, as far as I can ascertain, lived after the fashion of the old philosophers. A great many worship the sun, some the moon." " Out of the nine religious sects which may be said to exist in Japan, only one denies the immortality of the soul. That sect is regarded by all the rest as disreputable; and it contains the most abandoned and infamous characters." " The original founders of the religions are said to have been Xaca and Amida."* Xavier says he searched diligently into the histories to ascertain whether these were men; but finding that they were said to have lived for one, two, or even eight thousand years, he concluded that they were devils. (IV. 2. Fr. 94.)

Xavier was much struck with the prevalence of a monastic life in Japan, and this not in one sect, but in all, and extending to female as well as male communities. The members of these monasteries Xavier calls Bonzes and Bonzesses. The communities comprised three or four, or several hundred members. They abounded in every part of the country. They were regarded as the priests and priestesses of religion, and were generally the most learned among the people. The order of dis-

* The name of Xaca represents that of Siaka, which is given by Kæmpfer as the Japanese name of Buddhu. Amida, in the Buddhist creed, is the chief mediator and patron of the faithful followers of the precepts of Buddhu, which are the five precepts enumerated by Xavier in a subsequent extract.

cipline varied in different communities, but all acknowledged five fundamental precepts—not to kill, not to steal, not to commit adultery, not to lie, to abstain from wine. It was a common belief that these laws were obligatory upon all men, but that those who were engaged in worldly occupation could not always observe them; but that the Bonzes and Bonzesses were able to keep them in their stead, if they only paid them for so doing. Xavier describes, as remarkable points of similarity between the monastic life in Japan and in Europe, celibacy, the dress of a grey or black gown, the head being shaved, prayers recited by the help of beads.

Xavier gives a high character of the intelligence of the Bonzes. "The Bonzes are of a very subtle understanding. They meditate deeply on futurity—what will be their future condition, what will be the end of their being, and such like questions. Among their number there were many who were so shaken in their tenets as to be persuaded that their discipline could afford no safeguard for the salvation of the soul; for they thus reasoned with themselves: There ought undoubtedly to be a first principle of all things, but that no mention was made of it in their books. There is a remarkable silence in all their sacred writings respecting the creation of the universe. Certainly (they reasoned), if our sages had any knowledge of this first principle, they kept it to themselves, and concealed it from their posterity; probably because they could not allege any authority for it, either in ancient writings or in human reasons. Men of this class were therefore greatly delighted with the Divine law." (IV. 2. Fr. 94.)

Xavier soon discovered that the morality of these monastic institutions was far below that of common life. "The most learned (he writes) are the most wicked." The Bonzes were not only notoriously profligate, but gloried in their sins; yet the people honoured them the more the worse they became. He entertained hopes, on his first arrival, that he should be able to gain over the Bonzes to Christianity, and employ them in teaching others. But when he boldly rebuked their sins, and showed the folly of their supposed vicarious righteousness, they became his bitterest enemies, and everywhere endeavoured to counteract the truth. The Bonzes appear to have studied the art of popular preaching, and had large audiences on stated occasions. These opportunities were employed in denouncing the new religion.

SECTION 3. *Conclusion of Xavier's labours in Japan.*

After an interval of more than two years in the correspondence of Xavier, he resumes his pen in letters written from Malacca, at the close of the year 1551, and from Cochin, upon his return to India, at the commencement of 1552. From these letters, which are numerous and minute in their narrative, we gather notices of what befel him at Cangoxima, and during his subsequent residence in Japan. It is evident from them that Xavier's bright prospects of a speedy reception of Christianity had been considerably clouded over during this interval, and that his thoughts were chiefly turned to the establishing commercial and diplomatic relations between Japan and the crown of Portugal. Such measures he had projected even in his letters written at the close of 1549, for in one of them he had informed Peter de Sylva, the Governor of Malacca, who had so liberally furnished him for the voyage to Japan, that there was a port called Sacajus, the principal emporium of Japan, distant two days' journey from Miako, in which, by God's help, permission would be easily obtained for the king of Portugal to build storehouses, and to carry on a profitable trade in exchange for precious metals. He engaged, on his part, to negotiate with the King of Japan to send an ambassador to India. Xavier wrote also urgent letters to his friends at Goa, to prevail upon the Viceroy to send a vessel forthwith to open the trade, suggesting the kind of cargo likely to suit, and especially that there should not be above a certain quantity of pepper, which he had ascertained might be disposed of at Sacajus in a reasonable time.

As for the Mission, the whole Missionary party remained at Cangoxima for twelve months. Xavier gives this account of their leaving it:—" In the space of a year more than 100 were brought into the fold of Christ, and all, if they had been willing, might have entered, without giving any offence to their parents or friends. But the Bonzes stirred up the governor, who is lord of many cities, and showed him that, if he should suffer his people to embrace the religion of Christ, his whole power would be undermined, and the divinities of the country would come into contempt with the inhabitants; since the Divine law was contrary to the laws of Japan, so that whoever received it repudiated in fact the most sacred lawgivers of antiquity. But this would not take place without ruin to the government and the city. He should therefore have respect to the most holy authors of the Japanese laws; and as he would perceive that the Divine law was antagonistic to the law of their forefathers, he should issue an edict that no one in future should become a Christian on pain of death. The governor, excited by this speech, issued the edict which the Bonzes demanded. As soon as we saw that the governor of the city had thus decidedly set himself against the progress of Christianity, we determined to migrate elsewhere. We therefore bade farewell to the neophytes, who took our departure grievously to heart, weeping on account of their singular love to us, and giving us the warmest thanks for having laboured so much to show to them the way of eternal salvation. We left Paul, their fellow-citizen, amongst them, who is an eminent Christian, and will perfect the neophytes in the Christian life." (III. 24. Fr. 90.)

The three European Missionaries removed to a town

situated in the kingdom of Amanguchi. The Governor of this town received them with great courtesy, and there, after residing for some days, Xavier declares that nearly 100 persons embraced Christianity, though, in the next sentence, he acknowledges "No one of us could speak the Japanese: we drew many of them to the worship of Christ by nothing more than reciting from the semi-Japonic volume, and reading sermons to the people." The "semi-Japonic volume," to which Xavier here refers, he had previously explained to be a treatise on the chief articles of the Christian faith, which Paul had translated into the Japanese, and which the European Missionaries had written out in Roman letters. Converts so gained, and in so short a time, must be estimated accordingly. If, however, the biographies are correct in giving the name of this town as Firando, a sea-port with which the Portuguese had much intercourse, it is probable that a favourable impression of Christianity may have existed before Xavier's arrival; for he tells us, in a subsequent letter, that he received very great assistance, both in money and in acts of kindness, from his dear friend, Francis Pereira, who had with him a large company, who were all animated by a benevolent disposition.

An interesting memento of Xavier's visit to Firando is preserved in the Epistolæ Indicæ, in a letter from the King of Firando, in 1555, to Melchior Nunez, a Missionary of China, inviting him to come to Japan.

"When the Father Master Francis had come into this kingdom he made some Christians, much to my delight, whom I have taken charge of, and kept them from all injuries. Afterwards the Father who lives at Bungo (Cosmo Turrianus) twice visited us, and has baptized some of my relatives, and very many of the rest of the nobility. As often as I have heard that man and his doctrine, I have determined to follow Christ, so much have I approved of what I heard, so deeply has it penetrated into my soul. I am therefore desirous of seeing you in my kingdom. Once I deceived you, but I will not deceive you again. If you, therefore, come to us, you will do a thing pleasing in the sight of God, and will be treated in the most honourable and liberal manner by ourselves.

"Taqua Nombo, King of Firando."

Xavier, it will be remembered, had brought with him from Malacca valuable presents for the King of Japan. He repeatedly expressed his determination to make his way to the capital for the purpose of delivering them. He remained, therefore, but a short time at Firando, and, leaving Cosmo Turrianus to carry on the Mission, he took John Fernandez as his companion, and proceeded to Amanguchi, the capital of the kingdom of that name.

The city of Amanguchi was very extensive; it contained more than 10,000 houses, all built of wood.

"Here," he writes, "we met with many among the people and the nobility who were very desirous of knowing the Christian law; therefore, when we had deliberated upon what was best to be done, we determined to stand twice in the day in places of public resort, and recite the chapters of our book, and so address the people on the Christian religion. Some of the noblemen invited us to their houses, that they might more conveniently acquire a knowledge of our religion; and, of their own accord, gave us the promise that, if they should believe it to be better than their own, they would, without hesitation, embrace it. Many willingly listened to our addresses upon the Divine law; others were stirred up to enmity, and turned into ridicule whatever we said; so that, as often as we went through the streets of the city, a crowd of boys and of the dregs of the population pressed us with derisive shouts:—'These are the men who command us to embrace their Divine law if we would be saved, because we cannot be rescued from destruction except through the Maker of all things, and his Son: these are the men who declare that it is wrong to have more than one wife.' In a similar way they turned all the other articles of our religion into jest. We had been engaged for some days in these preachings, when we were called into the presence of the King, who was then in the city. To his inquiries from whence we came, and why we had come to Japan, we answered that we were Europeans, and sent there for the purpose of preaching the Divine law, as no one

K

could be safe or saved hereafter unless he would worship God and his Son, Jesus Christ, the Judge and Saviour of all nations, in piety and holiness. He then commanded us to expound to him the Divine law, upon which we recited the greater part of our book, and, as long as we spoke from the writing, which took us more than an hour, he listened to us with diligent attention. We were afterwards dismissed. We remained in that city many days, speaking to the people in the streets and market-places. Many earnestly listened to the great facts of Christianity, and they could not retain their tears when we described the most bitter death of Christ. Notwithstanding, very few were brought to accept baptism.

"When little fruit of our labours appeared in that place, we set out for Miako, the most celebrated city of Japan. We occupied two months in the journey. We were exposed to many dangers, because we had to pass through countries in which a civil war raged. I omit all account of the intense cold of these regions, and of the roads through which we passed, infested with a multitude of robbers. After our arrival at Miako we waited some days, till we could obtain permission of access to the King, and ask him to give us the license of promulgating the Divine law throughout his empire. We found every approach to the King utterly closed against us, and we discovered that his temporal authority was held in contempt by the other kings and rulers. We therefore dismissed the thought of seeking his permission, and determined to try and explore the feeling of the citizens, that we might ascertain how far that city was prepared to receive the worship of Christ; but as the citizens were all in arms, and were suffering from a grievous civil war, I judged that the time was inappropriate for preaching the Gospel. Miako was formerly a very large city: now, through the calamities of war, a great part of it is in ruins and wasted. Formerly, it is said, it consisted of 180,000 houses. That computation appears to me very probable, for the circuit of the walls shows it to have been one of the greatest cities of the East. Now, though a great part is in ruins, yet it contains 100,000 houses. As soon as we had ascertained that the state of Miako was sufficiently at peace, nor otherwise prepared for the Gospel, we returned back to Amanguchi."

As Xavier's splendid hopes of winning over the Emperor of Japan to patronize the preachers of the Gospel were thus dissolved by his visit to Miako, he determined to be content with the King of Amanguchi. He had, indeed, failed in his first visit, as he confesses, to influence the King or people by the message of the Gospel; but now he had recourse to other arguments. He determined to present to his Majesty the rich and attractive presents designed for the Emperor, which contained, among other rarities, a clock and a harpsichord. Xavier thus relates the result:—

"We delivered to the King of Amanguchi the letters and gifts, as tokens of friendship, from the Viceroy of India, and from the Bishop of Goa. The King was highly delighted with the gifts and the letters, and, for our recompense, he offered us a large amount of gold and silver. But we declined this offer, saying that if he wished to present what would be really acceptable to us foreigners, he must give to us the power of promulgating the Divine law throughout his dominions, and to his people the liberty of accepting it; that no gift would be so acceptable as this. With the utmost readiness, the King granted our wish. He published an edict, which was exhibited in the most important parts of the city, declaring his pleasure that the celestial law should be promulgated throughout his kingdom, and that it should be lawful to all to embrace it if they desired to do so. At the same time he assigned us a vacant monastery for our residence. Here numbers are accustomed to resort to hear of the new religion. We preach twice a-day. A long discussion always follows the preaching; so that we are fully occupied either in giving addresses, or in replying to questions. Many of the Bonzes are often at these meetings, and a great number of the nobility and common people. The house is always full, and many are excluded for want of room. Those who at first took the most bitter part in these disputes and controversies, were also the first to come over to us. Many of them are of good birth; and when they have adopted the Christian religion they show such devoted attachment to us as words cannot express. These new converts also explain to us the mysteries, or rather the follies, of the Japanese religion."

"The Japanese have a high opinion of the wisdom of the Chinese, in religious matters as well as in civil institutions and customs. They are accustomed to inquire—How is it, if what you preach is true, that the Chinese never heard of it? After much inquiry and dispute, the inhabitants of Amanguchi, both high and low, began to join the Church of Christ. In the space of two months 500 converts were easily made, and the number is daily increasing." (III. 24. Fr. 90.)

It appears from Xavier's letters that the lay assistant outstripped the two Missionaries in the acquisition of the Japanese language, and that Xavier failed to acquire it: all his information, therefore, was gathered through the uncertain means of interpreters. "Cosmo (Xavier writes) composes sermons in our own language, and Fernandez, who is well skilled in the Japanese, translates them into that tongue." (IV. 2. Fr. 94.)

Xavier's account, therefore, of "the 500 converts easily made in two months," must be received with the qualification arising from his uncertain means of communication with them. The probability is, that each party had imperfectly understood the other. At Xavier's first visit he made no converts. On his return from Miako, after the display of his presents, and the countenance shown him by the King, and the public proclamation in favour of Christianity, people flocked to him, and his sanguine disposition led him to reckon them as true converts. But Cosmo, describing the same circumstances, says more distinctly—"There was a great concourse of all classes at our house, partly drawn by a desire to know the truth, partly by the charm of novelty, partly by zeal to refute us." And speaking of the state of things, five months after Xavier's departure, in the same letter, he only employs the more cautious language—" The number of neophytes is large." (Letter of Cosmo Turrianus to the Society at Goa, Michaelmas-day 1551. Maffeus.)

Some instances, however, of individual success are recorded. Xavier specifies one remarkable case. "A learned man joined himself to Christ, who had studied many years at the university of Bandua, and enjoyed a great reputation for learning. He had contemplated becoming a Bonze before our arrival in Japan, but afterwards, changing his purpose, married a wife. He himself alleged this cause for his change, that he had discovered that the religions of Japan were all vain and false, and that he was bound to worship the Creator of the world. The Christians are greatly encouraged by the accession of this man, since he is, and is allowed to be, the most learned man in the city." (IV. 2. Fr. 94.)

Xavier set his heart upon sending some learned Jesuits to the university of Bandua, to which all the Japanese resorted for the knowledge of their laws, which were written in the Chinese language.

The letters from the Missionaries in Japan, written forty years after Xavier's death, commemorate also another remarkable conversion at Amanguchi. "Brother Lawrence was one of the first Christians baptized at

Amanguchi, in the time of Francis Xavier of pious memory. For several years he was an assistant to us, very useful in building up converts, and bringing in his neighbours. At length, after he was above twenty years old, he was received into our Society. He was the first of all our Japanese brethren who entered the Society;* and though an illiterate man, and the son of poor parents, yet He, who chooses the weak and contemptible things of the world to bring wonderful things to pass, made this man the instrument of converting to Christianity the wealthy classes of Miako; for many who are now our chief men, and men of power and influence in the state, were brought over to Christianity by his preaching." (Annual letters from Japan 1591: John Hayes.)

While the Mission was thus successfully advancing at Amanguchi, Xavier received an invitation from the neighbouring King of Bungo to come and advise with him upon the course he should pursue, in consequence of the unexpected arrival of a Portuguese ship in his harbour. Xavier immediately left Cosmo Turrianus and John Fernandez to carry on the work at Amanguchi, and hastened to Bungo; and he was there equally delighted by the reception which he received from the King, and by the sight of his countrymen.

Shortly after Xavier's leaving Amanguchi a civil war

---

* If Paul Anger became an Associate at Goa, this statement must imply that Lawrence was the first to enter the Society in Japan.

broke out in that city. A powerful lord expelled the King by force. The King, having no hope of escape, committed suicide, rather than fall into the cruel hands of his persecutors, and commanded his followers to kill his son, and burn both their bodies, that nothing might remain on which his enemies could wreak their vengeance. After the death of the King of Amanguchi the nobles sent a request to the King of Bungo to allow his step-brother to be their king, which was granted. His Majesty also promised Xavier that he would treat with his brother for the protection of Turrianus and Fernandez. The King elect of Amanguchi also promised that, as soon as he could put his foot in his new kingdom, he would provide for the safety of the Missionaries. The two Missionaries were providentially preserved in the midst of the revolution, through the protection of a powerful lady. A letter of John Fernandez to Xavier, written from Amanguchi (20th October 1551), contains the following account of their escape:—

"The fighting in the city, which was only stopped by the death of the King, was so savage and universal, that for eight days the town blazed with incendiary fires, and the streets ran with blood. For as soon as law was powerless, the evil-disposed triumphed everywhere with impunity. On all sides was murder and rapine. During that time we were eagerly sought for to be put to death, both by those who hated us, and by those who had set their hearts upon possessing themselves of our property, such as it is. We were often in the most imminent danger of our lives. But out of all these dangers the most merciful mother of our Lord delivered us, who specially guards all who put their trust in her. When things were at the worst, Cosmo sent Anthony to the wife of Naetondo, to ask her counsel. She desired us to come immediately to her. On our way to her we fell into the midst of many armed mobs. They, as we passed through their ranks, cried out, 'Why do we not put out of the way these foreigners, who deny that images of wood or stone can help themselves or men? The gods, enraged at this their impiety, have brought upon our people this bloody catastrophe.' They were thus excited against us, because, in the midst of this commotion, the incendiary fires had consumed many monasteries, with the images; and also because the reverence for their idols and charms had been very greatly impugned, when it was seen how little a King, most idolatrous, as you well know, had profited by his idolatry. Having escaped, however, this danger, we arrived at the house of Naetondo, whose wife gave us a servant to accompany us to a monastery of Bonzes, whom she supported by her own purse, and to whose care she committed us. But the Bonzes were greatly offended at the sight of us, and refused. They said that we were devils, and that they had no room for such a reprobate class of men. 'Why,' they asked, 'did not the God who dwells in heaven, and whose laws we expound, snatch us up to heaven out of these dangers.' Yet at last, either through fear of the lady, or induced by the entreaties of the servant who accompanied us, they assigned us as an abode a small corner of the temple. After having remained there two whole days, the lady called us again to her house, and allowed us to refresh ourselves with exercise in the grounds behind her house. But I shall be tedious, and therefore I will pass over in silence, for the present, all the risks and the troubles we have endured. ("Maffeus de Japonicis rebus.")

Xavier writes that the King of Bungo was very powerful, and that as soon as he knew the character and resources of the King of Portugal, he addressed letters to him to request admission into the number of his friends, and sent him a cuirass as a pledge of friendship.

This disposition of the King of Bungo afforded Xavier the opportunity which he had so greatly desired of opening diplomatic relations between Portugal and Japan. He arranged with the King of Bungo to send an ambassador to the Viceroy of India; and without revisiting his companions at Amanguchi, he finally quitted Japan, to sail in the same ship with the ambassador. Xavier acted now in his capacity of Royal Commissioner, and made all arrangements for the Ambassador's voyage to India, sending directions from Singapore to the Governor of Malacca to detain one of the Indian ships for their conveyance. Xavier wished to take with him from Japan, and to send to Europe, some of the Bonzes, that he might prove to his friends their mental acuteness and power, but none would consent. He tried, also, to persuade several neophytes to visit Europe, but he only succeeded with two, Matthew and Bernard, whom he afterwards sent on to Portugal, entreating Simon Roderick to make them fully acquainted with the power and riches of that country, and then to send them on to Rome, that they might witness the Christian religion in all its magnificence, and return to Japan with higher notions of Christianity, and afterwards persuade some of the superior classes of the Japanese to visit Europe.

The following curious letter from the King of Bungo respecting Xavier's visit, which his Majesty sent to the Viceroy of India, is given in the Travels and Adventures of Ferdinand Mendez Pinto, who visited Japan shortly after Xavier's death.

"Illustrious Lord, and of Great Majesty, Viceroy of the limits of the Indies, the dreadful lion in the floods of the sea, by the force of thy ships and artillerie: I, Yacataaandono, King of Bungo, Facataa, Omangucha, and the countries of the two seas, Lord of the petty Kings of the Islands of Tosa, Xemenarequa, and Miaygina, do give thee to understand by this letter, that Father Francisco Xavier, having been not long since in this country, preaching to them of Omangucha the new law of the Creator of all things, I secretely promised to him, that at his return into my kingdom I would receive from his hands the name and water of holy baptism, howsoever the novelty of so unexpected a thing might put me into bad terms with my subjects. Whereupon he also promised me on his side, that if God gave him life, he would come back again unto me as speedily as he could. And forasmuch as his return hath been longer than I looked for, I have sent thus expressly to know both of him, and of you, the cause of this retardment of his. Wherefore, my Lord, I desire you that he may hasten away to me with all the speed that the first season which shall be proper for navigation will permit. For besides that his arrival in my kingdom is greatly important for the service of God, it will be also very profitable to myself for the contracting of a new league with the great King of Portugal, to the end that, by this amitie, my country and his may hereafter be but one thing."

This letter having arrived at Goa some time after Xavier's death, another Jesuit Father was sent in his place, who, after various delays, reached the town of Fucheo, in the kingdom of Bungo, June 1556; but the King said that "the state of his country was such that he could not be baptized," and the father quitted the place in despair after five months. The Jesuits, however, in subsequent years, met with better success in the kingdom of Bungo. (See Travels of Ferdinand Mendez Pinto, translated into English 1692.)

Xavier's letters give us some idea of the expenses of the Mission in Japan. He writes:—"As long as we were in Japan, which was two years and a half, we were supported by the pecuniary aid of the most munificent King of Portugal. He directed more than a thousand gold pieces (doubloons, *Cutilla*) to be assigned to us under the name of alms. It is scarcely credible how much that excellent sovereign favours us, and what sums he has expended, and daily expends, on our colleges and houses." (IV. 2. Fr. 94.) Without investigating the precise value of the gold coin, or its equivalent in money of the present day, it is evident that the Missionaries were amply provided for, and had the means of exercising a large charity; especially as Xavier and Cosmo abstained from animal food while in Japan, lest they should seem less self-denying than the Bonzes.

In another letter of this series there occurs one sentence, which gives a transient insight into Xavier's own spiritual experience; a sentence of far more value than all his rapturous and inflated sentiments of spiritual joy in the midst of trouble. For in this instance he speaks the language of a sinner seeking the salvation of his soul; though even here, alas! he flies for refuge from an accusing conscience rather to a distant arm of flesh than to a present and living Saviour. The extract is from a letter to Ignatius Loyola, Cochin, 29th Jan. 1552:—

" I can never describe in writing how much I owe to the Japanese, since God, through their means, penetrated my mind with a clear and intimate conviction of my innumerable sins. Hitherto my thoughts ever wandered beyond myself: I had not searched into that abyss of evil lying deep in my conscience, until, amidst the troubles and anguish of Japan, my eyes were a little opened, and the good Lord granted me to see clearly, and to have, as it were, a present and tangible experience of the necessity of having a friend to keep up an ever-attentive and sedulous care over me. Let your holy charity, therefore, suggest to you what you may do for me whilst subjecting to my government the souls of fathers and brethren of our Society. For, through the infinite mercy of God, I have lately discovered that I am so ill furnished with the necessary qualities for discharging this government, that I ought rather to hope to be myself commended by you to the care and supervision of my brethren, than that they should be committed to my guidance." (IV. 1. Fr. 93.)

Xavier's affection for Ignatius was of the most ardent, and even romantic kind. After the words just quoted, he writes :—" Your holy charity has led you to say that you entertain a great desire of once more seeing me before our departure out of this life. Our Lord, who sees my inmost soul, knows how this kind signification of your continued love for me penetrated my heart with a sweet but violent emotion of tender affection. Indeed, as often as I think over your words—and I think them over very often—unbidden tears fill my eyes; nor can I restrain them till they are quenched by that dear imagination which my thoughts create, that it is possible that I may be again embraced by you. Though I see that this will be most difficult, yet there is nothing which holy obedience cannot accomplish."

Xavier's letters respecting the Japanese Missions contain fervid expressions of joy in his work, and energetic invitations to brethren in Europe to join the Mission, similar to those on which we have already remarked. One specimen may, however, be introduced.

"Though my hair is white, yet I am as strong and vigorous as ever; for the labours we endure in giving Christian instruction to a civilized nation eager to receive the truth and to embrace salvation, bring with them a rich recompense of joy. Even at Amanguchi, when the people began to resort to us in great numbers, after the King had granted us permission to preach the Gospel, I had such an enjoyment of life, and such satisfaction of mind as I never before experienced; for here I saw the spirit of the Bonzes broken by God, through our word, and a noble victory gained over the bitterest of our enemies. Again, I saw the joy of the neophytes at the humiliation of the Bonzes, and their burning zeal to confound the heathen, and to bring them to baptism, as well as their exultation in success, and in the recital to each other of their conflicts; whilst on every side I saw the superstitions of the people dissipated and overthrown. These things turned such a flood of joy into my soul as extinguished every sense of care. I wish that I could so set before the universities of Europe the heavenly consolations imparted to us in the midst of our labours,—such is the divine goodness!—that they might not only listen to, but, as it were, taste these delights. Then, indeed, multitudes of our younger students would transfer all their care and study to the conversion of the heathen, as soon as they had once tasted of the heavenly joy which accompanies the work. If it were universally known and understood how fully the Japanese are prepared to receive the Gospel, I am persuaded that very many would lay aside their favourite studies, and that canons, priests, and even rulers in the Church would abandon their benefices, however rich and ample, that they might embrace our mode of life, though a hard and anxious one, on account of its true sweetness and pleasure; and for the sake of this they would not hesitate even to sail to Japan." (IV. 2. Fr. 94.)

If we inquire into the results of Xavier's labours in Japan, we must remember, that though he spent more than two years in the study of the language, he was obliged, even to the last, to employ his lay-helper as an interpreter. He has himself expressed, in emphatic terms, the insufficiency of his personal efforts. Looking forward to a visit to China, he says—" I shall succeed in opening it for others, for I can do nothing myself— *quoniam ego ipse nihil ago."* (IV. 3. Fr. 94.)

This single sentence, beautiful in its humility, nevertheless points to the simple fact that his personal attempts to evangelize the natives were a failure everywhere, but that he led the way for others to follow, and encouraged numbers to do so. So, here, he devised the plan of a Jesuit Mission to Japan, chose his companions, conducted them into the country, encouraged them in their work for two years, conciliated the confidence of the King of Amanguchi by his presents, and afterwards won the still more important patronage of the King of Bungo by his diplomacy, and established a political intercourse between Portugal and Japan. In other words, Xavier erected a Mission upon the treacherous foundations of secular support. With the honest intention of promoting Christianity, he introduced into the work the elements of political intrigue and complications, which soon sprang up and choked whatever " good seed" such simple Missionaries as Paul, Cosmo, and Fernandez were labouring to disseminate.

The Mission, after Xavier's death, was carried on with great vigour, and was abundantly supplied with labourers, other denominations besides the Jesuits entering upon the field. Vast numbers of the natives are reported to have professed the Christian faith, but I have in vain sought for any reliable accounts of these successes. No such contemporary history or biographies exist of the Japanese Mission as the letters of Xavier. I have looked into the various collections of Epistolæ Japonicæ, but, like the Epistolæ Indicæ, they are filled with legends; and it is impossible, after reading Xavier's letters, to open those pages without the conviction that we have passed out of the regions of truth into those of exaggeration, suppression, and fiction. At the close of the sixteenth century, a fierce and bloody persecution commenced against Christianity, on the part of the political Emperor, upon the old plea of persecutors, that the peace of the state was endangered. From the great number of influential persons said to have been involved in this persecution, it may be inferred that the profession of Christianity had been very widely extended; and from the length of time, amounting to forty years, for which the struggle was continued, it is evident that multitudes firmly held to their adopted faith. In the year 1637, the reigning Emperor discovered, as he affirmed, a traitorous correspondence for dethroning him, between the native Christians and the King of Portugal. He therefore issued orders for the butchery of the remnant of Christians, estimated at 37,000. This order was barbarously carried into effect. Thus the Mission planted by Xavier was extinguished in blood, after existing for nearly ninety years; and this *through the political power on which Xavier had leaned in all his Missionary enterprises.* The fuller details of the extinction of the Japanese Mission, and the reflections which it suggests, must be reserved for a future chapter.

SECTION 4.—*Legends of Xavier's labours in Japan.*

The biographies record many legends of Xavier's successes in Japan. On his first journey from Cangoxima to Firando they tell of his visit to a famous castle, where a prince received them with great honour, and where they made many converts, of whom, upon his departure, the aged house-steward was constituted chief pastor. Xavier gave this man as a present, an old whip, which he had been accustomed to apply to his own back. "The old man," says Bohours, "kept it religiously as a relic, and would not allow the Christians in the assemblies where they chastised themselves to make common use of it. At the most he suffered not any one to give themselves above two or three strokes with it, so fearful he was of wearing it out. It was the instrument which God commonly employed for the cure of sick persons in the castle. The wife of the prince being in the convulsions of death, was instantly restored to health after they had made the sign of the cross over her with the whip."

The biographies report, also, a series of wonderful successes during Xavier's residence at Bungo: that he was received with the highest honours by the King; that he had several discussions with the Bonzes in the presence of the King; and that he convinced the King and the whole audience of the truth and excellency of the Christian doctrine. We are told that the most learned and considerable of the opposing Bonzes was converted in the midst of one of these discussions, and declared his faith in Christ. Père Bohours assures us that "vast multitudes of people from the very first renounced their idols, and believed in Jesus Christ; that the saint employed whole days together in baptizing idolaters, or in teaching new believers," though Xavier had left his companion Cosmo and his interpreter Fernandez at Amanguchi.

Xavier's own account of the events at Bungo is comprised in two lines:—"The King received me with great favour (*liberaliter accepit*): I derived much pleasure from my intercourse with the Portuguese." It is utterly incredible, after the particularity with which

Xavier relates all other circumstances connected with his visit to Japan, that he should suppress such important success at Bungo. And a letter, preserved by Maffeus, settles the matter. A Jesuit Missionary, Peter Alcaceva, writing to the Society in Portugal from Goa, December 1554, describes his journey with a brother Missionary to the city of Bungo, in June 1552, where they had an interview with the King, who told them that he was not ignorant of Cosmo Turrianus being at Amanguchi, and that he lamented *that there were no Christian neophytes in the cities under his own rule*, as there were in Amanguchi. He therefore gave them an edict of toleration, and full permission to preach. This was in October 1552, which was less than a year after the legendary report of Xavier's great successes at Bungo. ("Maffeus de Rebus Japonicis.")

The biographers seem to have reserved their most extravagant legends for the last year of Xavier's life. In their accounts of his voyage from China to India, they tell of his encountering a violent storm; that the ship, called "Holy Cross," was carried about in darkness for three days and three nights; that the ship's smaller boat, containing some of the crew, broke loose in the midst of the storm, and would infallibly have sunk, but that Xavier miraculously kept them from sinking, and appeared at the same moment at the helm of both vessels, though they were far separated, and brought back the smaller, in a straight course, to the "Holy Cross," against a head wind; that, in consequence of Xavier's prediction, no storm could harm the "Holy Cross" while it kept at sea; that for twenty-two years it weathered the most furious storms, and floated, notwithstanding the springing of leaks; but that, according to the same prophecy, it went to pieces, of its own accord, upon its touching land; that "George Nugnez, who thought within himself that there might be yet remaining in the planks somewhat of the virtue which the blessing of the saint had imprinted in them," nailed one of these planks to his own vessel, which enabled it to escape all perils while at sea, and, like the original vessel, to fall to pieces of itself on touching the shore. Such are the idle tales which disgrace the biographies of Francis Xavier.

CHAPTER VII.

Internal Dissensions of the Mission in India.

XAVIER'S BITTER DISAPPOINTMENT AT THE STATE OF THE MISSION — DISSATISFACTION WITH HIS ASSOCIATES — HIGH CHARACTER OF GASPAR BARZEUS — EARNEST INJUNCTIONS TO BROTHERLY LOVE — FINANCIAL AND ECONOMICAL ARRANGEMENTS — SPANISH DESIGNS ON JAPAN.

XAVIER left Japan in November 1551, and reached Cochin at the end of January 1552. He thus spent three months in India; during which period he wrote no less than twenty-one voluminous letters, some from Cochin, but the greater part from Goa, where his last two months were spent.

In a former chapter we contemplated the character of Xavier as the Director of the Jesuit Missions in India. Upon his departure for Japan he had assigned to each Missionary his sphere of labour, and an exact schedule of his duties. He had clearly defined their respective jurisdictions, and had earnestly enjoined upon all the duty of perfect harmony and mutual support. But his arrangements completely broke down. A letter from Cochin to Paul Camerte, at Goa, reveals his bitter disappointment at the state in which he found the Mission upon his return from Japan.

"I had hoped, on my return from Japan, to enjoy some repose after all the fatigues I had undergone. But no! There was no comfort for me. Far from that, I found only grief upon grief, and each in succession more poignant than the preceding. I found law-suits arising from a quarrelsome temper. Nothing is stirring around me but squabbles, disputes, divisions, to the great scandal of the people. Alas! this was not the work I so earnestly enjoined at my departure for Japan. What do I find? Insubordination; little or no obedience! Oh, my God! may thy holy name be always praised!" (IV. 4. Fr. 96.)

In the same letter he sends a priest, Emmanuel Moralez, and a layman, Francis Gonsalez, to Goa. Camerte was to take the priest to the Bishop, and to tell the Bishop that Emmanuel was no longer a Jesuit, as Xavier had expelled him from the community; and that he now, therefore, belonged to the jurisdiction of the Bishop, who might deal with him as he pleased. In modern Missions a question has sometimes arisen upon the relations between a Missionary Society and a Colonial Bishop. Xavier's expedient of getting rid of a troublesome Missionary, by casting the responsibility of his employment upon the Bishop, introduces a new element into the settlement of these relations.

The layman was simply to be told by Camerte that he might go where he chose, as he was turned out of the

Society. Xavier then bursts out into this complaint:—
"I am deeply grieved that their conduct has forced me to these extremities: but it gives me greater pain to think that they are not the only ones whom I shall have to treat in the same manner. God only knows the pangs it has cost my heart to have recourse to such measures."

Dissensions amongst Missionaries, alas! have not been confined to early, or to Romish Missions; yet it is remarkable that the presence of a Bishop, the strong will and personal influence of a Xavier, the previous training of a Missionary college, and the discipline of the Jesuit order, were all insufficient to restrain this propensity amongst the early Jesuit Missionaries in India. The cure for dissensions in a Mission is not from without, but from within; and the best office which external authority can perform, is to enjoin an internal settlement of disputes, upon the principles of mutual forbearance and love.

Tursellinus, in his Life of Xavier, relates that, immediately after Xavier's back was turned, Anthony Gomez assumed supreme power over the College at Goa, and transformed it from a Missionary Institution into a regular Jesuit novitiate establishment; that, after a time, Gomez removed to Cochin, and forcibly took possession of the Franciscan College there, with the same view; that Xavier, with the assistance of the Viceroy, banished Gomez to a distant fortress, which he never reached, as the ship was wrecked, and he was drowned on the way there.

It is not easy to reconcile this account with Xavier's letters. The letters, however, state, that upon his arrival at Goa, Paul Camerte was displaced from the headship of the college and from the dictatorship of the Missions, and that Gaspar Barzæus was put in his place.

Xavier does not notice these troubles in any of his letters to Europe; and they are only partially divulged in his letters to persons on the spot, who must have been cognizant of the circumstances. But his letters to Europe sufficiently show that he was not satisfied with his associates: they were not men of sufficient calibre for the management of colleges, or for disputing with acute Bonzes in Japan. Gaspar Barzæus was the only powerful preacher for the Portuguese settlements. He was therefore ordered to Goa, and made head of the College. Several refractory members were turned out of the Society, and the remainder were visited with severe rebukes for their self-will and disobedience. Gaspar was also made supreme and absolute Superior of all the Jesuit Society between the Cape of Good Hope and Japan.

Barzæus appears to have been a man of considerable talent, and the one good preacher; and Xavier, after addressing to him several letters respecting his appointment and duties, adds another in most fervid language, to warn him against pride and self-sufficiency, or depreciation of his brethren; reminding him that all his gifts are but entrusted to him for the glory of God and the good of the Church, and that his daily sins and infirmities do far more to hinder God's work than all his talents, whatever they may be, can effect for its advancement.

L

Barzæus was a Belgian by birth. He had been an officer in the army of the Emperor Charles V. He afterwards studied at Coimbra, and arrived in India about the time that Xavier went to Japan. He died within a few months after his appointment to Goa, having made a great impression upon the people by the few sermons he preached in that city.

Xavier earnestly entreated his friends in Europe to select superior men as Missionaries. To Ignatius he says—" By the zeal with which you burn for accomplishing the will of God, I conjure you to grant me this petition, which, were I present with you, I would ask, as a suppliant upon my bended knees at your holy feet, that you will send here a man, thoroughly known and approved by your holy and loving spirit, to be made Rector of the College of Goa; for that college urgently needs a man of your choice, and one whom you have fitted by your own hands, so to speak, for the post." (IV. 1. Fr. 93.) He assigns as the reason why superior and learned men were so much needed for Japan, that none others could encounter the learned men of that country, so as to win the confidence of the people by their superiority, or to expose their weakness in public controversy. Xavier put far too much confidence in the wisdom of this world, as the instrument for converting the heathen. "Give me," he says, "these able and learned men, and the Fathers now labouring in Japan shall become their interpreters." He did not sufficiently enter into the spirit of the great Apostle, who said to a more acute and learned race than the Japanese—" When I came to you I came not with excellency of speech, or of wisdom, declaring unto you the testimony of God. For I determined not to know any thing among you, save Jesus Christ and Him crucified;" or he would not have so summarily degraded Cosmo and Fernandez, then in Japan, of whom he himself testifies in the same letter—" They are gathering crowds in the streets of Amanguchi, and telling them the wonderful works of Jesus Christ, and calling forth the tears of multitudes by the recital of His sufferings."

It must be added, however, that Xavier's anxiety to have learned Missionaries did not blind him to the value of other essential qualities. He was equally urgent that his learned men should be also men of self-denial, severe virtue, diligence, and perseverance. He was dissatisfied with the choice of men made by his old friend Simon Roderick in Portugal, and earnestly besought Ignatius Loyola to allow the men selected by Roderick to be sent on a pilgrimage to Rome, that they might be in a measure tested by that journey, but still more by the scrutiny of Loyola himself. Xavier also expresses his conviction that Germans or Belgians would be found much more capable of enduring hardness than Italians or Spaniards, and suggests that many natives of those countries would be found in the Universities who might be more useful in Japan than at home.

Xavier's general instructions to the Missionaries are, for the most part, of the same kind as those of which specimens have been given in a former chapter. But he now becomes far more urgent upon them to avoid giving offence, and to live in love with one another. Many excellent maxims are enunciated, and many touches of tenderness and affection are interspersed with his rebukes. Writing to the Missionaries of a station he says—

"Let love, benignity, and a sincere charity towards an erring brother, shine forth in your words and your looks. Everywhere men like to be cured tenderly; but in no country more than in India. The Indian constitution is, when offended, as brittle as glass: it resists a sharp stroke, or breaks into shivers: by kind treatment it may be bent and drawn out as you will. By entreaties and mildness you may, in this country, accomplish any thing: by threats and severity, nothing at all."

In respect of their behaviour towards the brethren of another order, or to brother Missionaries, he enjoins—

"Even when your own conscience tells you that you are in the right and they in the wrong, never desire any other revenge upon those who unjustly vex you than that of silence,—humbly and modestly foregoing the defence of your rights as soon as you perceive it is to be maintained before one who is entrenched behind wrath and prejudice. Retiring within yourself, pity the condition of those who rush madly forward, regardless of right and wrong. Be assured that, sooner or later, divine vengeance will overtake such—a vengeance heavier and more bitter than either you or they suspect. Therefore pour out earnest prayers to God continually on their behalf, compassionating their infirmities and rashness; taking special care that you do not soothe your grief by meditating revenge of any kind whatever, or, by silent thought or wish, imprecate evil upon them, or reveal their evil deeds to society by conversation, or in sermons; far less should you do any thing which may return upon them evil for evil." (IV. 21. Fr. 113.)

In a letter written to two quarrelsome Jesuits stationed at Madras, Xavier dictates a most severe reproof to the elder, who was a priest, charging him with undoing with the left hand all that his right hand performed; setting before him the terrors of the day of judgment, and of the gulf of perdition into which he was hastening, unless he repented and humbled himself, which he was to do in the presence of the bishop's vicar at that place. But the letter closes with this fine touch of fraternal affection, mingled with the stern sentence of the Superior. "The above I have dictated. Recognise in what follows my own hand and heart. O Cyprian, if you knew with how much love to you I write these things, you would thank me day and night, and perhaps you would not be able to restrain your tears while reflecting upon the very tender and fervent love with which my soul burns to embrace you. Would that the arcana of the heart could be laid open in this life! Believe me, my brother Cyprian, you would clearly see yourself engraven in my inmost soul. Farewell." (IV. 20. Fr. 112.)

In a letter to Father John Roderick, stationed at Ormuz, occurs an excellent specimen of fidelity united with tenderness and with skilful reproof. It is also a curious instance of enforcing moral persuasion by the help of the eye. After urging various considerations for a profound submission and "blind" obedience to the orders of the vicar-general, he concludes thus:—"Be well persuaded that the good which you do without noise and without offence, though it be as short as this stroke of my pen ——, which is but a small fraction of a whole line, will give me much more pleasure than a great amount of good, which I compare to this long stroke ———————————————————————— if it has been accomplished in the midst of quarrels, offences, and the complaints of one or, perhaps, many persons who regard themselves as injured. . . . . . All the functions of the ministry, and especially of the priesthood, are to be discharged with calmness, with love, with the soft expressions of charity, without roughness, without murmur, without impatience, without brawling." (IV. 6. Fr. 98.)

To Gaspar, as a Director of Missions, Xavier addresses this admirable advice:—

"Take care that you obtain frequent and faithful reports from the brethren who go forth to preach, or who reside at various and distant stations, of all they do and of their welfare. Take care that you are fully acquainted with their circumstances. Write to them frequently, not in a perfunctory style, but explaining every thing exactly. Direct them also to write back to you frequently and fully. Give the most earnest attention to this correspondence, pondering at your leisure upon the letters you receive. Never dictate your replies without careful consideration: settle it in your mind that your diligence in this matter is a main part of your duty. In addition to this, take advantage of interviews with any of our countrymen who come from the same parts, to enquire minutely how the brethren behave, in what estimation they are held, what is commonly reported of them by the people." (IV. 22. Fr. 114.)

Xavier discovered that there had been a great laxity in the accounts of receipts and expenses. He gives many practical suggestions about book-keeping, and advises the Missionaries, where it was possible, to put the accounts into the hands of pious laymen, especially if they were rich men, and able to advance the money required if the funds should not be received in time. He gives important directions for uniting a strict economy with a liberal and exact supply of that which was really necessary for the comfort and efficiency of the Missionaries. He condemns the practice which had sprung up of allowing a particle of the funds devoted to the propagation of the faith being applied to cases of common charity. He interdicts all leniency in collecting the rents and dues of the college as a false compassion, and denounces as little better than robbery the diversion of funds, or neglect in collecting them, while souls are perishing through such neglect or diversion.

In the same spirit he checked the tendency within the Mission of spending Missionary funds in expensive churches. "With regard to the revenues of the college, take care that you expend them rather in the building up spiritual temples than material buildings. In buildings of this latter kind, whether of wood or stone, lay out nothing which is not absolutely necessary. . . . . It is by spiritual temples that God is chiefly honoured, such as in training up children in Christian doctrine."

Xavier complains bitterly of the delay and evasion of the payments assigned to the Mission by the King of Portugal, through the remissness of his officers, giving this energetic advice upon the subject:—

"Expedite the payments assigned by the King to the Colleges of Goa, Ormuz, and Bassein; urge the royal officers, especially the governors, to see to the matter: do not go about the business in a soft and inoffensive spirit: matters of this kind must be carried forward with vigour, and almost obstinately. The whole class of pay-masters, treasurers, or whatever other name the officers bear who preside over the royal treasury, are a hard race. They elude the most just demands, when preferred in a soft and bashful manner. They will give up nothing that is not wrenched from them. You must go and speak to them with a stern countenance, and an outspoken tone. You must not take delays patiently, for they know how to protract them *ad infinitum*, and to enrich themselves thereby, and to boast of their skill. Therefore, to give way to them is to sanction their prevarication. Rather than this, demand the payment of your dues with obstinacy and boldness." (IV. 26. Fr. 118.)

The art of bullying or teasing Government officers into a compliance with Jesuit demands seems to have been a standing practice in the Society. Dr. Geddes relates of Ignatius Loyola, who wished to obtain from the King of Portugal the means and authority for sending a Jesuit Mission into Abyssinia—" This he plied so closely as to carry it; for besides that he himself was indefatigable in the pursuit thereof, he commanded all the Jesuits that were in Lisbon to wait upon the King at least once a month about it; and one Lewis Goncalves da Comara, a Jesuit, who was of a noble family in Portugal, was not to fail to speak to the Portuguese Ambassador at the Court of Rome once in three days concerning it; which that father observed so punctually, and teased the Ambassador so much about it, that the Ambassador's servants, when they saw him coming, used to say of him, 'Here comes our lord's tertian ague.'" (Geddes' Church of Ethiopia, p. 150.)

Amongst the letters written at this period is one which relates to Spanish politics. Xavier had heard that Spain had an eye upon Japan. Probably the fleet which had brought Cosmo Turrianus to the Moluccas may have had a design upon that country, which was defeated by their loss of 400 men, and their consequent detention at the Moluccas, from whence they could not get back to New Spain, as stated in the letter of Cosmo already referred to. In the midst of all his Missionary affairs, Xavier wrote to Simon Roderick (IV. 18. Fr. 110.) to entreat him to draw up a memorial and transmit it to the King or Queen of Portugal, to warn the Emperor Charles the Fifth of the impossibility of his approaching Japan, either for trade or war, from Mexico. Xavier had previously written himself on this subject to the King of Portugal, but fearing that the pressure of other affairs had put it out of his Majesty's thoughts, he wished Simon Roderick to renew the subject. Xavier authorizes him to say that ships sailing from New Spain through the Pacific could find no safe anchorage upon the coast of Japan, and that every ship would be destroyed by storms or rocks; that even if they could succeed in landing an expedition on that wide extent of sterile country, the men would all perish with hunger; or if they should attempt to cover their warlike designs by entering some harbour and proposing trade, the Japanese would prove themselves as suspicious as they were avaricious, and would cut them off to a man. When we remember that, at the time Xavier thus dissuaded Spain from attempting to open Japan, he was using every exertion to secure the monopoly of trade to Portugal, it is evident that he was acting in a diplomatic spirit, rather than in the frank and sincere character of a Christian Missionary.

Many of the maxims and reflections given above are of great intrinsic value; but truth compels us to add, that, as they stand in Xavier's letters, they are too often the exceptions to the general tone and drift of his correspondence, and that they are alloyed by an alliance with very inferior and questionable advice. The inconsistency of Xavier's character, on which we have had occasion several times to remark, is here also sadly apparent. At times he speaks in the language of a Bible Christian, the result, it may be, of his early Protestant associations. But too soon he relapses into the true tone of a Jesuit, whose policy it is to aim at gaining a personal influence over men by flattering their vanity, even at the expense of sincerity, and by engaging in such good works as may best secure human applause and admiration We close this chapter by giving one letter in full, as a specimen of the usual style of Xavier's correspondence, which will sufficiently illustrate these remarks.

"*To Father Melchior Nugnez, at Bazain.*

"*Goa, 3d April* 1552.

"MY VERY DEAR BROTHER,

"May the love and the grace of our Lord Jesus Christ be with you evermore. Amen.

"I earnestly pray and beseech you, by your love to Christ, and by your zeal for the Divine glory, that you study to diffuse on all sides the good savour of Christ, and set yourself forth as an example of all virtues in the city in which you live; especially that you give no offence. This you will accomplish if moderation and Christian humility be conspicuous in all your conduct.

Therefore begin by undertaking diligently the most humble and the lowest offices; thus the people will be prepossessed in your favour, and will receive in good part whatever you say or do; and the more so, if they see that you persevere in such offices with increasing zeal. I therefore earnestly implore you to aim at progress in virtue, for you are well aware that he who does not make progress falls back.

"Again I entreat and beseech you, in the name of God, that you will stir up the people to piety by your example. When you are adorned with wisdom and humility, you will, I doubt not, see much fruit of your labour, and become a good preacher; for those virtues are the parents and teachers of many great works. Often visit the hospitals and the prisons, for such exercises of Christian humility are not only pleasing to God and useful to man, but they obtain among the people uncommon respect and influence, even for such as have neither the office nor the abilities of a preacher. Conciliate the favour and affection of the Governor, the Vicar-general, the priests, the confraternities of mercy, and the whole city; and be equally careful to retain what you have once secured; for this is the great secret of swaying men's minds, whether in your preaching, or in the confessional, or in conversation. I wish you to interest the Governor, Vicar-general, and the brothers of mercy, in the good work of cherishing and augmenting the little company of Christian converts; and so manage, that whatever accession to Christianity you make, may seem to redound to their credit. Thus they will the more assist your efforts, and put fewer impediments in the way.

"By pursuing this course you will have plenty of friends and patrons in any difficulties or contests in which you may be involved, and fewer enemies; perhaps none at all; for who will dare to assail a man when they see him surrounded with such a guard of patrons? On the same principle, whenever you write to the King of Portugal upon the progress of Christianity, make honourable and grateful mention of their excellent aid to the Christian cause, and show your letters, if you think fit, to the parties themselves; and ask the King to signify that their services to us and to the Christian religion give him pleasure; and also, in his royal letters, so to praise their zeal, as to seem to set down to their account, under God, all the increase of the Christian religion.

"Never put any thing in your letters to the King of Portugal except what concerns the conversion of the heathen: all other matters of business should be written to the Society in Portugal.

"To avoid giving offence, I wish that neither you nor any one of our Society should collect the dues appointed for the sustentation of the college and the neophytes, but that it should be transacted, if possible, by some other fit person. It will not be difficult, I think, to find a person of some property, so that there may be no risk of loss, and that poor contributors may not be too rigidly pressed for payment. You may make a man willingly undertake the office by preparing him by a course of meditation on divine things, and by a frequent attendance upon the holy sacrament.

"May God of his mercy unite us together in heaven!"

"Francis."

(IV. 9. Fr. 101.)

CHAPTER VIII.

Xavier's attempt to reach China—Death and Character.

SECTION 1. *Xavier's voyage to China, and Death.*—PLAN OF EMBASSY TO CHINA—JAMES PEREIRA—ARRIVAL IN MALACCA—EMBASSY ARRESTED BY GOVERNOR OF MALACCA—BITTER DISAPPOINTMENT—DENUNCIATION AGAINST THE GOVERNOR—DETERMINATION TO GO ALONE TO CHINA—ARRIVAL AT SANCIAN—ILLNESS—EXCOMMUNICATION OF THE GOVERNOR OF MALACCA—DEATH OF XAVIER—REMOVAL OF HIS CORPSE TO GOA.

SECTION 2. *Xavier's personal character reviewed.*—XAVIER'S GREAT NATURAL ABILITIES AND FAVOURABLE OPPORTUNITIES—EXEMPLARY POINTS IN HIS CHARACTER—DARKER SHADES OF HIS CHARACTER—CONTRAST WITH THE HEROISM OF PROTESTANT MISSIONARIES.

SECTION 1.—*Xavier's voyage to China, and Death.*

XAVIER first conceived the idea, during his residence in Japan, of opening a Mission in China. Having failed, as we have seen, to acquire the Japanese language, he felt, as he tells us, that he could be more useful as a pioneer in a new field, than by remaining in Japan. Besides which, he found that the respect of the Japanese for China was so great, that, if China could be gained, Japan would follow. The Japanese regarded China as the fountain of their arts and of their literature. Xavier incidentally mentions various other circumstances which increased his desire to visit China. Among these, he says that he had ascertained that there were Jews residing in the interior, and that there was a road from China to Jerusalem.

Xavier's discovery of Jews in China is thus related:—
"I met at Malacca with a Portuguese merchant who had recently returned from China. He told me that he had been asked by a grave and honourable Chinese resident in a royal city, whether Christians fed upon swine's flesh. To this the merchant answered that Christians did not refuse; but why was the question asked? The Chinese replied that there was a certain tribe in the interior of China, shut in by mountains, whose customs and manners were widely different from the Chinese, and that they abstained entirely from swine's flesh, and celebrated with solemn observances many festivals. When the merchant explained these things to me, I could not sufficiently satisfy myself whether this tribe were Christians, of the class of those who unite an observance of the Hebrew ritual with the Christian religion, as we know to be the case with some of the inhabitants of the coast of Africa and on the Red Sea, or whether they are Jews, who are dispersed over the whole face of the earth." (II. 17. Fr. 58.)

The fact of a settlement of Jews in China was first

verified by the Missionary Ricci, at the commencement of the seventeenth century. He opened communications with them, and several Jesuit Missionaries afterwards visited them. The present condition of the settlement has been investigated through the liberality of a lady in England, who entrusted a sum of money to the London Society for Promoting Christianity among the Jews, for the purpose. The Bishop of Victoria and the late Dr. Medhurst undertook the investigation, and sent two native Chinese Christians from Shanghae, at the close of 1850, to the Jewish settlement at K'hae-fung-foo, 700 miles in a north-west direction from Shanghae. The condition of the Jews is thus described in a tract published at the time*:—

"Here, in the midst of a surrounding population, two-thirds of whom were professors of Mohammedanism, and close adjoining to a heathen temple dedicated to the 'god of fire,' a few Jewish families, sunk in the lowest poverty and destitution, their religion scarcely more than a name, and yet sufficient to separate them from the multitude around, exposed to trial, reproach, and the pain of long-deferred hope, remained the unconscious depositaries of the oracles of God, and survived as the solitary witnesses of departed glory. Not a single individual could read the Hebrew books: they had been

---

* A Narrative of a Mission of Inquiry to the Jewish Synagogue at K'ae-fung-foo, with an Introduction by the Lord Bishop of Victoria. Shanghae, 1851.

without a Rabbi for fifty years. The expectation of a Messiah seems to have been entirely lost. The rite of circumcision, which appears to have been observed at the period of their discovery by the Jesuits two centuries ago, had been totally discontinued. The worshippers within the sanctuary faced towards the west; but whether in the direction of Jerusalem or towards the suspended tablets of the emperors, no clear information was obtained. The synagogue itself was tottering in ruins: some of the ground had been alienated to pagan rites, and a portion of the fallen materials sold to the neighbouring heathen. Some time previously they had petitioned the Chinese emperor to have pity on their poverty, and to rebuild their temple. No reply had been received from Pekin, but to this feeble hope they still clung. Out of seventy family names or clans, only seven now remained, numbering about 200 individuals in all, dispersed all over the neighbourhood. A few of of them were shopkeepers in the city; others were agriculturists at some little distance from the suburbs; while a few families also lived in the temple precincts, almost destitute of raiment and shelter. According to present appearances, in the judgment of our native messengers, after a few years all traces of Judaism will probably have disappeared, and this Jewish remnant have been amalgamated with, and absorbed into, surrounding Mohammedanism."

"Although the messengers were afterwards suddenly interrupted in their researches within the synagogue, and their departure from the city itself was subsequently hastened by fear, they remained for a period sufficient to enable them to accomplish the main object of their visit. They copied many interesting inscriptions in Chinese, and a few in Hebrew, which are appended to their journals."

" They brought back, also, eight MSS., of apparently considerable antiquity, containing portions of the Old-Testament Scriptures, comprising portions of the Pentateuch, Psalms, and Hagiographa."

" The temple, or synagogue, at K'hae-fung-foo is said to have been built about A.D. 1190; but the Jews themselves assert that their race entered China as early as the period of the Han dynasty, which would correspond with some time about the Christian era."

Our knowledge of the last portion of Xavier's history is derived from eighteen letters written between June and November 1552, *i.e.* from his arrival at Malacca till within three weeks of his death. Five of these letters are to James Pereria, who was to be his companion to China; the rest were to brethren in India.

James Pereria is only noticed once before in Xavier's letters. He was a merchant at Malacca, and Xavier, after his return to India from the Spice Islands, wrote to him from Goa, April 2, 1548, expressing his regret that they had not met before Pereria's departure to China, as Xavier regarded him as his best friend in respect of a Mission to Japan. In this letter

Xavier advises his friend to take with his cargo to China the most precious of all commodities, a good conscience, which the Chinese and Malacca merchants greatly neglected. He expresses his confidence that his very dear friend Pereria had furnished himself with this best guarantee for his commercial success.

James Pereria is now again introduced to our notice, after four years' interval, in connexion with Xavier's expedition to China. Xavier thus announces to the King of Portugal his plans and hopes, on the eve of his departure, in a letter dated Goa, April 10, 1552:—

"I go from hence in five days to Malacca, on my way to China, with a brother of our Society, and James Pereria, an envoy to the King of China. We carry with us many precious gifts to the king, which Pereria has bought, partly by the royal funds, and partly by his own. We carry, also, a precious gift, such as I doubt whether ever king sent to king within the memory of man, namely, the Gospel of Jesus Christ, which, if the King of China knows its value, he will place far above all his treasures, however great. I have a good hope that God will look in mercy on that vast region and people, and will open the eyes of men, made in His own image, that they may know their Maker, and Jesus Christ, the one Saviour of all mankind.

"The objects of our going to China are to obtain liberty for the Portuguese captives, to establish friendship between the Kings of China and Portugal, but to carry on war against Satan and his worshippers. We shall denounce, first to the King, afterwards to all others, in the name of the King of Heaven, the worship of the devil, and call upon them to worship only God their Maker, and Jesus their Deliverer and their Lord. It may appear a bold enterprise to go to a barbarous people, and a most powerful King, to reprove their sin, and to preach the truth. Such an enterprise, in this age would be a dangerous one, even in the case of Christian Princes and Kings; how much more in the case of barbarians! But that which gives us strength and courage is our confidence that God has put it into our minds to go. His glory is the scope and end of all my thoughts. He, too, has filled us with a good hope and with a firm assurance; so that, trusting in His mercy, we confide in His power, which infinitely exceeds that of the Emperor of China, and the potentates of the whole world.

"Since we have put the whole affair into the hand and power of God, there is no place for fear or doubt. All we have to fear is, lest we offend the God of heaven, and incur the punishment of the wicked." (IV. 19. Fr. III.)

It is impossible to withhold the expression of our admiration of these noble sentiments, and of our regret that false religion, and inconsistency of character, should have frustrated their high influence.

In other letters Xavier informs us that he had the sanction of the Viceroy of India for this enterprise, who had furnished the ship. Yet the style of Xavier's letter to the King of Portugal would seem to indicate that the whole scheme was one of Xavier's own devising, and that it was regarded by the Viceroy as rather of a private than of a public character, for the Portuguese were not wanting in a parade of military force when they designed to negotiate with kings. A royal envoy to the Emperor of China would not have been sent in the person of one of the merchants trading with that country.

No sooner, however, had the "Legation" arrived at Malacca, than the Governor of Malacca seized the ship, and forbade the projected embassy to China. The Governor was Don Alvarez Gama, brother of Don Peter Sylva, who had been so helpful to Xavier in his expedition to the Spice Islands; and Xavier bitterly regrets that the friendly brother was not now in power.

This unexpected and sudden frustration of Xavier's scheme for the evangelization of China threw him into a state of agitation, which, he assures his correspondents, they were unable to imagine. In Xavier's letters there is now a sudden transition of tone from the last letter, written from Cochin, full of hope and confidence, to the next letter, written from Malacca to James Pereria in the following terms:—

"It is all my fault! On account of my great sins, God has frustrated our Chinese enterprise. My sins have been so many and great, that they have not only stood in my own way, but in your way also, and rendered useless all the merchandize and money which you have collected for this legation. God is my witness how sincere was my desire to serve Him and yourself: had this not been so, I should now have felt far more bitter sorrow. I will go on shipboard at once. There I will await its time of sailing, that I may escape the sight of your people, who come to me in tears, and complain that they are themselves miserably ruined by the stoppage of the legation. One thing I have to ask of you. Do not come and see me. You will only increase my sorrow by the recital of your own grief and calamity, though I trust that this present evil will turn out for your future benefit; for I do not doubt but that the king of Portugal, as I have asked him by my letters, will repay to you the worth of your zeal for the religion of Christ. I have bid farewell to the Governor who has thus dared to put a stop to a Mission so well calculated to enlarge the Christian faith. May God pardon the man! I truly grieve over his condition; for he will suffer far heavier retribution than he thinks of. May our Lord be your guardian, and the leader and companion of my present enterprise!" (IV. 27. Fr. 119.)

James Pereria had comforted Xavier by providing him a berth in one of his ships trading to China, and had abundantly supplied him with money, and with all other requisites, and Xavier had determined to attempt to enter China, even without a single Associate, for he sent one of the Fathers who was then at Malacca, to Japan, and another to India. He only took with him on shipboard a native interpreter. A fatal epidemic soon broke out at Malacca, and Xavier's ship dropped down to the Bay of Singapore, where she remained a month or six weeks, and from whence Xavier wrote several letters.

The very trite remark, that misfortunes try the substance of a man, and render true greatness of character more than ever conspicuous, may now be applied to the history of Xavier. He had planned the "legation" to China, in the hope of obtaining entrance into the country as a Missionary through that means; knowing that in his true character he was precluded by the strictest laws of the Chinese empire, and under the penalty of death. But upon the failure of the legation, instead of receiving this check with submission, as coming from the hand of God, and laying out his plans for evangelizing China with a band of competent Associates, apart from the prop of temporal influence which had so often deceived him, the course which Xavier pursued indicated a hasty and angry temper, and an inordinate self-importance. He obstinately determined to carry out the plan, notwithstanding the altered circumstances, and to seek an interview with the Emperor of China! His most earnest thoughts were directed to the devising of punishment for the Governor of Malacca. He sent off Jesuit Fathers to India, with letters to various parties there, and he wrote letters to the King of Portugal, endeavouring to bring down both ecclesiastical and civil vengeance upon the Governor's head. Writing to his friend Gaspar, at Goa, from the bay of Singapore, he says—

"You will hardly believe, my Father Gaspar, into what paroxysms I have been thrown at Malacca. I cannot write of it myself. I have desired F. Perez to write to you. Whatever he says, however incredible it may seem, you must believe. I am on my way to the Chinese islands which are near Canton, denuded of all earthly, but surrounded, as I hope, with heavenly defences. I have imbibed the hope that heathen men in the continent of China will open to me the entrance which Christian men have denied me—men who have no fear of ecclesiastical censures or of divine wrath, which they miserably provoke. Take special care that the Bishop sends to his Vicar at Malacca a formal excommunication, by which the Governor of Malacca, and all others who have contributed to frustrate so good and Christian a work, may be publicly, and by name, interdicted from sacred things.

"I desire that, in that form of excommunication, it should be distinctly stated that I was sent into India as Apostolic Legate, by Pope Paul III, under diplomas which the Bishop has himself recognised. I insist on this, that no one hereafter may oppose the propagation of the Christian religion, and the efforts of pious men. As an individual, indeed, I would never ask any prelate to exclude a person from the communion of the faithful; but when persons have incurred the penalty of exclusion by virtue of pontifical decrees and diplomas, I will spare no pains to secure the proper recognition of their condition; nor will I for a moment suffer any connivance at the fault of such men, so that they may too easily find consolation when they are visited with compunction; which might encourage others in future daringly to impede the brethren of our Society going to Molucca, China, Japan, or anywhere else, in the cause of religion. Hence you must by every means secure the arrival of this edict." (IV. 30. Fr. 122.)

Another object of Xavier's displeasure at this time was the King of the Moluccas, who had opposed the progress of Christianity in his dominions, notwithstanding certain benefits which he had received upon his promise to assist that cause. John Beira was therefore sent to India to induce the Viceroy to revoke these benefits.

The letters thus written by Xavier, while waiting in the Bay of Singapore, exhibit his unabated activity of mind and his habits of business. Among other things, he explains to Gaspar the necessity of making his remittances to the Missionaries in Japan in gold of the purest kind, which he understood to be the Venetian coin. He sends back to Goa one of the Japanese interpreters, John Japan, whom he had brought with him, in order that he might return the next year as interpreter with some father to Japan; and to hold John to his engagement, he promised that he should have 30 "pardoes" to trade with, and to carry back a profitable investment to Japan. He wrote letters to the King of Portugal in favour of James Pereria, and sent them open, in duplicate, through the hands of James Pereria, that he might see the light in which Xavier had placed his merits: he was at liberty also to gratify the good brother of the Governor, by showing him the terms in which he had spoken of him to the King. He advises James Pereria, also, to write a full and well-considered account of all the advantages to Portuguese trade if an official residence for the Portuguese were obtained at Canton. His letters to his royal correspondent were to be put into a bag, and directed "To our Lord the King, from Father Master Xavier;" and were to be sent by a confidential person, who should deliver them personally into the hands of the King, but whose interests in India would oblige him to return without delay, and so bring back early replies.

At length the vessel left the Bay of Singapore, and reached the island of Sancian, a low sandy island off the coast, near Canton, where the Portuguese ships were accustomed to lie at anchor, and to barter their goods with the Chinese merchants, who brought their's in their junks to the same rendezvous.

Here Xavier was seized with fever, which lasted fifteen days. Then he recovered, and for the next three weeks renewed his active habits of correspondence and of scheming. Nine letters, written during these three weeks, are preserved.

To James Pereria he writes, on the first and on the last day of that period, telling him of his plans for entering China, and of the dangers which were predicted.

The last letter is full of gratitude to him for the ample provision he had made for all his wants, and for far more than he wanted, and assures him that the master of his ship, Thomas Scandal, was as zealous in his attentions as it was possible for a man to be. Xavier reckons confidently upon Pereria's executing his legation the following year, authorizes him to bring with him a Jesuit father from Goa, and begs him also to bring the beautiful ecclesiastic vestments which Xavier had prepared for his own use in China, but which he had left in the hands of Father Perez at Malacca, when the legation was arrested. He adds, "If any way is opened to me through divine favour of entering China, you shall find me there in one of two lodgings, which differ much in kind, either a captive in the dungeon of Canton, or in Pekin, where the Emperor is said to reside, preparing for your arrival, and as your courier, or as a forerunner in the office you will have to discharge."

To Father Francis Perez, whom he left in charge of the Jesuit house in Malacca, he writes a peremptory direction to quit that city, and to shut up the house. "I command you irrevocably to depart from Malacca. I forbid you to hesitate, whatever entreaties or fallacious promises may be addressed to you. Do not bestow any more labour upon a community so ungrateful, and so unworthy of the benefit of our establishment. That labour may be far more usefully bestowed anywhere else." Perez was to go by the next ship to India, and to take charge of the Jesuit college at Quilon; but especially he was to expedite, and to publish, the edict of excommunication.

Xavier informs his friends in these letters that he had procured the building of a small hut upon the shore, where he daily celebrated divine offices till he was too ill; and that he had plenty to do in hearing confessions, in composing quarrels, and in other such employments.

Xavier's last scheme for entering China was one of questionable morality. He learnt upon his arrival at Sancian that any attempt of the Chinese to smuggle an European into the country would be visited with the death of themselves and of their families. Nevertheless, he tried to bribe the Chinese to run the risk. Numbers refused. He found, at length, a merchant whose junk only contained his own family and servants, who was willing to run this risk of life. The desperate nature of the risk is evident from the greatness of the bribe, Xavier calls "enormous." It was to consist of twenty "pics" of pepper, valued at 200 moidores, which, Xavier adds, would be to the Chinese merchant worth 350. In English money this would have amounted to nearly £300, even at that day, a sum representing many times the amount at the present time. Such was the liberality of James Pereria, that Xavier was able to offer this sum. The courage, however, of Xavier's interpreter failed him, and he deserted. A lay brother whom Xavier was to take with him proved, he says, false, and was expelled by Xavier from the fraternity.

This desperate risk of his own life and of the lives of

others,—in point of morality very questionable, was the last scheme which occupied the living thoughts of Xavier; and this he describes, in fine language, as an act of faith in God.

The only two letters remaining to be noticed were addressed to Gaspar Barzæus, one to Gaspar personally, the other to Gaspar and Francis Perez conjointly. In each there are the most vehement injunctions to obtain the excommunication of the Governor of Malacca. In the last of the two Xavier dictates the full form of the accusation, and terms the conduct of the Governor treason against the King, as well as disobedience to the head of the Church. He gives minute directions respecting the publication of this excommunication in the pulpit of Malacca, and in other places. He paints in vivid language the efforts of the devil and all his legions to prevent the Jesuit Society from getting a footing in China. Again and again he repeats his solemn injunctions to the fathers to carry out all his commands to the very letter, which he had given, *vivâ voce*, or which he had subsequently written in his letters. And, in the last place, he guards Gaspar against admitting the thought that Xavier was dead, and that therefore he might exercise his own judgment, being no longer amenable to his commands. "I remember," he writes, "on a similar occasion, some fell into this error on account of my long absence; but I shall not die before God wills my death. Long since, indeed, I have desired death, and life has been a weariness. But let not human curiosity indulge in useless disputes about the hour of my decease. It is fixed in the eternal decree, and vain thoughts can neither hasten nor delay it. Take this warning, that you must not act upon your own judgment, as once happened, if you recollect: you then yielded somewhat to your own sense of what was right, though contrary to my directions. God knows whether, in that affair, you were wise or foolish. I hope that when I shall return, probably next year, I may find nothing of this sort to censure and correct."

Within three weeks of writing this letter, on Dec. 2, 1552, Xavier died. That teeming and anxious head ceased to think; that fervent heart ceased to throb. No companion was near to whom he could breathe out his dying thoughts. No priest gave the last offices of the Church, or committed his body to a Christian grave. He expired in a crowded mart of traders and mariners, and was hastily buried in the sand beside the sea shore. He died, says one of the narratives, in a shed constructed of stakes and branches of trees. Portuguese merchants found him there, ere the last spark of life had been quenched, and were present when he drew his last breath.

The earliest account, as far as I can find, which exists of Xavier's death, and of the subsequent circumstances, is that recorded by Maffeus in a letter of Arias Blandonius, a Jesuit, dated Goa, 23d Dec. 1554. It is addressed to the Jesuit Society in Europe, and states that a long letter had been written, which had been returned to Goa after the vessel which carried it had been shipwrecked; and that Melchior Nugnez had therefore desired him to write again. After other things, Arias states that Melchior Nugnez came from Bassein to assume the duties of Gaspar; that he then went to visit Francis Perez at Cochin, and afterwards Nicholas at Quilon; that while there he heard from sailors who came from Pegu of the death of Francis Xavier, and of the events which followed. Arias adds—" I will now relate what I have myself full knowledge of, respecting this event." He then relates that the embassy on which Xavier had reckoned for obtaining an entrance into China was stopped at Malacca; that Xavier went on alone, with no companion, not even a servant; that he died there of fever; that some Portuguese merchants who were there, and who greatly respected Xavier, buried him in his clerical vestments, in quick lime, that the flesh might be the sooner consumed, and that they might take his bones to India; that when they had waited, as they thought, long enough, they examined the body, and found it perfect; that they were astounded at the miracle. Yet when the time of their sailing arrived the merchants would have left the body, if one of them, who had been intimate with Xavier, had not determined to take it. The coffin, full of quick lime, was put into the ship, and carried to Malacca, where it was buried with great pomp by the inhabitants, and remained for a long time undisturbed; until one of the Jesuit brethren, whom

Melchior had sent to investigate the circumstances of Xavier and of the Mission in Japan, arrived at Malacca. This brother examined the body, and found it still perfect. He had it placed in a new and splendid coffin, provided at the expense of Francis Pereria, and it was deposited in the hermitage in which he himself lived. It remained there until Peter Alcaceva arrived at Malacca from Japan.

A letter from Peter Alcaceva in the same collection carries on the narrative. It states that his visit at Malacca was in November and December 1553, that is, about a year after Xavier's death. As there was a ship leaving Malacca for India, it was determined by the two brethren to take the body of Xavier with them to Goa, where they arrived in the spring of 1554.

"We at Goa," writes Arias, "had only heard that Xavier was dead, the ships from Malacca not having arrived. The first of the fleet announced that the body of Xavier was on its way from Malacca, and that the vessel was at Cochin. The admiral sent us word of this, and that by the virtue of the body it bore the ship had been delivered out of many dangers." Melchior immediately asked the Viceroy to send a fleet ship to receive the body; but the admiral objected that it was not fair to deprive the ship of its safeguard so near the end of the voyage. Melchior, however, and a company of choristers and brethren, took a vessel, and were for four days and nights out at sea. At last they met the ship off Baticola, twenty leagues from Goa. The body was then lowered from the ship into Melchior's vessel. The choristers in their surplices, and with branches in their hands, chanted the "Gloria in Excelsis." The ship fired a salute with its great guns. The body was dressed in splendid vestments, the hands in the form of a cross, the feet had on the sandals. It was brought to a chapel 1500 paces from Goa. It was afterwards conducted with a great procession, headed by the Viceroy, to the Jesuit house, and deposited in the chapel; and for weeks following crowds continually pressed to view the holy man.

SECTION 2. *Xavier's personal character reviewed.*

We have now before us the history of Francis Xavier. It remains to take a general review of his character and of his achievements. We have already marked the inconsistencies of his character, that great qualities were combined with great weaknesses. We will begin with the brighter parts of the picture.

The foregoing pages show that Francis Xavier was gifted by nature with a clear intellect, with a magnanimous heart, with a sanguine temperament, and with boundless self-reliance; yet this last quality was softened by its alliance with self-abasement and condescension towards others. He had also a compassionate and loving heart. All these great endowments were devoted with untiring energy to the work to which he conceived that he had been called of God. That work was to bring over native heathen Kings and their people to embrace the Christian religion, and to revive the religion of the Portuguese residents in the East. For the accomplishment of this work he was invested with very special civil powers, and the highest ecclesiastical sanctions. The position, the work, and the natural endowments and character of Francis Xavier, present a deeply interesting theme of contemplation. The following features may be studied with great advantage by all who are engaged in Missions to the heathen.

1. Francis Xavier affords an admirable example of *energy in his calling;* setting at once to work, from the first moment he placed his foot on a heathen soil, as at Melinda, Socotra, and on his arrival at Goa, before his particular field of labour was designated. The same energy never ceased till the day of his death. This was manifest even in the island of Sancian, amidst the intervals of his last fatal disease. All his letters show that the man was alive in every part, that nothing bearing upon his great object escaped his eye or his ear, and that he was ever ready to spend and be spent in his work. Having devoted himself to India for life and for death, the idea of a return to Europe, even to plead for fellow-labourers, was regarded by him as a simple impossibility. Where there is spiritual power in such a character the results are glorious. These men of persevering energy have been the most illustrious Missionaries in Protestant annals. Such men live two lives in one. If faithful to the Truth, God honours them by giving them great success in winning souls to Him.

2. Another point of view in which Xavier may be proposed as an example to Protestant Missionaries is in the maintaining *a bold position as a Christian Missionary.* It will, indeed, have been seen that he carried this conduct to an extravagant extent, and stretched the bow till it broke in his hand. He had also special worldly advantages for maintaining such boldness. But still there is much which may be imitated under better regulation, and in a more Christian spirit. Xavier was everywhere the Missionary. In the suite of an Ambassador, in the palace of a King, among the crew of a ship, in the busy sea-port while waiting for a passage, among civil and military officers, in the neighbourhood of native Kings, and even in their courts, Xavier was the Missionary, known and read of all men as such, and therefore enforcing attention, and exercising an important influence in favour of Missions. More especially in respect of the native races he acted the part of a true Missionary, maintaining their rights against the oppression and injustice of his own countrymen, and treating them as possessing the same feelings and capacities as their more civilized fellow-men.

3. Xavier's example is equally striking in *his sympathy for all his fellow-labourers* in the Mission field. Though placed by his political and ecclesiastical status prodigiously above all of them, and also invested with autocratical power over all the Jesuit Missionaries, he yet manifested in all his communications the most delicate attention to the feelings of a Missionary, and a

prompt zeal in ministering to their wants. The secret of this bright feature in his character was perhaps in the experience which he had gained by his first year's personal labours on the Fishery Coast. The section which is devoted to an account of his management of a Mission, affords many valuable hints to all Missionary Committees, and to the Bishops and other ecclesiastical authorities presiding over a Mission field. There is indeed much to avoid in the practice of Xavier, but much also to imitate.

4. An eminent and bright feature in Xavier's character was also his zeal as a *peace-maker*. He regarded it as a part of his office, wherever he was, to compose quarrels. His energetic remonstrances, affectionate entreaties, and sound, practical counsels, by which he strove to make his brethren dwell together in unity, deserve the highest praise. He knew, as he tells us, the peculiar irritability of Europeans in a tropical climate, and he spared no pains to secure the preservation of harmonious co-operation and brotherly love amongst all fellow-workers in the Christian ministry.

5. One more excellency in Xavier's Missionary example may be pointed out, namely, *the fulness and frequency of his communications with the Church at home.* In his day, letters to India were only sent and received once a year by the annual fleet: he had also renounced Europe for ever. Yet he continued to write to the last year of his life with all the freshness and fullness of his first impressions. He stood between the Church at home

and the Church abroad as the representative of both. He wrote with all the confidence and authority of one who was still identified with his old University at Paris, with the Missionary College at Coimbra, which he had never seen, and with Rome as the metropolis of his Church. Much as we must lament the "dressing" which his letters to Europe received at his hands, yet we cannot but wish to receive from those Missionaries to whom God has given the pen of a ready writer, letters as full and as fresh, though more consistent, than those written by Francis Xavier.

With such excellent features in the character of Xavier, it is much to be regretted that his admirers have had recourse to fictions in order to exalt him to a superhuman eminence. In the sober realities of his history there is enough to entitle him to a high rank in the roll of self-devoted philanthropists. But his eulogists claim for him the title of a Christian hero upon grounds which are untenable. We refer not to his reputed miracles: a worker of miracles is placed beyond criticism: but we refer to such legends as the conversion of a myriad of heathen in a few months, as his encountering and overthrowing a hostile army by his look and presence, as facing the most horrible dangers in the Spice Islands, and such like. The facts of Xavier's history show that he was less exposed than Missionaries generally are to personal dangers. In India, in the Spice Islands, in Japan, his ministrations were confined to the sea coast, which was under the command of the Portuguese navy. When the Badages were abroad upon the Fishery Coast, he did, indeed, run some personal risk, in his desire to secure the protection of his converts. His immediate successor in this work, Anthony Criminal, on a like occasion, threw himself into the midst of his converts, covered their flight, and perished under the darts of the enemy. But Xavier had no encounter with the Badages, and had only to attend to the wounded after the battle was over. Neither was Xavier's fortitude put to the test by any formidable opposition or persecution, except in his last scheme of reaching China, when his deportment has little in it of the heroic.

Yet we often hear the name of Xavier put forth as a great hero, to the disparagement of Protestant Missionaries. Reduce his history to its true dimensions, and Protestant Missions have no reason to shun a comparison. His pretensions fall short of those of Samuel Marsden and his two European Catechists in New Zealand, spending their first Sunday amidst a crowd of warlike cannibals, upon a coast which had been shunned for many previous years by every merchant-ship; or of Henry Martyn, the solitary witness for the word of Christ in Shiraz, disputing with the most learned Mahometans in their own tongue, and winning their admiration for his person, notwithstanding their bitter enmity to his religion; or of Williams, in his visits to the islands of the Pacific, where no European before himself had landed, and persevering in his efforts to impart to them the Gospel of Christ, till his life was sacrificed at their hands;

or of Judson in the prisons of Burmah; or of many other names which might be selected from the list of Protestant Missionary heroes. And when this list shall be exhausted, we have a reserve of heroic deeds in a class which has no existence in the Church of Rome. Let us compare Xavier with the Missionary's wife Rosine Krapf, who accompanied her husband, Dr. Krapf, into the heart of Abyssinia, shared his flight when expelled through the intrigues of Romanists, re-entered with him the wilderness of Shoho, to regain the province of Tigrè, though with the prospect before her of the birth of her first-born child in that wilderness. See her comforting her husband under the shade of a wilderness tree, as he took the dying babe in his arms to dedicate it to the Father, Son, and Holy Ghost. Hear her, while he hesitated for a name, pronounce the Amharic term for "a tear!" And then she was forced by the savage natives to pursue her journey after three days' rest. See the same valiant lady accompanying her husband through the perils of shipwreck in native boats, till they reached the more civilized settlement of Mombas, an island lying off the East Coast of Africa, as Sancian lies off the coast of China, each island within sight of the land sought to be evangelized. There listen to the last accents of this genuine female Missionary, while sinking into the arms of death, enjoining her husband to carry her body to the opposite continent of Africa, and to bury her on the sea shore, that the pagan Wanikas who passed by her tomb might be reminded of the object which had brought her to that country, and that her grave might be the starting-point for future Missionaries to carry the light of the Gospel through the Galla country into inhospitable Abyssinia.* How does the romance of Xavier's last scene at Sancian, off the coast of China, and of the transfer of his remains to the chapel at Goa, sink in the presence of this parallel story of a Missionary's heroic wife !

The cause of truth compels us also to notice the dark shades and great defects in Xavier's character.

Xavier's impulsiveness, and his frequent and sudden changes of purpose, contrast very unfavourably with the patient endurance and perseverance of the true Missionary.

A want of thorough truthfulness is also conspicuous in all Xavier's European correspondence. Whatever charitable allowances may be made for the opposite representations given in letters to friends in Europe, and to friends on the spot, concerning the work in which he was engaged on the Fishery Coast, it must be confessed that a sincere regard for truth should have saved him from such contradictions as his letters exhibit. The advice also which he gives to a Missionary to exercise a delicate flattery towards those parties whose goodwill he wished to secure, by representing the result of his own labours as due to them, bears the mark of insincerity. The same stamp rests upon his instructions to Missionaries for

* Church Missionary Record, April 1845.

maintaining their ministerial influence over others by a specious appearance of humility, and by an espionage into their private affairs. How far removed are all such expedients from the Apostolic maxim, " by manifestation of the truth commending ourselves to every man's conscience in the sight of God."

Xavier's Missionary reputation labours, also, under the capital defect of his failure to acquire any native language; whether from inability, or from undervaluing the means of preaching the Word of God.

A far darker shade in Xavier's history, viewed as a Missionary of the Gospel, was his attempts to advance the kingdom of Christ by the sword of the magistrate, by the terrors of persecution, and by the bribe of temporal advantages. The name of Xavier became identified in future generations with this anti-Christian system. "The Jesuits," says Dr. Geddes,[*] in his Church History of Ethiopia, "were all to a man of the same opinion with that great apostle of the Indies, Francis Xavier, whose maxim, as Ravaretta informs us, was, that Missionaries without muskets do never make converts to any purpose. The truth of which maxim John Bolunte, a Missionary Jesuit, tells us is confirmed by universal experience; for neither in the Brazils, Peru, Mexico, Florida, the Philippines, or Molucca, have any conversions been made without the help of the secular power."

[*] Dr. Geddes, Chancellor of Sarum, was for many years British Chaplain at Lisbon, and there studied the Portuguese Histories of Missions.

This fault, it may be said, was rather one of the age in which Xavier lived, and he might plead the prescription of Church history for centuries past in its vindication. But when he proposed to the King of Portugal to avow that it was the business of civil authorities, and not of Missionaries, "to make Christians," he carried a false principle to an unusual length. Besides which, it is our present purpose to bring the character of Xavier to the test of Christian principles; and by these Xavier stands convicted of an unchristian spirit in his military expedition against Jaffnapatam, in his threats of the Inquisition against those who opposed his work, and especially in the vengeance which he invoked with his last breath upon the Governor of Malacca, for his interference with the political part of a scheme which Xavier had devised for promoting a Missionary object.

The most serious charge against Xavier, however, remains to be stated. He undertook a great spiritual enterprise without the right means and preparation for the work. God's inspired volume in the language of the people was no part of his Missionary agency. He did not arm himself with that Gospel which is "the power of God unto salvation." It is melancholy to find throughout his writings, amidst many noble religious sentiments, little which tends to exalt Christ, or to honour the work of the Holy Spirit. The Virgin Mary and the Saints are obtruded into an idolatrous position. The religion which he attempted to propagate was not according to the Gospel of Christ. He has left on record his manual of instruction, and it proves to be a mixture of legends with the truth of God. Hence the elements of a great character were dwarfed and crippled by inferior motives and anti-christian principles. Great natural endowments and precious opportunities were wasted in the vain attempt to extend the kingdom of Christ by unauthorized expedients, and by "will-worship." Hence the contradiction between Xavier's natural force of character and his spiritual inefficiency; between the expectation which would be formed of his success in any secular pursuit, and his utter failure in the Missionary enterprise.

Failure is not alone a proof of the unsoundness of the principles on which an enterprise is conducted. But when the failure may be traced to sources of inherent weakness which might have been avoided; and when others have succeeded in the same enterprise by furnishing themselves with more adequate resources, then failure may be fairly alleged as a proof of defective preparation, and as partaking of the folly of the man who did not "sit down first and count the costs."

Xavier's failure in the enterprise he undertook has been proved by abundant evidence. Though he lived in an atmosphere of hope, and of large expectations, success always eluded his grasp. He could neither work alone nor control his associates. At last he turned his back upon all his comrades, and sacrificed his life in attempting a solitary and impracticable enterprise. If we compare him with that class of Missionaries to whom we have alluded—Schwartz, Martyn, Marsden, Johnson, Judson, Williams, and many other modern Evangelists, the results of his personal labours, and of his Missionary usefulness, sink into insignificance.

It may perhaps be urged that we should give Xavier the praise of having been the leader in the great Jesuit Missionary enterprise of the sixteenth century, which was sustained for two hundred years, and extended over all the chief regions of the world. Before, however, we can fairly estimate the reflex glory or reproach which Romish Missions cast upon the leadership of Xavier, it will be necessary to discuss, somewhat at length, the history of Romish Missions; and it will be better to close the review of Xavier's personal character and labours, and to make the proposed discussion the subject of a separate chapter.

CHAPTER IX.

The Failure of Romish Missions to the Heathen.

SECTION 1. *Sources of Information respecting Romish Missions.*—LETTERS OF MISSIONARIES—LETTRES ÉDIFIANTES—ANNALS OF THE FAITH.

SECTION 2. *Vast extent of Romish Missions.*—INSTITUTIONS IN EUROPE FOR THE SUPPORT AND GOVERNMENT OF MISSIONS—THE PROPAGANDA AT ROME—THE CONGREGATION OF THE PRIESTS OF THE FOREIGN MISSIONS IN PARIS.

SECTION 3. *Failure of the principal Romish Missions since the time of Xavier.*—SOUTH INDIA—THE MISSION IN CEYLON—EXTINCTION OF THE MISSION IN JAPAN—FAILURE OF MISSION IN CHINA—ABYSSINIA—THE MISSION IN PARAGUAY AND THE PHILIPPINE ISLANDS.

SECTION 4. *Concluding Remarks.*

SECTION 1.—*Sources of information respecting Romish Missions.*

THE present chapter will be devoted to a far wider subject than the personal history of Francis Xavier, namely, the character and success of Romish Missions in general. We have seen Xavier's confession, after seven years' residence in India, of the failure of Romish

Missions in his day. He undoubtedly communicated a new impulse to Romish Missions. But it is a question whether this new era was for good or for evil, in respect of the progress of Christian truth throughout the world. The history of Romish Missions before the era of Jesuitism is very scanty. Fabricius mentions a Latin work of authority on this subject, by Raymond Caron; but I have not been able to meet with that book.

The Jesuits undoubtedly introduced practices and dissensions into the Mission field, which were in the highest degree disgraceful and disastrous to the cause.

It will be well to commence our inquiry by some reference to the sources from which the history of Romish Missions may be obtained. The earliest original authorities from the time of Xavier are the volumes of Letters of Missionaries, published from time to time in various countries of Europe. I have already shown the suspicious character which attaches to these works. Xavier's letters are distinguished from such collections by their general sobriety and ingenuous disclosures, as well as by their number and variety. All that could be found of his writings have been presented to us in their genuine condition, having been collected from time to time, and published by careful editors. No such materials have appeared of any other Romish Missionary. Father Ripa's narrative of his residence as a painter at the Court of Pekin from 1710 to 1723 is the nearest approach which I have found to the autobiography of Xavier.

I have looked through many volumes of letters of Missionaries, published in the sixteenth and seventeenth centuries, but they contain such stereotyped accounts of hundreds and thousands of converts, such boastful assertions of miracles and martyrdoms, such vague and disconnected statistics of success, that I have regarded it as a hopeless task to attempt to draw any satisfactory conclusions from this source.

Towards the close of the seventeenth century, French Missionaries began to be numerous. Many of these were sent out and supported by a Missionary Institution in Paris. The letters which they sent to France relating to their labours were published in French from time to time. At the commencement of the eighteenth century, the letters of French Missionaries were brought into notice and repute by the famous series of "*Lettres édifiantes et curieuses, écrites des Missions étrangeres, par quelques Missionaires de la Compagnie de Jesus.*" Selections of these letters were printed in English by Mr. Lockman, 1742, who gives the following succinct account of the work in his Preface.

"The original consists of 25 volumes 12mo., which were printed at Paris at different times, as the several letters came to hand, or as the editors thought proper to send them to press. The first volume was made public in 1717, and the earliest letter is dated 1699. The 25th volume was published in 1741, and the last letter is dated in 1740. The first eight volumes of the original were communicated to the world by Father Le Gobien; and the succeeding volumes by Father Du Halde, both Jesuits, who compiled the four large folio volumes, containing a general history of China."

The fidelity of the glowing accounts of successes contained in the "Lettres édifiantes," &c., has been disproved by Romish, as well as by Protestant writers. But it requires much moral courage in a Romanist to risk the enmity of the Jesuits by publishing any thing to their discredit. A Capuchin Missionary, who was bold enough to run that risk, even though supported by the Pope, was hunted like a hare, according to his own account, throughout every country in Europe. P. Norbert went out as a Missionary from Rome to South India in 1737. He afterwards held the office of "Procureur général en Cour de Rome des Missions aux Indes Orientales." He began to expose, after his return from India, the falsity of the Jesuit letters from the East. In one of his published volumes, (vol. iii. p. 60,) he states that "he was often solicited by the Cardinals of the Propagation of the Faith to unveil in the face of the Church the numerous falsehoods contained in these letters." He therefore prepared a work for the press, containing a history of the Madura Mission, and of the visitatorial Mission of the Cardinal de Tournon, a Papal legate, who was sent to China, and perished in the attempt to carry out the Papal decrees in opposition to the Jesuits. The work is highly condemnatory of the conduct of the Jesuit Missionaries in Madura and in China, and contains all the Papal examinations, decrees, and documents on the questions at issue between the Jesuits and other Missionaries. As soon as it was known that Norbert was engaged in this work, a persecution against him began, so severe, that Pope Benedict XIV. issued a brief, warning all persons not to molest him. He left Rome to avoid the hostility of the Jesuits, he escaped to Venice, then to Lucca, then to Holland, then to England, where he supported himself by a tapestry manufacture; then he removed into Prussia. He procured a brief from the Pope to wear the habit of a secular priest, and took the assumed name of Abbé Platel, under which name he published his first volumes. From Prussia he sought refuge in France, then in Portugal, and then returned to France, where he died about 1770, being 73 or 75 years old.

Another Romish witness to the untruthfulness of the Jesuits' reports of their Missions, as well as to the unchristian character of their proceedings, was M. Favre, a Swiss priest, who was chosen by the Bishop of Halicarnassus, M. de la Baume, as his secretary, on a special commission, in 1740, from the Pope, to inquire into the state of the Jesuit Mission in Cochin China. This Papal commissioner, like the Cardinal de Tournon, paid the forfeit of his life, through the persecutions of the Jesuit Missionaries, whom he attempted to curb. M. Favre, after his return to Europe, published a volume of letters, in which he details these circumstances; (Venice, 1746,) in the preface of which he thus speaks of the Lettres édifiantes: "What do these letters principally contain? Choice eulogies upon their Missions and their Missionaries—

eulogies which are not in the least founded upon truth. What else? Marvels which have no existence except in the imagination of the writers. To believe them, how many conversions have been effected by their ministry! what progress has the Gospel made in their hands! Yet I say it with as much grief as truth, I found on the spot not the least vestige of these fine things, these "edifying" achievements. I found only scandalous profanations of the divine worship, and the dissemination of discord, which it is now almost impossible to suppress." The volume contains a variety of documents and reports, which abundantly prove the disorders and fierce disputes amongst the Missionaries of this Roman-Catholic Mission.

Romish testimonies to the untruthfulness of the letters of Romish Missionaries might easily be multiplied. But whoever will carefully study the letters with a view to the information which they contain, will soon discover, I apprehend, that the statements are so vague and fragmentary, that it is impossible to weave them into any connected history, or to collect from them any tolerable account of the actual results of the Missions, even if their honesty had never been impeached.

A new series of letters, in French, upon the plan of the Lettres édifiantes, named "The Annals of the Propagation of the Faith," was commenced as a monthly publication by the Missionary Institution at Lyons, in 1823. This work contains extracts from the correspondence of Missionaries in the various Roman-Catholic Missions which receive pecuniary assistance from that

Institution, which has been of late years the main support of Romish Missions.

Numerous histories of particular Missions have been published from time to time since the close of the sixteenth century. But I have not been able to meet with any, from Maffeus downwards, which do not reproduce the statements of "The letters" and partake of the same character.

Two thick volumes, containing 3000 columns of print, have lately been published in French, which give a general history of Romish Missions in all countries. "Historie des Missions Catholiques, depuis le XIII$^{me.}$ Siècle jusqu'a nos jours, par M. le Baron Henrion. Paris, 1840." In the preface the Baron states that this is the first attempt to compile such a general history. These volumes contain all legendary tales, miraculous relations, and martyrdoms of Romish Missionaries, strung together into an entertaining narrative; and illustrated by 320 engravings. From these, however, it is impossible to pick out a connected history of any one Mission, or the general results of Romish Missions.

Yet such Missionary records have too often served the purpose of misleading Protestant writers. In many Protestant histories of the progress of Christianity, the romance of Romish Missionary legends is preserved, and the most palpable extravagencies are pared down to the standard of Protestant credulity, and then put forth as historical truth. Take as an example—"Xavier," it has been said, "claims 10,000 converts in one month:

say half that number. What Protestant Missionary can show 5000 converts in a month?" Thus are many unwary Protestants caught in Romish meshes.

There is, however, a class of Protestant writers on Romish Missions, such as Fabricius and Mosheim, who have not only had an extensive knowledge of the subject, but who have exercised much skill and patience in unravelling original authorities. Though these are secondary authorities, I cannot hesitate to avail myself of them for the purposes of a review of the most famous Romish Missions.

SECTION 2.—*Vast extent of Romish Missions..*

In estimating the success or failure of Romish Missions, it is important to remember that the efforts put forth by the Church of Rome for the conversion of the heathen to the Christian faith, have been of the most powerful and extensive character. If only a few adventurers had gone forth upon the enterprise, their failure would not bring reproach upon the Church from which they went out. The case is, however, far different from this. The Church of Rome has organized and sustained its Missions for centuries upon a magnificent scale. It will have been seen that Xavier and his associates were chiefly supported by the munificence of the King of Portugal, and by charges upon his revenue in India. The different religious orders in Europe have also sent out and supported many of their associates in various parts of the Missionary field.

In the early part of the seventeenth century, *Missionary Institutions* sprung up in the Romish Church, which enjoyed the highest ecclesiastical sanction and patronage, and largely promoted the extension of Missions. I extract from Mosheim's Ecclesiastical History some account of these establishments.

"Gregory XV., by the advice of his confessor Narni, founded at Rome, in the year 1622, the famous Congregation for the propagation of the Faith, and enriched it with ample revenues. This Congregation, which consists of thirteen cardinals, two priests, one monk, and a secretary, is designed to propagate and maintain the religion of Rome in all parts and corners of the world. Its riches and possessions were so prodigiously augmented by the munificence of Urban VIII., and the liberality of an incredible number of donors, that its funds are, at this day, adequate to the most expensive and magnificent undertakings. And, indeed, the enterprises of this *Congregation* are great and extensive. By it a vast number of Missionaries are sent to the remotest parts of the world; books of various kinds published to facilitate the study of foreign and barbarous languages; the sacred writings and other pious productions sent abroad to the most distant corners of the globe, and exhibited to each nation and country in their own language and characters; seminaries founded for the sustenance and education of a prodigious number of young men, set apart for the foreign Missions; houses erected for the instruction and support of the pagan youths that are yearly sent from abroad to Rome, that they may return from thence into their respective countries, and become the instructors of their blinded brethren; not to mention the charitable establishments that are designed for the relief and support of those who have suffered banishment, or been involved in other calamities on account of their zeal for promoting the glory of its pontiff. Such are the arduous and complicated schemes, with the execution of which this *Congregation* is charged; but these, though the principal, are not the only objects of its attentions: its views, in a word, are vast, and its exploits almost incredible. Its members hold their assemblies in a splendid and magnificent palace, whose delightful situation adds a singular lustre to its beauty and grandeur.

"To this famous establishment, another, less magnificent, indeed, but highly useful, was added in the year 1627, by Pope Urban VIII., under the denomination of a *College, or Seminary for the Propagation of the Faith.* This seminary is set apart for the instruction and education of those who are designed for the foreign Missions; and they are brought up, with the greatest care, in the knowledge of all the languages and sciences that are necessary to prepare them for propagating the Gospel among the distant nations. This excellent foundation was due to the zeal and munificence of John Baptist Viles, a Spanish nobleman who resided at the court of Rome, and who began by presenting to the pontiff all his ample possession, together with his house, which was a noble and beautiful structure, for this pious and generous purpose. His liberality excited a spirit of pious emulation, and is followed with zeal even to this day. The *Seminary* was at first committed by Urban to the care and direction of three *Canons* of the *patriarchal* churches; but this disposition was afterwards changed, and ever since the year 1641 it is governed by the *Congregation*, founded by Gregory XV.

"The same zealous spirit reached France, and produced there several pious foundations of a like nature. In the year 1663, the *Congregation of Priests of the Foreign Missions* was instituted by royal authority; while an association of Bishops and other ecclesiastics founded the *Parisian Seminary for the Missions abroad*, designed for the education of those who were set apart for the propagation of Christianity among the pagan nations. From hence apostolical vicars are still sent to Siam, Tonquin, Cochin China, and Persia, Bishops to Babylon, and Missionaries to other Asiatic nations, and all these spiritual envoys are supported by the ample revenues and possessions of the *Congregation and Seminary*. These *priests of the foreign Missions*, and the apostles they send into foreign countries, are almost perpetually involved in altercations and debates with the Jesuits and their Missionaries. The former are shocked at the methods that are ordinarily employed by the latter in converting the Chinese and other Asiatics to the Christian religion. And the Jesuits, in their turn, absolutely refuse obedience to the orders of the apostolical Vicars and Bishops, who receive their commissions from the Congregation above mentioned, though this commission be issued out with the consent of the Pope, or of the *College de Propaganda Fide*, residing at Rome. There was also another religious establishment formed in France during the seventeenth century, under the title of the *Congregation of the Holy Sacrament*, whose founder was Antherius, Bishop of Bethlehem, and which, in the year 1644, received an order from Urban VIII. to have always a number of ecclesiastics ready to exercise their ministry among the pagan nations, whenever they should be called upon by the Pope, or by the *Congregation de Propaganda*, for that purpose. It would be endless to mention other Associations of less note, that were formed in several countries, for promoting the cause of Christianity among the darkened nations, as also the care taken by the Jesuits and other religious communities to have a number of Missionaries always ready for that purpose.

"These congregations and colleges sent forth those legions of Missionaries, who, in the seventeenth century, covered, in a manner, the whole face of the globe, and converted, to the profession of Christianity at least, if not to its temper and spirit, multitudes of persons in the fiercest and most barbarous nations. The religious orders that make the greatest figure in these Missions are the *Jesuits*, the *Dominicans*, the *Franciscans*, and the *Capuchins*, who, though concerned in one common cause, agree, nevertheless, very ill among themselves, accusing each other publicly and reciprocally, and that with the most bitter reproaches and invectives, of want of zeal in the service of Christ, nay, of corrupting the purity of the Christian doctrine to promote their ambitious purposes. But none are so universally accused of sinister views and unworthy practices, in this respect, as the Jesuits, who are singularly odious in the eyes of all the other Missionaries, and are looked upon as a very dangerous and pernicious set of apostles by a considerable part of the Romish Church. Nor, indeed, can they be viewed in any other light, if the general report be true, that, instead of instructing their proseyltes in the genuine doctrines of Christianity, they teach them a corrupt system of religion and morality, that sits easy upon their consciences, and is reconcileable with the indulgence of their appetites and passions; that they not only tolerate, but even countenance, in these new converts, several profane opinions and superstitions: that by commerce, carried on with the most rapacious avidity, and various other methods little consistent with probity and candour, they have already acquired an overgrown opulence, which they augment from day to day: that they burn with the thirst of ambition, and are continually grasping after worldly honours and prerogatives: that they are perpetually employing the arts of adulation and the seductions of bribery to insinuate themselves into the friendship and protection of men in power: that they are deeply involved in civil affairs, in the cabals of courts and the intrigues of politicians: and, finally, that they frequently excite intestine commotions and civil wars in those states and kingdoms where their views are obstructed or disappointed, and refuse obedience to the Roman Pontiff, and to the Vicars and Bishops that bear his commission. These accusations are indeed grievous, but they are perfectly well attested, being confirmed by the most striking circumstantial evidence, as well as by a prodigious number of unexceptionable witnesses.

"Among these we may reckon many of the most illustrious and respectable members of the Church of Rome, whose testimony cannot be imputed to the suggestions of envy, on the one hand, nor considered as the effect of temerity or ignorance on the other: such are the Cardinals, the members of the *Congregation de Propaganda Fide*, and even some of the Popes themselves. These testimonies are supported and confirmed by glaring facts, even by the proceedings of the Jesuits in China, Abyssinia, Japan, and India, where they have dishonoured the cause of Christianity, and hurt the interests of Rome in the most sensible manner by their corrupt practices." (Mosheim's Ecclesiastical History, cent. xvii. sec. 1.)

Now in these institutions in Rome, France, and other countries, we see a Missionary apparatus and force far beyond that which has as yet proceeded from the Protestant Churches. We may therefore well ask, What have been the results? Many may be disposed to reply at once, What can be expected when Missionaries themselves fall into contentions and persecutions one against another? This reply, however, would too summarily dispose of the question. It deserves a deeper research.

We return, therefore, to the inquiry, What have been the results of Romish Missions, put forth on the vast scale we have described, during the last three centuries? What have been their conquests over heathenism and Mohammedanism throughout the world? To what country will Rome point as exhibiting the triumph of its Missions? If we examine some of its chief scenes of early hope and promise, we shall discover only signal failures, notwithstanding much boasted success at times. If we turn over the 3000 closely-printed columns of Baron Henrion, and notice the multitude of illustrious names and deeds of Romish Missionaries through successive centuries, and then ask, Where are the present results of these Missions?—where are the native Churches which have sprung from them? the proof of the failure of Romish Missions becomes perfectly astounding.

Yet the Church of Rome perfectly understood the importance of the Missionary element in a true Church. For Cardinal Bellarmin, in his rules of a true Church, makes her "efficacy upon infidels," or Missionary success, one of his fifteen notes of a true Church.

We have already noticed the comparatively small success in the region of Cape Comorin, and the extinction of the Japanese Mission. But we will examine somewhat more in detail these and other of the most celebrated Missions of the Church of Rome.

Section 3.—*Failure of the principal Romish Missions since the time of Xavier.*

South India.

From Goa, as a centre, Romish Missionaries of several religious orders extended their Missions throughout South India and Ceylon. What have been the results of these Missions?

If we are to judge by the numbers of their reputed converts, the results will exhibit failure, rather than success. We have seen that soon after the death of Xavier, the number of converts in the western portion of South India alone were reckoned at 300,000. We have seen also how these statistics were made up; and what was the low character of the converts: that they were for the most part not real, but mere nominal converts. The Abbé Dubois, who laboured in India two centuries and a half afterwards, so late as up to 1815, gives the number of converts in all India, particularizing the several dioceses. That number was 635,000,* including half-castes and the descendants of the Portuguese. He asserts, also, that he had seen the lists which were dated seventy years before his time, from which it appeared, that in the Carnatic, Mysore, and Madura, the number of converts had fallen off from 245,000 to 81,000. † I fully allow the uncertainty of these statistics. But Romish statistics never erred on the side of under-

---

* Letters on the State of Christianity in India. p. 54.
† *ib.* p. 7.

reckoning. The calculations in both cases would be made upon the same principles; and therefore they are fair subjects for comparison. It appears, from the comparison, that the extension of the Missions throughout all India, during two centuries and a half, had only gathered 335,000 additional converts; which would imply that the number of converts in the original fields of labour must have been nearly stationary. And the Abbé further states, that within the last seventy years the numbers had been rapidly diminishing.

I am well aware that other numbers may be found in "Letters," &c., and that of late years the statistics of Rome have been prodigiously augmented. But the comparison I have given above must speak for itself as far as it goes.

The success, however, of Missions is to be reckoned rather by the quality of the work, than by statistics. Judging by this rule, it is to be observed that the most extensive and influential Mission of the Church of Rome in South-India was that of the Jesuits, and the glory of their South-Indian Mission was the Madura Mission. We have already noticed the principles of fraud and compromise with idolatry upon which that Mission was founded by Robert de Nobili, nephew of Card. Bellarmin, and his successors. These practices and principles were resolutely maintained for more than 120 years, against the protests of other religious orders and the decrees of Popes. At length, in 1744, Benedict XIV. issued a Bull which bears the name of *Omnium sollicitudinum*, in which he condemned, on the authority of his predecessors as well as his own, the practices and principles of the Jesuits in South India. He describes the Mission as all but ruined. (*Eo rem adduxerant, ut tot verbi Dei præcones eximii sine causâ adhuc laborasse, largosque sudores et sanguinem ipsam frustra effudisse viderentur.*) These Missions had long been repudiated by all Protestant Missionaries; and now the condemnation of their paganized Christianity was pronounced by the Church of Rome itself.

The subject of the Madura and other South-Indian Romish Missions has been very ably treated, and their failure has been demonstrated, in an Article entitled "The Jesuit Mission in India," in the Calcutta Review, vol. ii. 1844.

The quality of the Christianity in these South-Indian Missions has been also revealed by the Abbé du Bois, in the letters already referred to. His experience as a Romish Missionary extended over thirty years; and his intelligence and knowledge of India are attested by a volume of established reputation, published by him, on the scientific and ethnological history of South India, which is largely quoted by Baron Henrion. His sympathies were much drawn out towards the people of India, and his letters contain severe strictures upon Protestant Missionaries for depreciating them. Yet the following are extracts from his work.

In the advertisement of his volume, the Abbé thus speaks:—

"The author has vainly, in his exertions to promote the cause of Christianity, watered the soil of India with his sweats, and many times with his tears, at the sight of the quite insurmountable obduracy of the people he had to deal with; ready to water it with his blood, if his doing so had been able to overcome the invincible resistance he had to encounter everywhere, in his endeavours to disseminate some gleams of the evangelical light. Everywhere the seeds sown by him have fallen upon a naked rock, and have instantly dried away.

"At length, entirely disgusted at the total inutility of his pursuits, and warned by his grey hair that it was full time to think of his own concerns, he has returned to Europe, to pass in retirement the few days he may still have to live, and get ready to give in his accounts to his Redeemer." (Letters, &c. Page 7.)

After a brief review of the work of the Jesuit and other Missionaries in India, the Abbé adds:—

"Such is the abridged history of the rise, the progress, and the decline of the Christian religion in India. The low state to which it is now reduced, and the contempt in which it is held, cannot be surpassed. There is not at present in the country (as mentioned before) more than a third of the Christians who were to be found in it eighty years ago, and this number diminishes every day by frequent apostacy. It will dwindle to nothing in a short period; and if things continue as they are now going on, within less than fifty years there will, I fear, remain no vestige of Christianity among the natives." (Page 12.)

The following is a specimen and illustration of his general statements.

"In order to give you a striking idea of the religious dispositions of the Hindoo, and as a strong instance of what I asserted above, that there was to be found among them nothing else but a vain phantom of Christianity, without any real or practical faith, I will, with shame and confusion, quote the following scandalous instance—

"When the late Tippoo Sultan sought to extend his own religious creed all over his dominions, and make, by little and little, all the inhabitants in Mysore converts to Islamism, he wished to begin this fanatical undertaking with the native Christians living in his country, as the most odious to him, on the score of their religion. In consequence, in the year 1784 he gave secret orders to his officers in the different districts to make the most diligent inquiries after the places where Christians were to be found, and to cause the whole of them to be seized on the same day, and conducted under strong escorts to Seringapatam. This order was punctually carried into execution: very few of them escaped; and I have it from good authority, that the aggregated number of persons seized in this manner amounted to more than 60,000.

"Some time after their arrival at Seringapatam, Tippoo ordered the whole to undergo the rites of circumcision, and be made converts to Mohammedanism. The Christians were put together during the several days that the ceremony lasted; and oh, shame!—oh, scandal! will it be believed in the Christian world?—no one, not a single individual among so many thousands, had courage enough to confess his faith under this trying circumstance, and become a martyr to his religion. The whole apostatized *en masse*, and, without resistance or protestations, tamely underwent the operation of circumcision, no one among them possessing resolution enough to say 'I am a Christian, and I will die rather than renounce my religion!'" (Page 73.)

The Abbé also gives this confession of the failure of his own personal labours.

"For my part, I cannot boast of my successes in this holy career during a period of twenty-five years that I have laboured to promote the interests of the Christian religion. The restraints and privations under which I have lived, by conforming myself to the usages of the country; embracing, in many respects, the prejudices of the natives; living like them, and becoming almost a Hindoo myself; in short, by 'being made all things to all men, that I might by all means save some,'—all this has proved of no avail to me to make proselytes.

"During the long period I have lived in India, in the capacity of a Missionary, I have made, with the assistance of a native Missionary, in all beween two and three hundred converts of both sexes. Of this number, two-thirds were *pariahs*, or beggars; and the rest were composed of *sudras*, vagrants, and outcasts of several tribes, who, being without resource, turned Christians, in order to form new connections, chiefly for the purpose of marriage, or with some other interested views. Among them are to be found some, also, who believed themselves to be possessed by the devil, and who turned Christians, after having been assured that, on their receiving baptism, the unclean spirits would leave them, never to return; and I will declare it, with shame and confusion, that I do not remember any one who may be said to have embraced Christianity from conviction, and through quite disinterested motives. Among these new converts many apostatized, and relapsed into paganism, finding that the Christian religion did not afford them the temporal advantages they had looked for in embracing it: and I am verily ashamed, that the resolution I have taken to declare the whole truth on this subject forces me to make the humiliating avowal, that those who continued Christians are the very worst among my flock.*

"I know that my brother Missionaries in other parts of the country, although more active and more zealous, perhaps, than myself, have not been more fortunate, either in the number or the quality of their proselytes. For my part, I have, until now, struggled, though in vain, with the numberless difficulties stated in these

*The late mutiny in India brought out a very different Christianity in the Protestant converts—men who confessed Christ, and were willing to die rather than embrace Mohammedanism.

letters, and exerted myself to the utmost not to sink under so many disadvantages. If a great many persons of my profession have discharged their duties with more ability, I believe that I may boast that few have done it with more patience and perseverance than myself; and in spite of every kind of disgust and contradiction—in spite of the inutility of my pursuits—I am determined, after having embraced the profession of a Missionary, to continue the desperate struggle, and persevere in it to the last." (Page 133.)

It is impossible to read these statements without reverting to the words of Xavier recorded in a former chapter—"If you will, in imagination, search through India, you will find that few will reach heaven, either of whites or blacks, except those who depart this life under fourteen years of age, with their baptismal innocence still upon them." Some modern Protestant writers have doubted whether the Abbé has not given a gloomy and splenetic colouring to his description. But Xavier and the Abbé must stand in the same category.

Let us now contrast the account of Roman-Catholic Missions in South India, after the labour of three centuries, with the results of Protestant Missions in the same district after an efficient labour of half a century. A Protestant Mission was, indeed, commenced at the beginning of the eighteenth century, by two Danish Missionaries: but the Protestant Missionaries remained a mere handful, till increased during the last half century. The statement I present was drawn up at a Conference of Protestant South India Missionaries, held at Ootacamund in May 1858, by thirty-two Representatives of Protestant Missionary Societies of England, Scotland, Germany, and America, of various forms of ecclesiastical government. A happy contrast did this Protestant union exhibit to the sad dissensions and violent oppositions which chequer the histories of the South-India Romish Mission under Rome's boasted unity! The united testimony of these various Missionaries is given in these words:—

"Let us, then, cast a rapid glance at the success which, through God's blessing, has crowned the labours of his servants in the South-Indian field.

"In the Tinnevelly, Travancore, Tanjore, and Madura Provinces, 'the Lord hath made bare his arm in the sight of the nations, and this end of the earth hath seen the salvation of our God.' Here He is saying to his Church, 'Lift up thine eyes and behold: all these gather themselves together, and come to Thee.' Here are numerous congregations of men and women who have renounced idolatry and demonolatry, sitting at the feet of the Christian Missionary to learn of Jesus and his salvation. Here are many infant Churches, with a goodly band of their own pastors and teachers. Here are many thousands of children who have been preserved from the polluting and soul-destroying influences of idolatry, and who are now being trained in the nurture and admonition of the Lord. Behold their newly-built churches and chapels and school-houses, and see how delightfully they contrast with the hoary shrines of false gods and hideous demons, and silently but surely indicate their approaching doom! Listen to the many thousands of infant voices early taught to lisp the Saviour's name! Look at the goodly number of adults who from time to time meet together to remember Him who shed his precious blood on the cross for the remission of their sins; and at the multitudes who congregate each Lord's-day to hear the wondrous story of man's redemption! Count up their contributions to the cause of the Gospel, and see how, like Macedonian Christians of primitive times, 'their deep poverty has abounded unto the riches of their liberality!' Contrast the lives and actions of those professors who are established in the Christian doctrine, with those of the heathen around them, and learn that 'the righteous is more excellent than his neighbour!' Stand by their dying couch, and see how their faith in Christ imparts peace and confidence, and lights up the dark valley, in which their heathen neighbours can see nothing but confused images of the dismal and the terrible!

"That many of them have first put themselves under Christian instruction from very imperfect motives, and with very slight knowledge of what they were doing; and that many of them long continue very feeble and imperfect, even as nominal Christians only, is not denied; but then they are no longer worshippers of abominable idols, no longer under the dominion of a crafty and lying priesthood, no longer groping in the thick darkness of heathenism, and no longer entirely ignorant of God and futurity, of Christ and his salvation.

"That the majority of them are not the rich and great of this world is true; but this is the 'sign from heaven' that Jesus is the Messiah, and that it is indeed his Gospel which we preach and they believe. Here we see realized the prophetic description of the seer, 'an afflicted and poor people shall trust in the name of the Lord.' Such hath the great Sovereign Ruler ever chosen, to bring down all the loftiness of man, and to make low all his haughtiness and pride, that He alone may be exalted. Among these the Lord is raising up the faithful heralds of his cross, whom He will clothe with the might of his Spirit, and send forth to gather out from among the heathen around a people for his name, and whom He will appoint to feed his sheep and his lambs. But we rejoice to find that this great work is not confined to the lower orders of the people. The Gospel is now reaching the more educated and respectable classes, some of whom have made an open profession of the Christian faith.

"Let us now turn to the Missions of the German brethren on the western coast, where we see many proofs that the hand of the Lord has been with his servants, and that many have believed their report. Here, in addition to congregations, and Churches, and Schools, similar to those we have already described, though on a smaller scale, we see the Gospel in its benevolent aspect towards the industrious labouring poor—the brethren having taught many of them how to improve their temporal condition, while they are also teaching them to seek first the kingdom of God.

"Leaving this field, which is already become a fruitful one, and where more than forty devoted brethren are labouring in the Gospel, and already rejoicing over the tokens of God's gracious approval of their toil, we may visit in succession the many stations of various Societies of Britain and America, scattered over the land. At each we may look upon an infant Church and congregation; at most on boarding and day-schools, both in the vernacular and in English; on a staff of native teachers, with here and there a seminary for their efficient training; on printing-presses, with stores of books and tracts, and translations of the Holy Scriptures, in the various languages; on churches, and chapels, and school-houses, and Mission dwellings, and thus behold a complete system of appliances for carrying on the work of the Lord. And if we stop at each station, and inquire what has been done to bring the Gospel to bear upon the surrounding masses, we shall be everywhere furnished with ample proof that the truth has fully enlightened the understandings and gained the approval of many, and is powerfully leavening the community at large.

"By means of scriptural education many a youth has lost his faith in Hinduism, and learnt that Christianity is both true and divine; while by means of preaching, conversation, and the perusal of tracts and portions of the Scriptures, many an adult has done the same, being no longer Hindu in conviction, though not yet Christian in profession.

"At some of these stations, and in the surrounding districts, the heart is gladdened by the sight of prosperity similar in kind, though not yet equal in degree, to that of Tinnevelly and Travancore. At some others it is cheered by the delightful intelligence, that, after a long night of toil and weeping, the first-fruits of the harvest have just been gathered in, and the brethren are rejoicing in the dawn of the morning.

"And now let us visit the great city of Madras. Here, in addition to the usual machinery of bringing the Gospel into contact with the native mind, we behold a large and powerful system of Anglo-vernacular education—based upon the Bible, and entirely pervaded by its soul-transforming truths—steadily at work, moulding the minds of several thousands of youths of the middle and upper classes; and, through the divine blessing, touching the hearts of not a few, and leading them to Christ. Several of these we see becoming efficient preachers of the Gospel, and often do we witness crowds of heathen attentively listening to their earnest and telling words.

"Great has been the power put forth by this system on a class of native minds, scarcely to be reached by any other instrumentality, and great are the results it has already accomplished; while a greater still seems to await its progress. But it involves most arduous and persevering toil, and, in such a climate, often do the labourers literally groan under 'the burden and heat of the day.' But they see that in their work which bids them go forward, and not be weary in well-doing, knowing assuredly that the rich harvest-time will certainly come in its appointed season.

"But let us now collect our statistics, and state what at present is the result of Missionary operations; not for our own praise, but for the glory of Him without whose blessing all our works would end in vanity and confusion.

"We have, then, as the fruits of Missionary labour in Southern India, and the entire island of Ceylon—

"1. More than one hundred thousand persons who have abandoned idolatry, and are gathered into congregations receiving Christian instruction.

"2. More than sixty-five thousand who have been baptized into the name of Christ, and have thus publicly made a profession of their Christian discipleship.

"3. More than fifteen thousand who have been received as communicants, in the belief that they are sincere and faithful disciples of Christ.

"4. More than five hundred natives, exclusive of schoolmasters, who are employed as Christian teachers of their countrymen, and who are generally devoted and successful in their works.

"5. More than forty-one thousand boys in the Mission schools learning to read and understand the Holy Scriptures, which are able to make them wise unto salvation.

"6. More than eleven thousand girls rescued from that gross ignorance and deep degradation to which so many millions of their sex in India seem to be hopelessly condemned.

"Looking at these leading results, may we not exclaim, 'What hath God wrought!' 'Surely, 'this is the finger of God!' Here are the palpable evidences of the divine power of the Gospel—evidences which are yet destined to constrain many a heathen to abandon his idols, and turn to the now despised and hated name of Jesus."

Ceylon.

The failure of Roman-Catholic Missions in Ceylon, in the middle of the seventeenth century, cannot be fairly cited for our present purpose; because, when the Dutch expelled the Portuguese from the island, the profession of the Roman-Catholic faith was suppressed by penal laws; and the adoption of the Protestant form of religion was promoted by civil rewards and distinctions; and the education of the children in that faith was made compulsory. The history of Christianity in Ceylon, in its external relations, has been ably treated in a volume, published in 1850 by Sir James Emerson Tennent, for some time Colonial Secretary. The Missions were established in Ceylon, as Xavier testifies, by Franciscan and Dominican Missionaries, and were subsequently supplied from Goa. Their greatest success was amongst the Tamils of Jaffnapatam, and in the Island of Manaar. Their progress among the Singhalese population seems scarcely to have extended beyond the neighbourhood of the Portuguese forts. There are no reliable accounts of the number of converts. But in 1658 there were no less than forty or fifty churches in Jaffnapatam, besides numerous churches throughout other parts of the Tamil district.

Upon the conquest of the Portuguese possessions by the Dutch the churches were transferred to the reformed worship, the priests were driven away, and chaplains were sent from Holland to instruct the natives in Christianity. The profession of the reformed religion by those who had lately been Romanists was so rapid, that within five years of their arrival the Dutch reckoned the number of "Protestant" native Christians in Jaffnapatam at 65,000. In 1684 they were reckoned at 141,456, and a few years later the number had risen to 180,364, out of a population of 278,759. In 1722 the whole number of Protestant native Christians in all Ceylon was estimated by Valentyn, a Dutch chaplain, at 424,392. The education of the children was always a chief branch of the Dutch Mission. The number of children under instruction rose to 85,000. Facts, however, show how little value can be placed upon these statistics. In 1684 there were only four Missionaries over 141,456 converts, and a proportionate number of schools; and the native ministry had been scarcely commenced. In 1722 there were only fourteen Dutch clergymen to superintend 424,392 souls; and out of these clergymen, very few, comparatively, were able to preach in the vernacular languages. Valentyn gives a list of ninety-seven Dutch clergymen sent to Ceylon between 1642 and 1725, of whom only eight qualified themselves to preach in the native tongues! The knowledge and superintendence of the native flock must have been therefore merely nominal. Hence the Romanists were able, after the first rigour of their exclusion was past, to return by stealth, and to win back the greater part of the native Christians to the practice of their rites. In 1796 the English expelled the Dutch from Ceylon, and took possession of the island. The number of native Protestants in Ceylon was estimated at that period as 342,000, and the members of the Roman-Catholic Church were still more numerous. But as soon as a free toleration of all religions, and equal civil rights, were proclaimed by the British Government, the numbers on both sides began to fall off. At the present time about 150,000, less than half the reputed number seventy years ago, are claimed by the Romanists; while Protestant Missionaries have happily reduced their statistics so as to comprise those only to whose Christian consistency, and separation from heathenism, they can bear testimony.

This most painful review may well be a warning to all Protestant Missions, as showing that wholesale baptisms, and mere nominal converts, are as worthless in Protestant as in Romish Missions. The subject deserves a very careful study. As far as I have been able to investigate it, I am inclined to think the great mass of nominal converts, whether Romish or Protestant, never cast off heathenism; but that among the Dutch converts there were very many individuals, who, by the inculcation of pure Scriptural truth, and by the help of an open Bible, became living members of Christ: whereas in Romish Missions I have found no indications of the like blessed result.

Japan.

The facts of the final expulsion of Romish Missionaries from Japan, and of the massacre of the native Christians, have been already noticed in a preceding chapter. It will be important, however, for our present purpose, to review some of the causes which led to this terrible catastrophe. I borrow a passage from the Church History of Mosheim.

"The ministerial labours of the Romish Missionaries, and, more especially, of the Jesuits, were crowned in Japan with surprising success towards the commencement of the seventeenth century, and made an incredible number of converts to the Christian religion. But this prosperous and flourishing state of the Church was somewhat interrupted by the prejudices that the priests and grandees of the kingdom had conceived against the new religion; prejudices which proved fatal, in many places, both to those who embraced it, and to those who taught it. The cause of Christianity did not, however, suffer only from the virulence and malignity of its enemies; it was wounded in the house of its friends, and received, no doubt, some detriment from the intestine quarrels and contentions of those to whom the care of the rising Church was committed: for the same scenes of fraternal discord that had given such offence in the other Indian provinces, were renewed in Japan, where the Dominicans, Franciscans, and Augustinians were at perpetual variance with the Jesuits. This variance produced on both sides the heaviest accusations and the most bitter reproaches. The Jesuits were charged, by the Missionaries of the three orders now mentioned, with insatiable avarice, with showing an excessive indulgence both to the vices and superstitions of the Japanese, with crafty and low practices unworthy of the ministers of Christ, with an ambitious thirst after authority and dominion, and other misdemeanours of a like nature. These accusations were not only exhibited at the Court of Rome, but were spread abroad in every part of Christendom. The disciples of Loyola were by no means silent under these reproaches, but, in their turn, charged their accusers with imprudence, ignorance of the world, obstinacy, asperity of manners, and a disgusting rusticity in their way of living: adding that these circumstances rendered their ministry rather detrimental than advantageous to the cause of Christianity among a people remarkable for their penetration, generosity, and magnificence. Such, then, were the contests that arose among the Missionaries in Japan; and nothing but the amazing progress that Christianity had already made, and the immense multitude of those that had already embraced it, could have prevented these contests from being fatal to its interests. As the case stood, neither the cause of the Gospel, nor its numerous professors, received any essential damage from these divisions; and if no other circumstance had intervened to stop its progress, an expedient might have probably been found out, either to heal these divisions, or, at least, to appease them so far as to prevent their noxious and fatal consequences." (Mosheim's Ecclesiastical History, vol. ii. p. 300.)

For a further account of the Japanese Mission, I refer to the "History of Japan" by Dr. Kæmpfer, a writer of high repute for his scientific attainments and accuracy of his narratives. He spent several years in the East as a physician and naturalist, and was more than two years in Japan, about fifty years after the final destruction of the Christians. Among many other curious works, which are preserved in the Hans Sloane MSS. in the British Museum, he brought home a Japanese account of this event. The following is Dr. Kæmpfer's account of Christianity in Japan in his published work:—

"This new religion, and the great number of persons of all ranks and qualities, who were converted to it, occasioned considerable alterations in the Church, prejudicial in the highest degree to the heathen clergy; and it was feared that the same might be attended with fatal consequences, even upon the state; for which, and for several other reasons to be mentioned hereafter, the secular Emperor thought it necessary to put a stop to this growing evil, and to forbid all his subjects, under pain of death, to embrace a religion likely to prove so detrimental. For this purpose proclamations were issued in 1586. The same year the persecution began, and several persons were executed for having disobeyed the imperial commands. This unexpected turn, however, was not able to stop the progress of Christianity. The common people continued openly to embrace and to profess the same, and many persons of quality, out of fear and circumspection, did the same in private. Not even the raging flames of a persecution, the most dreadful of any mentioned in histories, seemed at first to have that effect which the heathen government expected it should. For although, according to the letters of the Jesuits, 20,570 persons suffered death for the faith of Christ, only in the year 1590, yet in 1591 and 1592, when all the churches were actually shut up, they made 12,000 new converts. The Japanese writers themselves do not disown that the young Emperor, Fide Jori, who, in the year 1616, was put to death by his tutor Ijejas, who usurped the throne upon him, was suspected of being a Christian, and that the greatest part of his court, soldiers, and military officers, professed the same religion. The cheerfulness with which the new converts suffered all imaginable torments and the most cruel death, rather than renounce their Saviour, excited the curiosity of many people to know what doctrine it was that could make its followers so joyful even in the pangs of death; and they were no sooner instructed in the same, but it manifestly appeared so full of truth and comfort, that many resolved to embrace it." (Kæmpfer's Japan, Book iv. cap. v. p. 313.)

Kæmpfer thus records the sad conclusion of the Japanese Mission:—"About the year 1635, the Dutch being at war with Portugal, took a homeward-bound Portuguese ship from Japan, on board of which they found some traitorous letters to the King of Portugal, written by one Capt. Moro, who was chief of the Portuguese in Japan, himself a Japanese by birth, and a great zealot for the Christian religion." The letters were sent to the Emperor, who, by these means, discovered a plot which the Japanese Christians, in conjunction with the Portuguese, had laid against his life and throne. The Portuguese had promised them ships and soldiers, " and, to crown all, the Papal blessing." Upon this discovery, large numbers of the Christians were put to death, and in the year 1637 an imperial proclamation was issued, by which Japan was shut to foreigners. The edict is given by Kæmpfer, of which the following are articles:—

"Whoever discovers a priest shall have a reward of 400 to 500 shuets of silver (about £500 sterling), and for every Christian in proportion. All persons who propagate the doctrines of the Christians, or bear this scandalous name, shall be imprisoned in the common gaol of the town. The whole race of the Portuguese, with their mothers, nurses, and whatever belongs to them, shall be banished to Macao."

The Dutch were allowed a restricted trade, and were

confined to a few houses built up in the harbour of Nagasaki, and communicating with the town by a bridge strongly guarded.

The final extinction of the native Christians is thus related:—" About 40,000 Christians, reduced to most desperate counsels by the many unparalleled cruelties and torments which many thousands of their brethren had already suffered, and which they themselves had, till then, very narrowly escaped, rose up and retired into an old fortified place in the neighbourhood of Simahara, with a firm resolution to defend their lives to the utmost of their power. The Dutch, upon this, as friends and allies of the Emperor, were requested to assist the Japanese in the siege of this place, and in the total destruction of the besieged Christians." "To the disgrace of the Christian name, the Director of the Dutch trade complied with the request of the Emperor, and bombarded the fort until it was so far reduced, that the Japanese were able to take it by assault, and put all the inhabitants to death."

Thus we witness the melancholy spectacle of a Mission torn by internal dissensions; and, subsequently, the complete extinction of a native Christian church, which had flourished for three generations. The presence of Christ must depart from a church before the gates of hell can prevail against it. The warnings given to the Seven Churches of Asia to repent, or else their candlesticks should be removed, confirm this truth. The Japanese Christianity must have been unsound from its origin, or it must have degenerated from its first condition. If the martyrdoms were, as Kæmpfer reports, such as to prove the genuineness of the martyrs' faith, how great must have been the degeneracy of the mass! But the history of the earlier martyrdoms, it is to observed, comes to us through the testimony of the " Letters from Japan," and must therefore be received with caution. It is clear, also, that the last 40,000 who sustained a siege, and perished fighting, can hardly claim the crown of martyrdom; for the edict of 1637 gave the Christians no alternative of saving their lives by renouncing their faith. Throughout the whole history of the Japanese Mission, the example of Xavier was the polar star, and his system of political intrigue, and of dependence upon an arm of flesh, was perpetuated in the Mission. We cannot, therefore, separate the overthrow of this Mission from the defective foundation which had been laid under the auspices of Francis Xavier.

China.

The great Roman-Catholic work on China, and on the Chinese Mission, is that of the Jesuit Father Du Halde. It consists of three or four folios (1725). But Du Halde had never been in China. He only collected and arranged the accounts given by Chinese Missionaries. He was joint Editor of the Lettres édifiantes et curieuses, &c., those very questionable authorities, as we have shown, upon Missionary results. As a Jesuit, he was also a supporter of the Jesuit Missionary principle of compromise with idolatry, which other religious orders and the Popes of Rome repudiated. These considerations cannot but shake our confidence in Du Halde's descriptions of Missions in China. It would be easy, also, to collect counter statements from Romish writers, which at least neutralize the more favourable statements of the Jesuits. For instance, Father Ripa, who was sent, in 1710, as a Missionary to China by the Pope and the "Propaganda," and resided at Pekin for thirteen years, during the most flourishing period of the Mission, makes the following astounding disclosure:—

"From 1580 to 1724 the number of Missionaries sent from Europe scarcely amount to 500. I also know, that however numerous and zealous the European Missionaries might be, they could not produce any satisfactory results, in consequence of the formidable barrier of the language, which up to my time none had been able to surmount so as to make himself understood by the people at large." (Memoirs of Father Ripa, during thirteen years' residence at the Court of Pekin in the service of the Emperor of China: selected and translated from the Italian by Fortunato Prandi. London, 1844. p. 94.)

Ripa also states that no attempt had been made to introduce an educated native ministry; he therefore commenced with a few theological pupils, but he says: "Finding all my efforts were maliciously counteracted by my enemies, and scarcely produced any thing but scandal and discord; considering how little I could effect in China for the propagation of Christianity, and how repeatedly I was exposed to the danger either of participating in idolatrous practices, or of perishing, I determined to leave China." (*ib.* p. 159.) Ripa, therefore, left China with three native pupils, and eventually established a Chinese seminary at Naples.

Putting aside, therefore, Du Halde, I shall avail myself of two works of established reputation, the one a volume by Mosheim, entitled "Authentic Memoirs of the Christian Church in China," translated from the German, published in 1748; the other, " China, its State and Prospects," by the distinguished Missionary, Dr. Medhurst, published in 1838; in order to present a brief sketch of Romish Missions in China.

More than twenty-five years elapsed after the death of Xavier before Romish Missionaries could obtain an entrance into China. In the year 1579, Matthew Ricci and two Associates commenced the Mission. Ricci was soon left alone, and spent seven years among the Bonzes, that he might obtain an intimate knowledge of their language and literature. He afterwards laid aside the habit of a Jesuit, and put on the dress of a Chinese philosopher. He was a man of great abilities and eminent attainments, especially in mathematics. Converts are said to have been made in the neighbourhood of Canton, and in various parts of that province. He afterwards travelled to Nankin, then the residence of the Emperor. "At court, his presents were received, and his person honoured; a house was assigned him, and he was taken into the service of the state A.D. 1601. Ricci was no sooner settled than he began to diffuse his doctrines, and in a few years succeeded in converting several persons of distinction. The number of Christians continued to increase, and the new doctrine soon spread from the capital to distant cities, particularly Nan-chang and Shanghae; at the latter of which a Mandarin, of great talents and influence, professed himself a follower of Christ. This man, on his baptism, took the name of Paul, as he wished to be the apostle of his countrymen. His exertions and example did much to promote the cause of Ricci, and his accurate knowledge of the language enabled him to throw the publications of his instructor into a neat and elegant style, which contributed to their acceptability with the higher classes of the people. He apologized for the Christian faith in a learned manner, and defended the cause in the presence of the Emperor: in short, his zeal, his wealth, his talents, and his influence, contributed much to the extension of the Romish faith in China, and his posterity trod in his footsteps." (Medhurst, p. 227.)

Ricci was joined by several devoted brethren, whom he established in various parts of China. He published, at Pekin, books in favour of Christianity, the number of converts increased daily, some of them were men of influence. Ricci died in 1610, but the work was sustained by the accession of numerous Jesuit Missionaries till the year 1630, when the Dominicans and Franciscans first entered that field of labour. The Missionaries of the new orders, soon after their arrival, denounced the Jesuit Missionaries as having been guilty, from the time of Ricci, of making unlawful compromises between the true and false religions, especially in respect of the worship of ancestors. A great controversy was also raised respecting the title which had been given to the true God. These dissensions lasted for one hundred years, through seasons of adversity and prosperity in the Mission. The Popes of Rome repeatedly interfered in vain attempts to decide the controversies. The history of these dissensions affords a remarkable instance of the futility of the pretensions of the Bishop of Rome to be regarded as the Supreme Head of the Church, and the arbiter of religious controversies. Pope Innocent the Tenth, in the year 1645, decided against the conduct of the Jesuits; Pope Alexander the Seventh, in the year 1656, reversed his predecessor's decision. The storm of controversy now began to rage in Europe as well as in China, and Pope Clement the Ninth, in the year 1669, decided that the decree of Pope Innocent, and the decree of Pope Alexander " were both to be observed." (Mosheim.) The prosperity of the Mission, however, continued greatly to increase: the national revolution which placed the Tartar dynasty upon the throne of China served only to give the Missionaries increased power, as they retained their influence over the new Emperor. Upon his death the education of his son, the next Emperor, then a minor, was committed to a German Jesuit named John Adam Schall.

A violent persecution broke out against the Missionaries

during the minority of the young Emperor, who bore the name of Kang-he, and many of them were banished or imprisoned; but when, in 1669, the young Emperor took the reins of government, the golden age of the Mission commenced. He was a prince of much talent, and a great patron of arts and sciences; and the Jesuit Missionaries were his friends and counsellors: "In short, they directed every thing at the court of Pekin." (Mosheim.) Louis XIV., King of France, sent a Mission to this Emperor, consisting of several learned men. In 1692 the Emperor published an edict, by which the Christian religion was declared to be good and salutary, and all his subjects were permitted to embrace it: he built a magnificent church within the walls of his palace, and sent an embassy to the Pope at Rome. During this era there was every prospect that the Emperor of China would declare himself a Christian, and that all China, Corea, and Tartary would be brought within the pale of the Roman Church. The dissensions among the Missionaries, however, rose in intensity. An Apostolic Vicar in China, Maigrot, issued a mandate in opposition to the Jesuits, which the Emperor censured as fallacious. The Pope supported his Vicar; and in 1705 the Papal Legate, Mons. Tournon, was sent to China to decide the disputes. The decree he issued being adverse to the Jesuits, occasioned his hasty deportation to Macao, where he was detained a prisoner, and died in confinement; the Pope having sent him, for his consolation, a cardinal's hat. After Tournon's death, the pope issued a Bull, drawn up in the severest terms, to support the injunctions of the Cardinal; but the Emperor took the part of the Jesuits, and the Pope's Bull became a dead letter. A second Papal Legate was sent from Rome, named Mezzabarba, who supported the Pope's authority in profession, but allowed of exceptions which nullified its substance. The Emperor died, unbaptized, in 1722, and at his death the Romish Mission in China rapidly fell away: the new Emperor repealed the edict published by his father in favour of Christianity. A violent persecution arose, and in 1723 " all the Missionaries were driven from their stations, three hundred churches were destroyed, or converted to a profane use, and three hundred thousand Native Christians were at once deprived of their pastors." (Medhurst.) A few Missionaries were permitted to reside at Pekin for the sake of their mathematical skill, but throughout other parts of the empire they were obliged to conceal themselves, and from time to time, when discovered, some were put to death. This state of things continued for a century. Medhurst, writing in 1838, describes the state of the Romish Missions in China, and gives the returns " from Marchini's map of the Missions presented to the Bishop of Macao in 1810," by which it appeared that there were at that time, in all China, six bishops, two co-adjutors, twenty-three Missionaries, eighty native agents, and 215,000 Native Christians. This return, presented to the Roman-Catholic Bishop of the city of Macao, which was the basis of all their operations, and from whence their supplies were received, bears upon the face of it an authority which cannot easily be disputed.

When Medhurst wrote, the number of Missionaries it appears had increased. He states that the expenses of the Missions were met by bills on Europe negotiated at Macao to the amount of £40,000 annually, and that all European Missionaries still remained in concealment, and wore the Chinese dress. .

The spiritual state of the Mission is thus described by Medhurst:—"Some idea of the doctrine taught by the Romish Missionaries may be gathered from the books which they have published in the Chinese language. Many of these are written in a lucid and elegant style, and discuss the points at issue between Christians and Confucians, in a masterly and conclusive manner. Their doctrinal and devotional works are clear on the Trinity and the Incarnation, while the perfections of the Deity, the corruption of human nature, and redemption by Christ, are fully stated: and though some unscriptural notions are now and then introduced, yet, all things considered, it is quite possible for humble and patient learners to discover, by such teaching, their sinful condition, and trace out the way of salvation through a Redeemer. It must not be forgotten, also, that the Catholics translated the major part of the New Testament into Chinese; and though there is no evidence of this having been published, yet large portions of the Gospels and Epistles were inserted in the lessons printed for the use of the congregations."

"The present race of adherents to the Catholic Missions in China, whatever the original converts may have been, are, it is to be feared, sadly deficient, both in knowledge and practice. Deprived, for the most part, of intelligent instructors; left generally to the care of the Native Catechists, who are not much better than themselves; and adopting the Christian profession mainly as the result of education or connection; it is hardly to be expected that they would excel, either in grace or zeal. The modern Missionaries, in admitting members, merely require an outward profession, without insisting on a change of heart, or scarcely a reformation of life. The Scriptures are not placed in the hands of the people; religious services are conducted in a language which the generality do not understand; ceremonies are frequent, and public preaching rare; while from the laxity of morals, too common in their communities, we we much fear that the Catholic converts, in the present day, are very little better than the surrounding heathen."

We have thus sketched the history of the Romish Mission in China during two centuries and a half. It is impossible to conceive any combination of circumstances more favourable for its success than occurred during the fifty years' reign of the Emperor Kang-he. The ablest Missionaries whom the Church of Rome could provide were sent to China. The reported number of their converts was prodigious. In 1671 no less than 20,000 baptisms were reported within the year. Yet, at the close of that period, Medhurst only reckons their converts at 300,000, and upon persecution arising, Christianity was virtually suppressed. A century later the number was reduced to 215,000. How complete is the proof of the inefficiency of Romish Missions;—that their vast apparent success under favourable external circumstances is hollow and deceitful, and vanishes as soon as those circumstances change! The dissensions among the Missionaries may in some measure account for their failure, but these dissensions exhibit the inherent weakness of the Romish system; and prove that the boasted unity of the "one Apostolic and indivisible Church" of Rome is a mere fiction.

Abyssinia.

Although the Romish Mission to Abyssinia was not a Mission to a heathen country, but to an ancient Christian Church, with a view to bring it under the domination of Rome, and although it was an abortive one, it must be briefly noticed on account of Xavier's reference to it, in his early letters from India, as the Mission to Ethiopia. It was, also, a Mission instituted by Ignatius Loyola, and was therefore, in its origin, a twin Mission with that of Xavier to India and the East.

The history of this Mission has been given by three Protestant writers of established reputation—Ludolph, Geddes, and La Crose. Dr. Geddes, while residing at Lisbon, took advantage of his knowledge of Portuguese, and of the opportunities of that situation, to make himself thoroughly acquainted with all the Portuguese Missionary histories then extant. Upon his return to England, he published his "Church History of Ethiopia" in 1696. La Crose published a similar history in French in 1739.

The leading facts of the Abyssinian Mission are these. A small band of Portuguese soldiers having assisted the Abyssinian Emperor Claudius to defeat an insurrection, which arose about the year 1542, the Emperor was urged by the Portuguese commander, and by an usurping Portuguese Patriarch, Bermudez, who had been consecrated to that office by Rome, to submit, with his whole kingdom, to the authority of the see of Rome. The Emperor, on the other hand, sent to the Patriarch of Alexandria for a new Bishop, or Abuna, of his appointment, which was the ancient practice of the Abyssinian Church. Into this complication of affairs Ignatius Loyola desired to plunge himself, by going, as a Romish Missionary, to aid the subjection of the Abyssinian Church to Rome. He was not allowed by the Pope to go himself, but it was determined to send a splendid Mission, in which none but Jesuits of Loyola's appointment should be employed. One Jesuit was consecrated Patriarch of Abyssinia, two others, Bishops *in partibus*, and ten Fathers were added as Missionaries. This expedition proceeded to India in 1554, but never reached Abyssinia. Some of its members maintained for a time a footing in the maritime provinces, where they stirred up rebellion against the Emperors, which occasioned the most bloody civil wars; till, after 1560, the attempt to establish a Mission gradually came to an end by the death of some and the expulsion of the rest of the Portuguese from the empire.

The Jesuit Fathers employed in this Mission, and the Jesuit historian who wrote an eulogistic account of the Mission, all concur in deploring the deficiency of Portuguese soldiers as the cause of its failure.

The last Portuguese Bishop and Patriarch, Oviedo, writing to the rector of Goa, June 3, 1566, says—" There was one thing they might be certain of, which was, that there was no other remedy for Ethiopia but a good body of Portuguese troops; that if they had but five or six hundred stout musketeers, he would undertake for the reducing of Ethiopia to the Church in a short time." And the Jesuit historian, Tellez, writes—" It had always been the opinion of such as had any experience in the affairs of Ethiopia, that unless the Catholic preachers were defended and authorized by dragoons, they would never have the success that was desired among those schismatics." (Geddes, 204—208.) "Thus ended," writes Geddes, "the first great Abyssinian Mission, from which Ignatius Loyola had promised so much honour to himself and his order; which, as it was no happy thing for the Jesuits, so, excepting the second (Romish) Mission, it was the worst thing that ever befel Ethiopia." (p. 223.)

A second attempt to bring the Abyssinian Church under subjection to Rome was commenced under the auspices of the King of Spain and the Pope, by a Jesuit

Missionary named Peter Pays, who effected an entrance into the country in 1603, and rose to great influence and power under successive Emperors. He was followed by many other Missionaries, and by usurping Patriarchs and Bishops appointed by Rome. On two occasions the reigning Emperor was induced to swear obedience to the Church of Rome, and to compel the nation to follow his example. Yet for thirty years a national struggle was maintained against these innovations, and deluges of blood were shed; till the Emperor, Seltem Saged, perceived the ruin of his country, and, therefore, though he determined himself to remain in communion with Rome, he issued a prolcamation in 1634 recounting the civil wars into which the interference of Rome had plunged his Empire, and granting liberty to all his people to resume their ancient form of religion. Upon this the whole population returned to their allegiance to the Abyssinian Church, and to its form of worship. The Romish Mission came to an end, and their Missionaries were expelled, or fell a sacrifice to popular fury. (Geddes p. 394.) Subsequent attempts have been made of a like kind, and with similar results.

Paraguay and the Philippine Islands.

The Paraguay Romish Mission has been often spoken of as a great success; and their industrial establishments have been, even in modern times, referred to as examples to be followed in Protestant Missions. The Spanish Roman-Catholic Mission in the Philippine Islands has been spoken of in the same terms of praise. These two distant and distinct fields of Missionary labour are classed together, because they have one feature in common. In each case it will be found that instead of a national conversion to Christianity by instruction and the willing reception of the truth, the Missionaries became possessed of supreme power, and enforced by law an external conformity with the rites of the Romish Church. The natural consequence followed, that the people combined these rites with their own heathen system. In the case of Paraguay, as soon as the authority which imposed the form of Christianity was abrogated, the people as naturally relapsed to heathenism.

The most celebrated panegyrist of the Paraguay Missions, M. Muratori, says of the first century of early Romish Missions in South America, and especially in Paraguay—"Formerly the Fathers of the Society (Jesuits) chiefly applied themselves to making frequent excursions into South America. From time to time they converted a few Indians, but no Christian colonies were settled, nor was there a Church of the true religion to be seen in Paraguay. The chief, and almost only fruit of so much labour, was the baptizing some dying infant. The adult, or grown-up persons, who embraced the faith, were usually removed from among the infidels, and persuaded to fix in places inhabited by Christians." It thus appears that here, as elsewhere, Roman Catholic Missions failed

P

when unsupported by the arm of temporal power. ("A Relation of the Missions of Paraguay, written originally in Italian by M. Muratori, and now done into English from the French translation, 1759." See Preface of Author.)

About the middle of the seventeenth century the Jesuit Missionaries began to collect the Indians into communities of 4000 to 6000 each, by the lure of large temporal advantages, and under a civil organization, well calculated to preserve order and diligence, in which the chief power rested with the Missionary, and in which the Indians were trained to military service. These communities were called "Reductions." In 1717 the Jesuits reckoned thirty-two very populous Reductions, with 121,168 baptized Indians. The form of the Romish religion was of course introduced, and no toleration was allowed to any other religion. Access to the territory thus occupied by the Jesuits was denied to independent witnesses, even though Romanists. As it would be unfair to judge of the internal state of the country from the violent abuse which the other Romish orders have bestowed upon the Jesuit Mission of Paraguay, it is impossible to form any opinion of its Christian condition. The Mission became a great Indian Republic, with an army of from 70,000 to 80,000, in which the Jesuits were supreme. In 1752, after the narrative of Muratori ceases, the armies of Spain and Portugal combined to invade Paraguay, and, after several bloody engagements, the province was reduced to a nominal subjection to

Spain. The Jesuit order was soon afterwards suppressed;—in Portugal in 1759; in Spain in 1767; and throughout the Romish Church in 1773, by Pope Clement XIV.

The sequel is thus concisely stated in the last edition of the Encyclopædia Britannica, article *Paraguay*.

"They (the inhabitants of Paraguay) had attained to a state of some civilization, when, in 1767, the Jesuits were suddenly expelled from South America; and Paraguay again became subject to the Spanish Viceroys. After this event, though some of the communities continued in existence till a later period, the greater number fell to the ground, and the inhabitants relapsed into a state of barbarism."

The isolated position of the Philippine Islands has enabled the religious orders who conduct the Missions in those countries to maintain a supremacy nearly approaching to that assumed by the Jesuits in Paraguay. The researches made at Manilla by the officers of the exploring expedition lately sent out by the Austrian Government, in the Novara frigate, furnish the information that various orders of monks divide the ministerial charge of the Islands, viz. the Augustinians, Dominicans, and Franciscans. The population of the Islands is reckoned to be 2,792,452. But the following statements of the unprejudiced author of the voyage of the Novara, forbid us to reckon the Philippines as a Missionary success.

"The Spaniards have conquered and have subjugated the islands, fanatical monks have, what they call, Christianized the people, but during the 300 years that the Castilian has held supremacy here, little, if any thing, has been done for the prosperity and development of the country, or the intellectual and moral advancement of the people." (Voyage of the Novara, p. 285.)

"The entire Archipelago is nothing but one rich church domain, a safe retreat for the legion of Spanish monks, who are able to lord it here with unrestricted power. There is a Governor-General of the Philippines only so long as it pleases the Augustinian, Dominican, and Franciscan friars." (p. 298.)

"Here apparently, as in the earlier dependencies of Spain, in Central and Northern America, the Roman-Catholic ritual has become mingled in the most extraordinary manner with ceremonies borrowed from paganism." (p. 345.)

These notices, few and imperfect as they are, exhibit the general character and results of Romish Missions to the heathen. But the subject is so large and so important, that it is hoped some writer of leisure, and of acquaintance with Missionary topics, may be induced to study it in all its bearings, and to test, by the common rules of historical fidelity, the credibility of the reports, which are from time to time boastfully put forth, of the success of Romish Missions. Contemporaneous records will serve to check each other. The disputes between the different religious orders often let us behind the scenes. The reports of travellers, and scientific histories, will throw some light upon various particulars. Such a careful and patient investigation would dispel the halo of delusion and romance which envelops many a Roman story. Till such a work appears, the author of these pages hopes that enough has been stated to caution Protestant writers against repeating loose statements, and exaggerated traditions, whether taken from the serials of " Letters from the East" in their ancient form, or as "Lettres édifiantes et curieuses," or as " Annals of the Faith."

Nothing is more striking, in reading Missionary records, than the contrast between the scanty, vague, extravagant, and unsatisfactory notices of Romish Missions, and the cautious, candid, and multitudinous records of Protestant Evangelical Missions.

Romanists have indeed endeavoured to turn to an evil account the caution and candour of Protestant statements, by collecting together the early accounts of tentative and immature Protestant Missionary operations, and by treating them as if they had been as old as their own. Dr. Wiseman began the work. A few subsequent years of Protestant Missionary labour have served to reverse the facts upon which he then relied. The Protestant Church may well bear such Romish attacks with patience; for each year is adding to the accumulated proof of the solid advance of Protestant Missions, of the manifest blessing of God which rests upon them, of the spiritual life of Native Churches, and of the testimony of independent witnesses to the beneficial influence of Protestant Missions upon the civil and social condition of the native population in every quarter of the globe.

It forms no part of the scope of these pages to describe at length the successes of Protestant Missions, else the comparison already made between the confessions of failure by Romanists, and the solid and unquestionable spiritual fruit of Protestants in South India, might be extended by a reference to the Native Churches established in Sierra Leone, in New Zealand, in many islands of the South Sea, in Burmah, in Madagascar, and elsewhere.

One leading point in the contrast between Protestant and Romish Missions must, however, receive a passing notice. Protestant Missionaries have never been charged with causing war and bloodshed. The genuine influence of true Christianity has always been manifest in conciliating, rather than irritating, the most savage passions of the heathen. A great statesman of India has put upon record this sound principle:—

"Christian things, done in a Christian way, will never, the Chief Commissioner is convinced, alienate the heathen. About such things there are qualities which do not provoke or excite distrust, nor harden to resistance. It is when unchristian things are done in the name of Christianity, or when Christian things are done in an unchristian way, that mischief and danger are occasioned." (Despatch of Sir John Lawrence, Chief Commissioner of the Punjab during the Mutiny of 1857.)

Even where the enmity of the natural heart against the religion of Jesus has for a time triumphed, as in Madagascar, to the expulsion of Missionaries, the word of Truth which they had sowed has maintained itself, and has flourished, even against the edge of the bloody sword of a persecuting tyrant.

Concluding Remarks.

The historical review now given will establish the conclusion, that the brightest prospects and the most confident hopes of Romish Missions to the heathen have vanished sooner or later, by one catastrophe or another:— that they have not contained within themselves the principle of permanent vitality. Where they are not upheld by the sword, they are overborne by opposition. Their apparent success for a time has been the result of favourable worldly circumstances; and when those circumstances have changed, the Mission has come to nothing. This conclusion is based upon the history of three centuries; during the greater part of which period the Church of Rome had the fields to itself. Rome put forth Missionary agencies to reap them far more numerous than the Protestant Church has yet been able to command. But Rome failed to gather in the harvest, and the fields are all now still unreaped, and open for the entrance of Protestant Evangelists. Romanists boast of Francis Xavier as the Apostle of the Indies; they erect altars and chapels for his worship; they invoke his aid in their Missionary efforts; and "verily they have their reward." The blight of Xavier's Missionary principles has rested upon them ever since; and the disappointment which pursued Xavier to his last breath has been the portion of many a sincere, able, and zealous Romish Missionary.

Where true religion has been once established, Romanism can extend itself, because it is essentially a declension from the truth, and it offers to partially awakened consciences an easier religion, and one more accommodated to the cravings of a fallen nature. Where Popery is adopted as an engine of the state, and can unsheath the sword of persecution, it can triumph over all opposition. But Popery, it has been seen, cannot plant or propagate itself in lands where true religion has not been first introduced. It cannot maintain its foot-hold there. Even the blood of its martyrs is in no sense the seed of its Church. Popery exists, therefore, only under the predicted character of the Apostacy; and all its fallacious boasts of success in Missions to the heathen, all its pretentions to miraculous powers, all its absurd legends, do but add another mark of "the Apostacy"—"speaking lies in hypocrisy."

If Romanism has nothing to hope for in unevangelized lands, have Protestant Missions any thing to fear through the extension of Romish Missions? Will the efforts of Rome materially impede Protestant Missions? Are the native heathen who have had Romish Missionaries settled among them less ready than other heathen to receive the Gospel? The inquiry practically relates to such countries as India, China, and Africa, where the Missions of both communities co-exist. What, in such countries, has been the mutual action of the two systems upon each other?

The foregoing pages sufficiently prove that the masses of nominal Christians, baptized by Romanist Missionaries, and admitted to the rites of their Church, must prove a hindrance to true Christianity, by exhibiting to their heathen countrymen a false standard of Christian truth, and of the Christian life; whilst in the eyes of the Mohammedan population, the Roman worship of saints and images, fixes upon Christianity the charge of idolatry. It is also often found that Romish native converts have been deeply prejudiced against the truth of the Gospel by slanders against Protestants. There are, moreover, incidental evils in the proximity of Romanists to a Protestant Mission. A ready asylum is opened for the converts who resent the restraints of Protestant discipline. In some few cases, also, the Romish Missionary has sided with the heathen or Mohammedan party, as well in political matters, as in religious questions. When a public controversy was held at Agra, in the year 1854, by Dr. Pfander and the Rev. T. V. French, M.A., late of Univ. Coll., Oxford, on the one side, and certain learned Mohammedan Mullahs on the other, the Romish

Bishop at Agra supplied the Mohammedans with arguments against the authenticity of the Hebrew and Greek texts in the Holy Scriptures.* But such unchristian antagonism cannot be expected often to occur.

On the other hand, a fact meets us in this inquiry—and it is a broad fact—that in South India, which has been one of the chief scenes of Romish Missions, Protestant Missions have had most success. This is at least a proof that the influence of Rome is limited in its operation; and that the heathen generally, in such neighbourhoods, are not more disinclined than others to listen to the Protestant Missionary. Some, indeed, seem prepared for the reception of the truth, by an acquaintance with the terms in which it is conveyed; and many con-

---

* "Another incident connected with this controversy (April 1854) deserves to be mentioned: it is the active assistance which some of the Roman Catholics have been lending to our Mohammedan opponents here, by supplying Wazir Khan, who knows English, both with books and arguments against us, or rather against the Gospel. The bitter spirit also, in which he spoke in his letters to me of the Protestants, and of Luther and Calvin, shows clearly the influence under which he has been; for the Mohammedans in general show a much greater regard for the Protestants than for the image-worshipping Roman Catholics, whenever they are aware of this distinction. We, of course, have nothing to fear from such combinations: neither Pilate nor Herod have prevailed against Christ and His Gospel, nor will any combination of error, not even the gates of hell, ever be able to overcome the truth." (Fourteenth Report of the Agra Church Missionary Association for 1854.)

verts have been gained from Romish Missions, who have been valuable witnesses of the identity of Romish and heathen idolatry from their intimate knowledge of both.

The conclusion which an extensive inquiry on this subject suggests, is, that Protestant Missions have little to fear from Rome; if only the Church of Christ puts forth its spiritual strength for the advancement of the Redeemer's cause. Romish interference may sometimes distress the individual Missionary, who is exposed to its annoyance, but he need not fear any permanent hindrance to the cause of truth, unless the Romish teaching be supported by the arm of secular power.

There may be, also, incidental benefit to Protestant Missions from the juxtaposition of Romish Missions. They afford a standing warning against trusting to a mere nominal Christianity. They serve to show the worthlessness of a formal profession of Christianity which is not grounded upon an open Bible, and spiritual life in the soul. There will be much mere formal profession in Protestant Missions, and the value of such formal profession differs little in the one case or the other. But the strength of a Protestant Mission is in " the truth of the Gospel," and in the spiritual operation of the truth in the souls which receive it. Converts who are alive to God through faith in Christ Jesus, and who live the life of faith in the Son of God, showing their faith by its fruits, are " the holy seed," and " the holy seed shall be the substance thereof." (Isai. vi. 13.) For the sake of these the Lord sustains and protects the external framework of a Mission, and bears with much longsuffering the nominal Christianity which will ever enter too largely into its composition.

It may be permitted to one who has had large opportunities and long experience in the supervision of Missions to state his firm conviction, that all attempts to lay the foundations of a Protestant Mission, without true conversions and spiritual life in individual souls, will be as unsatisfactory and as transient as those of Xavier and his followers. Christian education may be extended; a visible Church, in all its completeness, may be established; civilization may be promoted by Industrial Institutions; but there may be no " living" Church. For a season, especially in the early days of freshness and hope, the Mission may appear to flourish; but if the spiritual " substance" be wanting, the end will be disappointment, failure, and, too often, the apostacy of converts. The conversion of the heathen is hard work, even when the word is accompanied with power and demonstration of the Spirit. It is the testimony of every Missionary of spiritual discernment, even of the most soberminded, that Satan has a power in heathen lands, of which we in the Church at home have little conception. If the spirit of Christ be not with the Missionary, he will be baffled at all points, and wear out his strength in continuous and incessant, but profitless labour.

The compilation of these pages has served to deepen the conviction, in the mind of the compiler, of the truth and importance of these cardinal Missionary principles; and he will esteem his labour well repaid, if his work serve to uphold these principles in the Missionary efforts of all Protestant Churches.

The faithful Missionary, whose aims all culminate in the exaltation of "Christ crucified," will receive generally a few seals to his ministry; and if they stand fast in the Lord, he lives. His chief employment should thenceforth be to cherish them, as a nurse cherishes her children, to stir up the grace that is in them, to set them to work in gathering into the fold fresh converts, to make them the pivot upon which his Missionary operations turn. Their example of holiness and liberality will give a tone to the whole Mission which nothing else can supply: as their numbers increase, the strength of the Mission increases; its stability, its self-support, and its self-extension are secured. An open Bible keeps open the stream of the waters of life. Thus a Native Church is formed, from which the Word of God is "sounded out." God giveth the increase to the labour of the planters and waterers. Against such a living branch of the true Church the gates of hell shall never prevail: like the vine brought out of Egypt, it takes deep root, and fills the land.

To those who long for the day when Jesus "shall have dominion from sea to sea, and from the river to the ends of the earth," I confidently point, in the history of Protestant Missions, to the abundant evidences that the spirit of Christ is with them; that under His influences a native agency is in preparation which will have power and grace to carry on the work without foreign assistance. I point, also, to the providential removal of hindrances to the extension of Christianity, which has become a sign of the times, since Missions have been prosecuted in the spirit of the Gospel,—to the gradual preparation of the nations for the living Word of God, and to its multiplication in all languages. In these things we see the way of the Lord prepared, and may anticipate His predicted and universal dominion; when "all nations shall call Him blessed."

www.ingramcontent.com/pod-product-compliance
Lightning Source LLC
Chambersburg PA
CBHW021200230426
43667CB00006B/491